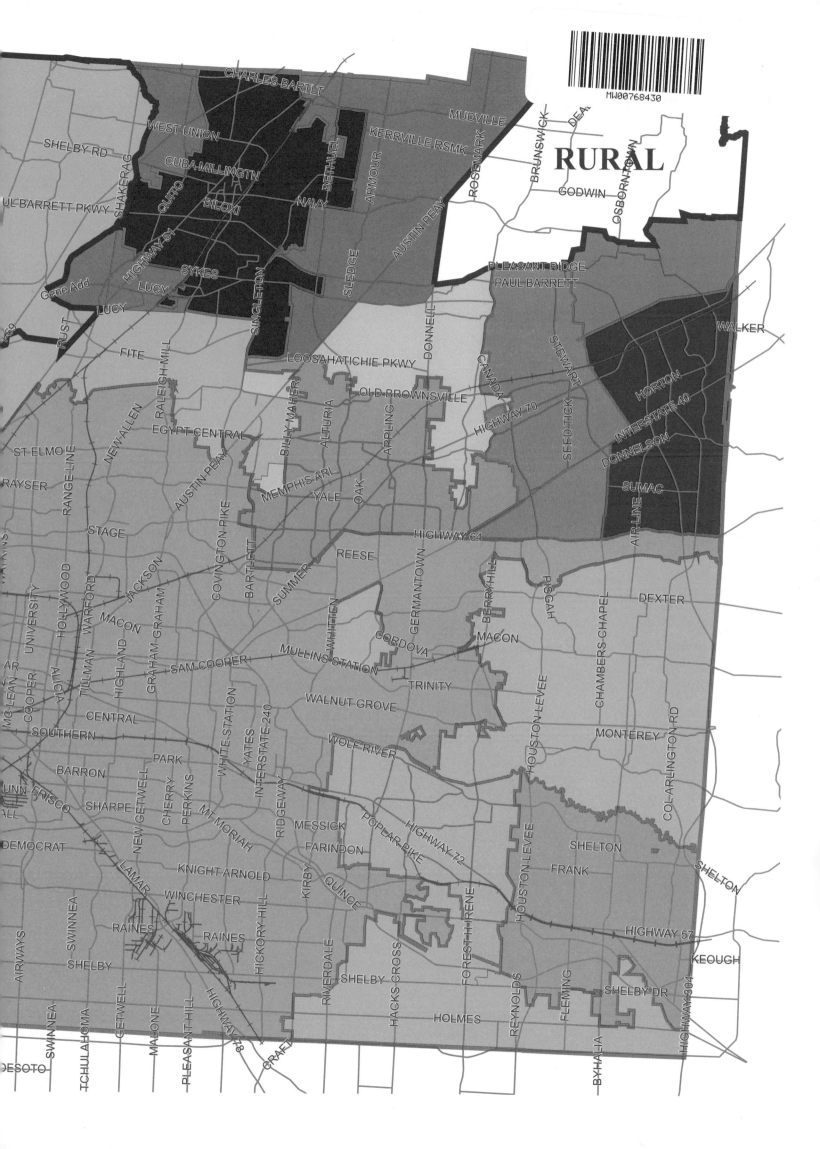

HISTORIC SHELBY COUNTY
An Illustrated History
by Dr. John E. Harkins

To Carol Morris
John E. Harkins

Commissioned by the West Tennessee Historical Society

Historical Publishing Network
A Division of Lammert Incorporated
San Antonio, Texas

CONTENTS

ISBN: 9781893619869
Library of Congress Card Catalog Number: 2008929431

Historic Shelby County: An Illustrated History

author: John E. Harkins, Ph.D.
contributing writers for "Sharing the Heritage":   Joe Goodpasture, Scott Williams

Historical Publishing Network

president: Ron Lammert
project managers: Wynn Buck, Curtis Courtney
administration: Donna M. Mata, Diane Perez, Evelyn Hart, Melissa Quinn
book sales: Dee Steidle
production: Colin Hart, Craig Mitchell, Jason Lively,
       Charles A. Newton, III, Roy Arellano

DEDICATION

This book is lovingly dedicated to the memory of my great, good friend, Judge John Brennan Getz (1934-2005). John taught me a great deal about Shelby County history. Had he lived longer, his knowledge, generosity, and acute perception would have guaranteed a better telling of our county's history. Through all of our adult friendship, John Getz was a very good friend to Memphis-area history, too.

ACKNOWLEDGMENTS

Thanks to the staff members of the Shelby County Archives, the University of Memphis Libraries' Special Collections Department, and the Memphis and Shelby County Room of the Memphis Public Library. Memphis Pink Palace Museum and First Tennessee Bank gave access to and permission to use images from their collections.

John Dougan, Ed Frank, and Ed Williams kindly read the manuscript and made numerous helpful suggestions. My wife, Georgia Harkins, always my first, best critic, reviewed the manuscript several times, editing it for clarity, grammar, and form.

In addition, each of the persons listed below has contributed to this book in one or more significant ways, beyond those whose aid is implicit in this book's bibliography and those working in repositories of Shelby County's history.

Terry Balton, Guy Bates*, Bess Barry*, Elva Bledsoe*, Annice M. Bolton, William C. Boyd, David Bowman, Ronald Brister, Rachael Burrow*, Shirley Sigler Chamberlin, Wyeth Chandler*, Richard Childers, Vincent Clark, Brenda Bethea Connelly*, Jeanne Crawford, Nancy Crosby, Douglas Cupples, Skip Daniel, William V. Davidson, Bettie B. Davis, Bill Detling, John Dougan, Robert Dye, A. W. "Bill" Fisher*, Jane Fisher*, Mary Lawrence Flinn, Laurence B. Gardiner*, John B. Getz*, Nick Gotten, Jane Hooker, Eleanor D. Hughes*, Betty Hughes, Denise Hunt, Ruth Wykoff Hunt*, Kenneth T. Jackson, Sarah E. Kaestle, Ranny Langston, Robert A. Lanier, Leslie Lee, Francis G. Loring, Paul Matthews, G. Edward McCarver*, W. Patrick McCarver*, Gwen McClain, John B. McKinney, Lee Millar, Mary Louise Nazor, Andy Pauncy, S. Caya Phillips*, Barbara Plyler, Charles E. Pool, Sr.*, Clark Porteous*, John Rea*, James E. Roper*, Clarene P. Russell, Judy Rutledge, Andy Saunders, John S. Shepherd, Jonathan Smith, John W. Spence*, Tara Tate, Martha P. Tibbs, Robert A. Tillman*, Marilyn Van Eynde, Joe Walk, Cliff West*, Jean A. West, Betsy Foster West*, Edward Foster Williams, III, and Walter D. Wills, III.

* indicates deceased

Despite having had so much help from so many sources, any errors of fact or tone in this study are my own.

John E. Harkins

PREFACE

The last general history of Shelby County to appear was Goodspeed's effort, published in 1887, six score years ago. Although a modern, comprehensive history of Shelby County is sorely needed, this book cannot fill that need. The pictorial format of a "coffee table history" dictates a suggestive, rather than a definitive treatment. Using the analogy of a portrait, our text supplies a highlight sketch or line drawing of its subject, rather than a full-length, full-color, oil portrait. It provides many of the major contours and configurations of the county and its primary lights and shadows, but recognizes that some features must be muted or merely suggested. On the premise that a picture is worth a thousand words, however, the book's rich illustrations speak volumes for themselves.

Despite the limitations imposed by format, this book is still ambitious. Although it is designed for the general reader, its research draws on such a wealth and variety of sources that it should be of significant interest to scholars and local history enthusiasts as well. Moreover, the subject has been painstakingly researched. Had reference notes been included in the book's format, one or more sources could have been cited for every statement. Likewise, knowledgeable students and scholars of Shelby County's history have vetted this book's text for accuracy and balance of content and tone.

The starter question for any study like this one should be "What is Shelby County?" The term "county" generally denotes administrative governing divisions of Great Britain and many of its former possessions, including the United States. In 2001, there were 3,141 counties and county-like (i. e. parishes, boroughs) divisions in America. Shelby County, Tennessee, ranked as the 41st most populous American county in 1980, but had dropped to 44th by the year 2000. Because Shelby County abuts two other states' boundaries, perhaps the Memphis Standard Metropolitan Area is a more accurate gauge of the metro area's size and importance than county figures alone. In the year 2000, Shelby Countians comprised 897,472 of the 1,135,614 persons (about 80 percent) living in the metro area and about 15% of Tennessee's nearly 6,000,000 residents. Tennessee, incidentally, is the sixteenth most populous state in the Union.

Shelby County is a geographical area, a political unit for representative local government, an administrative unit of the state government, a loosely knit community of persons who are neighbors, groups of more specific communities, the heart of a major metropolitan area, and a point of cultural identification of sorts. Its governmental functions include a school system, several levels of judicial structures, a law enforcement system, a penal system, a health department, a hospital system, and much, much more. (For a detailed compilation of Shelby County's historic authority, functions, and responsibilities between 1819 and 1960, see the book *The Private Acts of Shelby County*). In recent decades, starting largely with the administration of Mayor William N. Morris, Shelby County has also provided a much broader array of social welfare services to its less fortunate citizens, including the aged, the unwell, and various underprivileged groups. In this area of expanding functions, Shelby County has paralleled a nationwide expansion of county governments' services for their citizens. Ultimately, Shelby County is and reflects its people, individually and collectively.

Shelby County history is inextricably interwoven with that of its city of Memphis. Politically, economically, culturally, it is impossible to separate the two. But, the term "Memphis and Shelby County" contains ambiguities. The "and" as used here can be conjunctive or it can be disjunctive. The first meaning is Shelby County inclusive of Memphis. The second is those parts of Shelby County outside of the city's corporate limits. In this sense it often seems to express "Memphis versus Shelby County." The term Shelby County can even be used to refer to county citizens living a rural life style outside of any of the county's incorporated areas.

"Memphis and Shelby County" has meant vastly differing things geographically over time. In 1819, Memphis was just a tiny strip of a few streets laid off along the edge of the river-bluff. In 1826, Memphis became the only incorporated municipality in Shelby County. One hundred eighty years later, approximately 90% of Shelby County is either part of an incorporated municipality or is part of the future annexation areas agreed upon by the county's seven municipal governments. When the projected annexations have been carried out, about two-thirds of Shelby County will be within the Memphis city limits.

During the 1830s, Tennessee's boundary with Mississippi was resurveyed and corrected. The correction moved Shelby County's southern boundary approximately three and one-half miles further south and increased the county's area by about 88 square miles. In the early twentieth century, Shelby County was called "Big Shelby," symbolizing its machine politics and their profound impact on Tennessee gubernatorial elections and decisions by the state legislature. Shelby County delegates to the state legislature called their home base "the great state of Shelby." They block voted and arrogantly flaunted their power, to the distress of other Tennessee politicos. Once, during Prohibition, they allegedly swapped their votes on a particular issue for a case or two of scotch whiskey.

In recent decades, Memphis and Shelby County have come to symbolize high property and sales taxes. These and other problems have generated considerable middle class flight from their respective jurisdictions. Circumstances of growing affluence, the ease and low cost of commuting, a revolution in electronic communications, quality of life issues, and distress with tax rates have sent many Memphians scurrying to suburban municipalities, and many Shelby Countians moving across county and even state lines. For at least a time in the early twenty-first century, Collierville was the fastest growing municipality in Tennessee, and nearby Olive Branch was the fastest growing of Mississippi's cities. Recently, Bartlett, Collierville, and Olive Branch have each been rated highly for their quality of life environments.

Because of the ambiguities and con-tradictions cited above, one embarks on writing about Historic Shelby County with a good deal of trepidation. Deciding how much of Memphis history to exclude is vexing. It would be nice to be able to write a stand-alone history of Shelby County, but that is virtually impossible to do. The histories of Memphis and Shelby County are interwoven. The historian can scarcely remove one without mangling and distorting his account of the other. Moreover, even the county's other municipalities and its unincorporated communities can be given only passing inclusion. The limit of about thirty thousand words reduces boundaries for inclusion to the county's general historical flow and some of its more relevant and interesting anecdotes.

Despite such difficulties, there are a number of things that make a brief history of Shelby County easier to chronicle than it would have been just a decade or two earlier. Not only are numerous facts accessible via the Internet, but numerous secondary works on smaller communities in Shelby County are also now available. The latter works include books, articles, theses, and dissertations. Some of these are comprehensive and of very high quality. Those that are limited in scope and in quality still tend to be very helpful. Accordingly, and this is very important, this study includes a fairly comprehensive, very briefly annotated bibliography.

It is the author's sincere hope that this work will help inspire additional and more comprehensive historical studies on Shelby County in the very near future.

✧

This mid-1790s map of the Fourth Chickasaw Bluff shows the riverfront territory that the Spanish acquired from Chickasaw Indians and upon which they quickly built Fort San Fernando. The original is in the Spanish National Archives in Madrid and this is probably the first time that a copy has been published in a history of Memphis or Shelby County.

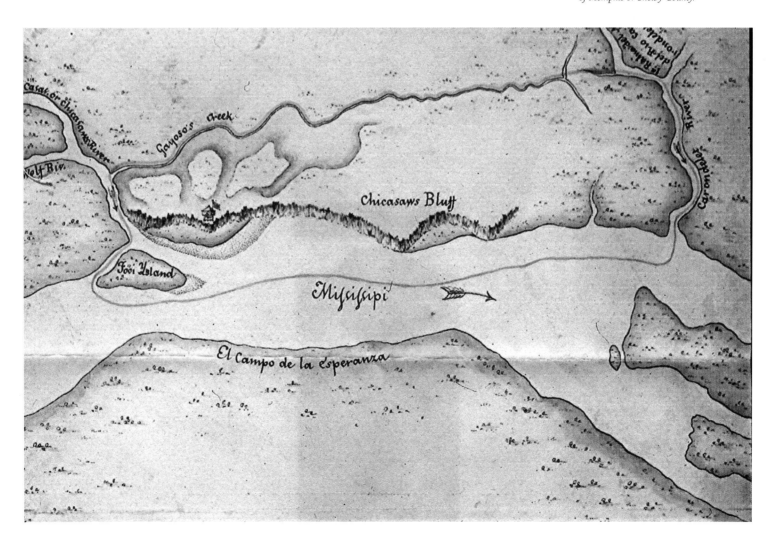

CHAPTER I: PROLOGUE

PREHISTORY THROUGH THE CHICKASAW CESSION

Historic Shelby County has the state's largest geographical area, 775 square miles. During the twentieth and into the twenty-first centuries, Shelby has been the most populous of Tennessee's 95 counties. It occupies the extreme southwest corner of its state and abuts the states of Arkansas and Mississippi. Created by an act of the Tennessee Legislature in November 1819, Shelby County Government began serving its citizens' needs the following May. Shelby was the first county completely within the boundaries of the Western District of Tennessee. The Tennessee Legislature named it in honor of General Isaac Shelby, a military hero and the first governor of Kentucky. Shelby had partnered with Andrew Jackson in negotiating the treaty through which some leaders of the Chickasaw "nation" sold the United States all of its lands above the 35th parallel of north latitude between the Tennessee, Ohio, and Mississippi Rivers. Counties in eight other states have also been named to honor Isaac Shelby. Of these, Shelby County, Tennessee is the most populous and the most prominent.

Of course, there was a lot of human activity on the site of Shelby County, Tennessee, prior to the "Chickasaw Cession." Thousands of years before European incursions into this area, native Americans had advanced through the Archaic and Woodlands stages and into the Mississippian cultural development. Agriculture, pottery making, mound building, and the development of city-states characterized the latter. Archeologists have uncovered, deciphered, and interpreted many of the area's prehistoric artifacts.

It would have been Mississippian Indians that Hernando De Soto's expedition encountered in 1541, in his failed expedition to find a new El Dorado. The location of the hospitable Indian town of Quiz Quiz and the point on the banks of the Mississippi River where DeSoto's men "discovered" the father of waters remain matters of speculation and contention. De Soto County, Mississippi, with its county seat of Hernando, is immediately south of Shelby County. Several areas further south also claim De Soto as their own.

The natives that De Soto encountered have yet to be precisely identified, but their culture does predate the presence of the Chickasaws and the Choctaws, the Indian groups present when the French began taking military control of the Mississippi River Valley in the early eighteenth century. Father Jacques Marquette, Louis Joliet, Robert, Chevelier la seier de La Salle, and other French travelers recorded their visits to the Fourth Chickasaw Bluff, the present site of downtown Memphis. La Salle led the French colonization of lower Louisiana, and by the 1730s the Chickasaws definitely controlled West Tennessee, including what became Shelby County. Governor Bienville led two unsuccessful expeditions against the Chickasaws in the late-1730, and built Fort Assumption just south of where the three bridges span the Mississippi today. Urban renewal programs helped finance the "French Fort" subdivision in that vicinity during the city's post-World War II building boom.

During the middle of the eighteenth century, Britain struggled against the Bourbon monarchies of France and Spain for hegemony in Europe and for control of the North American continent. Britain won the French and Indian War (1754-63), but, because of the accession of King George III, did not reap the full fruits of that victory. Accordingly, France awarded Western Louisiana and the "Isle of Orleans," to Spain in payment for her alliance in the war and in compensation for her loss of Florida to the British. Britain took all of Eastern Louisiana and Florida, between the Great Lakes and the Gulf, by right of conquest. Desiring to minimize friction with Trans-Appalachia's Indians, Britain forbade colonial settlement west of the crest of that mountain range. Early Anglo-American frontiersmen ignored this Proclamation Line of 1763, but the area of the Fourth Chickasaw Bluff did not get permanent European settlement until perhaps as late as 1795.

✧

Chucalissa is a reconstructed Mississippian Indian Village in Southwest Shelby County. Its culture is the one that greeted Hernando DeSoto, if he got as far north as Memphis.

COURTESY OF CHUCALISSA INDIAN VILLAGE AND ARCHEOLOGICAL MUSEUM, UNIVERSITY OF MEMPHIS.

Britain's efforts to integrate her Anglo-American colonies more thoroughly into her mercantilist world empire sparked sufficient resistance to ignite America's war for independence. France, Spain, and the Netherlands sided with the fledgling United States in the ensuing conflict, and this coalition won the war. However, the British, more or less, won the peace. They drove a diplomatic wedge among their foes by ceding their title to Trans-Appalachia to the USA. Spain, which had captured British forts and settlements along the Gulf Coast and up the Mississippi as far as Natchez, claimed the area between the Ohio River and the Gulf of Mexico by right of conquest.

The confusion rising out of the French Revolution greatly affected European diplomacy in the Mississippi Valley. In May of 1795, the Spanish governor of Louisiana had troops occupy the Fourth Chickasaw Bluff and build a frontier fort at the junction of the Wolf and Mississippi Rivers. Lt. Governor Manuel Gayoso de Lemos secured the permission of Chickasaw chiefs and had his men construct Fort San Fernando de las Barrancas or Saint Ferdinand of the Bluffs. (The fort was named to honor Spain's crown prince, who ultimately became the worst king in his country's modern history). This settlement began permanent European habitation in the area that a generation later became Shelby County, Tennessee. Ironically, locals celebrate Gayoso's impact on the origins of Mid-South settlement much less than they do the De Soto expedition, which in fact may never have gotten as far north as present-day Shelby County.

Fort San Fernando was a hardship post, garrisoned by Spanish subjects, about half of whom were ethnically French. Victor Callot's detailed map of this area shows the layout of Spain's fort and of its support

community. This outpost did not last long. In the very year that Spain's colonial officials were expanding their military control up the Mississippi Valley, the mother country negotiated "Pinckney's Treaty" (San Lorenzo) with the United States. In so doing, Spain ceded her claims to the area between the 31st and 35th parallels to the U.S. In March of 1797, following orders based on much broader international considerations, the San Fernando garrison destroyed its fort and withdrew across the river to Hopefield, Arkansas. America's diplomatic victory meant that her eastern seaboard states would control the destinies of the Trans-Appalachian West.

In the immediate aftermath of the Revolutionary War, North Carolina claimed the extension of its northern and southern boundaries all the way to the Mississippi River. The state began issuing warrants to lands in that area, soon to become Tennessee, to help pay down its war debts. Not long afterward, North Carolina ceded its western lands to the federal government. The lands

south of the Ohio River became the "Territory South of the Ohio River," later called the "Old Southwest Territory." Soon the northern portions of these lands went through the territorial stages and entered the Union as full-fledged states. Kentucky became a state in 1792 and Tennessee in 1796. Until 1818, however, the Chickasaws still controlled Western Kentucky, West Tennessee, and North Mississippi.

After the Spanish withdrew from Fort San Fernando and burned its stockade, American troops under Captain Isaac Guion arrived and built a fort on the same site. A short time later, the army moved its garrison to a more defensible location two miles further south. American soldiers occupied this post until well after the Louisiana Purchase.

There was also a government-sponsored trading post on the site and a few families of Anglo-American squatters trading and providing food and fuel to river craft traversing the Mississippi. Commandants at the area's American forts included Meriwether Lewis of Lewis and Clark expedition fame, future president Zachary Taylor, and Zebulon Pike, father of the explorer for whom Pike's Peak Colorado is named. The most noted "factor" or merchant at the federal trading post was Isaac Rawlings, later to become a prominent Memphis merchant and the city's second mayor. Some of the pre-cession squatters had been present under Spanish rule, and a few were still living in the locale when West Tennessee was opened to legal settlement. Among the pre-cession residents in the area were the families of Paddy Meagher, Jacob Bean, and Joseph Mizel. [Spellings of these earliest settlers' names vary greatly in the extant documents].

Francis Baily, passing the site in 1797, wrote of "five or six families settled [there] who may be called half-Indians, that is they are persons, who in habit and manners are nearly allied to them and have generally married into the Indian families." In 1805, John Graham visited at the American garrison and remarked on the scenic quality of the area's wildlife. The following year, Thomas Ashe recorded, "On [the Bluff] are erected a fort, barracks for a company of soldiers and a few artillery men, and houses and stores for

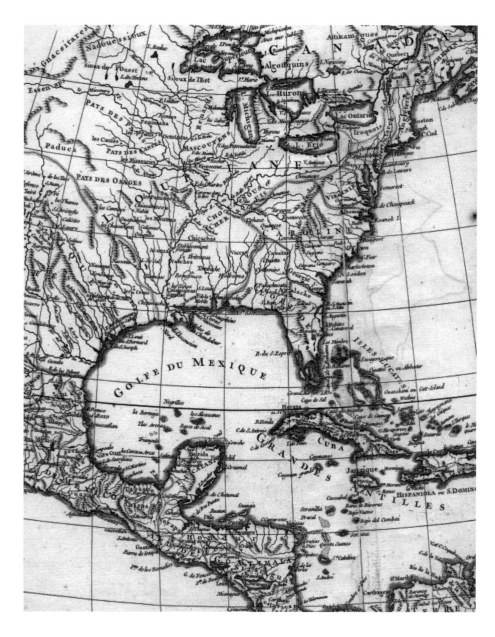

state [Indian?] commissioners.... [The Bluff] maintains about a dozen families, who raise corn, breed poultry and pigs, and supply boats descending the river with what common provisions they may want."

Until 1818, all of West Tennessee and Western Kentucky still technically belonged to the Chickasaws. In that year, James Monroe's administration acted to "extinguish" the Chickasaw's claims to the whole area. Andrew Jackson and Isaac Shelby, agents acting on behalf of the Federal Government and their respective states, met with Chickasaw leaders at "Old Town" and negotiated the agreement for the Indians to cede all lands north of the 35th parallel to the United States. However, Chickasaw and Choctaw Indians remained in the vicinity into

✧

This early French map shows the land of the "Chicachas" on the "left bank" of the Mississippi River, about halfway up to the junction with the Ohio River.

COURTESY OF SPECIAL COLLECTIONS, UNIVERSITY OF MEMPHIS LIBRARIES.

✧

Above: Spanish Governor General Bernardo de Gálvez captured all of the British military posts in the lower Mississippi Valley and along the Gulf Coast during America's war for independence. At the Treaty of Paris of 1783, however, Britain ceded its claims to Trans-Appalachia to the fledgling United States. Both Spain and the United States claimed the area between the Ohio River and the Gulf until the Treaty of San Lorenzo in 1795.

COURTESY OF WIKIPEDIA.

Right: French Governor Bienville built Fort Assumption on the heights where the three bridges cross the Mississippi River. French efforts to subdue the Chickasaws failed, and the French signed a treaty with the Indians, then abandoned their fort and withdrew.

COURTESY OF SPECIAL COLLECTIONS, UNIVERSITY OF MEMPHIS LIBRARIES.

Bottom, right: Before Spain relinquished her claims to what is now Kentucky, Tennessee, Alabama, and Mississippi, Spanish Louisiana's Governor Corondelet established an outpost on the site of Memphis. Lieutenant Governor Manuel Gayoso de Lemos got Chickasaw permission and built Fort San Fernando de Las Barrancas in early 1795.

COURTESY OF SPECIAL COLLECTIONS, UNIVERSITY OF MEMPHIS LIBRARIES.

4E   17

FORT ASSUMPTION

Near this point, at the highest part of the bluff, on Assumption Day, Aug. 15, 1739, this fort was erected by Bienville, French governor of Louisiana. This was the first structure built by white men in Shelby County, and the third such in Tennessee.

the 1830s, when subsequent treaties pushed them further west.

Although earliest white settlers into Southwest Tennessee left little in the way of description of the natives prior to the treaty of cession, memoirs reported in the *Old Folks of Shelby County's Record* give us renderings of how the settlers of the 1820s viewed them. An unattributed (but written by J. J. Rawlings, nephew of Isaac Rawlings) entry simply under "Eds. Record" reads:

In 1824 there were but three mercantile firms in the now city of Memphis—Winchester & Carr, Henderson & Fearn, and Isaac Rawlings. Their trade was principally with the

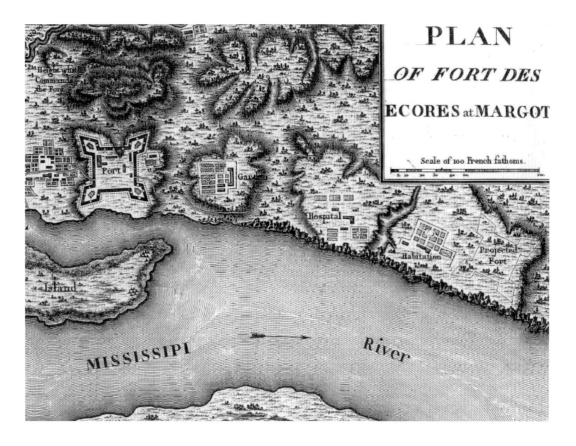

PLAN OF FORT DES ECORES at MARGOT

Scale of 100 French fathoms.

MISSISSIPI River

Left: During the wars of the French Revolution, French General Victor Callot descended the Mississippi River and drew a very detailed map of the Fort San Fernando settlement in 1796. Fort San Fernando was the beginning of permanent white settlement in Shelby County.

Below: The Chickasaw who most forcefully supported American designs on the Fourth Chickasaw Bluff was Piomingo (Mountain Leader). Because of Piomingo's role in getting Chickasaw acceptance of an American fort on the site, Samuel Cole Williams said of him, "Historic Justice will not be done until in Memphis there stands a statue of the great chief of the Chickasaws, Piomingo." In 1983, First Tennessee Bank commissioned Roy Tamboli to create a statue honoring that great chief.

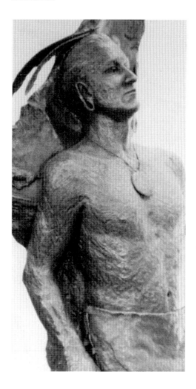

Indians, the Chickasaws and Choctaws, that inhabited the southern [probably should read northern] part of Mississippi and Alabama. This trade was valuable and there was a considerable struggle between the three houses for it.

The Indians came in caravans, with their ponies well packed with cow-hides, deerskins, beaver, bear and otter, and an innumerable quantity of coon-skins, which were exchanged for blankets, striped domestics (cloth yard-goods), tobacco, whisky, &c. Railroads, nor even country roads were known in that day. They [the Indians] traveled a path in single file through the wilderness.

In writing about a nation or tribes that have no history, we can only write from personal observation. The Chickasaws and Choctaws, in their primeval condition, were a happy set in their way. Their wants were but few, and a support was easily made. Nature had bountifully provided for them—the country abounded in game, such as they thought the Great Spirit had provided especially for their use. It was part of their means to supply their families with meat.

When they [the braves] started hunting they provided themselves with a little bag of "tomfuller," as they called it. It was parched corn, gritted into meal—a spoonful or two put into a tin cup, with a little sugar and water, made a very palatable beverage. A small bag, that they could stick under their belt[s], would last them a week.

By their [Indian] laws, they were entitled to as many wives as they could support. Good hunters generally had three or four wives. It was their business to do the housework and cultivate ground sufficient for the support of the family. Their cultivated patches were generally small and their products principally consisted of pumpkins, corn, beans, potatoes, with a small orchard consisting of peaches and plums; the women got along happily together—hardly ever disagreed; the men supplied them with meat, such as bear, venison, turkey, &c. There was nothing to interrupt their happiness as they said, until they became acquainted with white men.

Although, as a nation, they were treacherous and thievish, some were high-minded and honorable, proud and remarkably fond of dress. There is a great similarity of dress pertaining to all the different tribes of Indians. The leggings and moccasins worn by them, were manufactured by themselves. They

Isaac Rawlings

dressed in the skin of a deer, cut out the leggings in proper shape and sewed up with the sinews taken from the deer. In the same way were made the moccasins worn upon their feet—the [upper] body was always covered by a blanket.

There were among them some very ingenious workmen in brass and silver. Large silver ear-rings were worn in the ears and nose, and silver bands around their wrists. Some of these ornaments were curiously carved in the shape of eagles, owls, serpents, &c.

At a later point in the *Record*, a guest editorial, also attributed in a penciled note in the text to J. J. Rawlings, offers further information on "The Aborigines of the County: the Chickasaws and Choctaws." It reads:

Messrs, Editors:

In a former article published in your valuable little monthly, (January number) I expressed the opinion that it was best that these people moved west to a country better adapted to their nature, as no country can ever change the nature of an Indian, never.

When these people [the Chickasaws and Choctaws] were first discovered, they were complete children of nature; they knew nothing about the arts and sciences of more civilized countries. Their own native ingenuity invented the bow and arrow, which they used with great precision. They would hit a copper cent oftener than miss it at thirty or forty paces. When using the bow for hunting large game they used a bearded [barbed] arrow, and when once struck into a bear or deer it could not be pulled out, so they would capture the game with their dogs, of which they always had innumerable quantities.

They next became acquainted with the old flint-lock rifle, which they considered a great improvement over the bow and arrow. The first was probably presented to them by the first discoverers of the country. They learned the use of the rifle to great perfection—let it miss fire or snap as it would, they held it with a steady hand that carried death to its victim. Then came the percussion cap, which they valued highly as a great improvement on the old flintlock.

During the time these vast improvements were going on, Civilization was doing its work. They were becoming surrounded by a different class of people; the encroachments were daily increasing. They at first resisted these encroachments of the whites—but to no purpose; it was destined to accomplish its work; the progress of one nation was the destruction of another. They could not readily account for the effects that circumstances were producing. Game of all kinds was gradually disappearing; their hunting grounds were contracted. They would ask among themselves— 'Why is it that deer are so scarce in the hills? Why is it that [there are] no bear in the jungles?

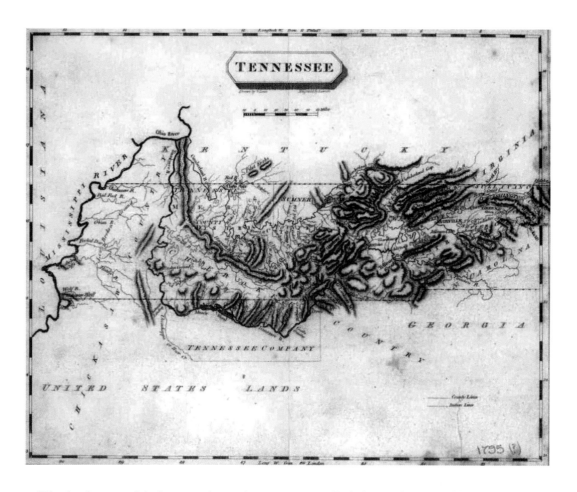

✧

Left: In 1797, the Spanish abandoned Fort San Fernando and moved their garrison across the Mississippi River to Hopefield Point. West Tennessee was then claimed by the newly admitted State of Tennessee, but still controlled by the Chickasaw Indians until 1818. The state's acquisition of West Tennessee is often called the Chickasaw Cession or the Jackson Purchase.

COURTESY OF SPECIAL COLLECTIONS,
UNIVERSITY OF MEMPHIS LIBRARIES.

Below: Marcus B. Winchester was the son of General James Winchester, one of the Memphis proprietors. M. B. Winchester was agent for the proprietors, merchant, postmaster, and the first mayor of Memphis.

COURTESY OF MEMPHIS & SHELBY COUNTY ROOM,
MEMPHIS PUBLIC LIBRARY & INFORMATION CENTER.

What has become of the beaver and otter that once abounded in our streams?' Exclaiming also: 'Our country is changing; it is fast becoming unfit for our habitation.'

Ah, and changed it has! You can imagine a poor lonely squaw, thinly dressed, barefooted, on a cold, bleak evening, with her little "pushcush" (a baby) upon her back, (probably not a fortnight old), treading a lonely path about two feet wide, hunting the camp-fire that the men have gone ahead to prepare. That camp-fire was on this bluff, where now stands large three and four story brick houses, groaning under the weight of supplies for a civilized people. Near by that little two [foot] path now runs a locomotive at twenty miles an hour; mysterious change that has occurred in my own time, and under my personal observation.

Civilization was the bane of these poor people. They had discovered its effects before they consented to move. The introduction of whisky at once carried many a one to another country—where they had no use for the bow and arrow—the old flint-lock, nor the percussion cap.

Early impressions are said to be the most lasting. When but a boy I was intimately associated with those people for five years. I had partially learned their language, studied their character, and become possessed in their favor. Their move to the West I think was best for them, and I hope they [are] doing well and prospering as a nation.

Your little volume professes to be devoted to historical facts and incidents pertaining to (old times in) Shelby County, I will avail myself of the opportunity to relate one or two incidents that nobody but myself knows.

When I first landed on this bluff, my preceptor had in his employ an interpreter by the name of Measels—Jack Measels. He was a half-breed Cherokee, but spoke the Chickasaw and Choctaw languages. Jack was a very stout robust man and weighed about two hundred pounds. He frequently boasted about his aquatic performances and proposed to bet

M. B. Winchester

✧

Above: This sketch shows an Indian coming in peace to a Tennessee settlement in order to trade what looks like an animal pelt. He seems to be received in peace as well.

COURTESY OF SPECIAL COLLECTIONS, UNIVERSITY OF MEMPHIS LIBRARIES.

Right: Over recent decades, the Chucalissa Indian Village and Archeological Museum has hosted many gatherings of Native Americans. In this shot, modern Indians are demonstrating their mastery of traditional crafts. The man is making arrowheads and the woman is grinding corn by hand.

COURTESY OF SPECIAL COLLECTIONS, UNIVERSITY OF MEMPHIS LIBRARIES.

HISTORIC SHELBY COUNTY

one hundred dollars that he could swim the Mississippi River at high tide. The boys soon made up the hundred dollars, though Jack had nothing to put up against it. When the river became very full, the time arrived for Jack to win or lose his bet. He crossed the river in a skiff, jumped off at Foy's Point (the present railroad landing) and landed at Fort Pickering, thus winning the bet and pocketing the hundred dollars—more money than he ever had had at one time before. I have never known the feat to be repeated.

In 1824, while at breakfast one Sunday morning, I was aroused by a noise, whooping, hallooing. I ran out to see what was the matter. A huge bear was making his way through town, and all the boys, black and white, dogs and terriers were after him. Old Paddy Meagher lived in a log house on the bluff. Old Paddy had two awful curs, that he kept chained in the day and turned loose at night, much to the terror of us boys who gave his premises a wide berth after [dark]. Old Paddy thought his two dogs could capture anything in the shape of an animal.

As the bear approached his house he turned loose his dogs. They had not learned the strategy of fighting a bear and, naturally they

seized him by the throat and ears. With one lick of his paw the bear cut one nearly in two, killing him immediately and wounded the other so badly that he died in a few days. [This was] much to the chagrin of old Paddy, but very gratifying to us boys, who thought we could now pay an evenings visit to his daughter Sally, unmolested by those infernal dogs.

The bear made his way through town, and just at the water's edge, Henry James shot him in the head with a rifle. He was butchered and divided out among the people of the village. All had bear [meat] enough and to spare.

Since his remarks were read to his fellow Shelby County residents, there is no reason to suppose that Mr. Rawling's descriptions are other than accurate or that his sentiments were other than typical. If so, then early Shelby Countians' attitudes regarding American Indians remained ambivalent, even conflicted, well into the nineteenth century. Like Jefferson and Jackson, Rawlings, who had lived among the Indians and sympathized with them, could think of no less horrendous response to the conflict between European and native cultures than to induce or force the Indians to move further west. Ultimately, this is what was done.

Left: Davy Crockett never lived in Shelby County, but he did represent its citizens in the U.S. Congress. Thus, he was in and out of Memphis with some frequency prior to leaving for Texas and death at the Alamo. There is also a strong possibility that he hunted into this area before the Chickasaw Cession.

COURTESY OF FIRST TENNESSEE HERITAGE COLLECTION.

Below: This 1775 sketch of a "Characteristick Chicasaw Head" depicts an unidentified warrior from before either the Spaniards or the Americans became a serious problem for the tribe.

FROM THE MUSEUM D'HISTORIE NATURELLE, LE HAVRE, FRANCE.

CHAPTER II:

THE CREATION AND COURSE OF
SHELBY COUNTY GOVERNMENT

In the wake of the Chickasaw Cession, settlers and speculators streamed into West Tennessee, many into the area at or near the Fourth Chickasaw Bluff. Speculators especially desired to advance the value of their properties by the quick establishment of county government, which would provide law, order, and other administrative services in the newly opened lands. Proprietors of the Rice grant provided a sample petition for residents at the Bluff to circulate for signatures and forward to the state legislature for its action. In the early 1980s, Shelby Countian Annice Bolton rediscovered the badly deteriorated original petition in the holdings of the Tennessee State Library and Archives (doc. #69-1812). She sent a copy to the Shelby County Archivist, who transcribed the document and published it with commentary in the *West Tennessee Historical Society Papers*, 37 (1983) pp. 96-102. The petition's signatures identify many of the county's earliest settlers. Their plea reads in part:

To the Legislature of the State of Tennessee Your petitioners beg leave Respectfully to show, that the only Settlement of consequence in the purchase of the Chickasaws south of the Tennessee River is at the Bluff and in its neighborhood. That the said petitioners conceive, and beg leave to represent to your Honorable Body, that most of them have emigrated latterly, from other parts, and selected the State of Tennessee, distinguished for the freedom of her laws, and bravery and patriotism of her people as their place of residence. To be a citizen of such a State is real cause of exultation, but this feeling is somewhat diminished in its enjoyment by the situation in which your petitioners find themselves. Some convenient Judicial Tribunal to settle their disputes, is a right that they claim of your Honorable Body, as due to freemen, and as an attribute to civilized Society. Reynoldsburg is the nearest Court of Justice and that is [150] miles from them, without a road, bridges or ferries across Water courses. They [residents] now have considerable trade disagreements and disputes, which could easily be corrected by a Court of Justice convenient to their homes, and to be obliged to attend Court at a distance through such country as that in which they live at present, they believe is tantamount to a denial of Justice which the Constitution secures to each citizen of the State of Tennessee. They therefore pray your Honorable Body's creating of a County Beginning, on the Mississippi where the Southern [state] boundary line strikes the same thence East along the line and up [missing text] as your Honorable Body may please to direct but your petitioners suggest the following bounds, which would [missing text] to all, and to which, they respectfully hope, there can be no objection, viz: Beginning on said river as above thence East along the Southern boundary of the state thirty miles to the 80 mile tree on said line, thence north twenty five miles, thence West to intersect the Mississippi River thence down with the meanders of said river to the beginning, containing six hundred and twenty five square miles as contemplated in the Constitution, which will more fully appear by the annexed plat.

And your petitioners pray that the place of holding Court should be fixed at the Bluff until the next or any subsequent Legislature, when such order, as the Legislature may think proper, may be taken thereon—

And your Petitioners will ever Pray

There follow about seventy signatures that correspond closely to the names appearing on the 1820 census for Shelby County. The legislature responded to the settlers' petition quickly and favorably. Its act of November 24, 1819 established the new county wording the act nearly verbatim as requested by the petitioners. The legislature named the county for Isaac Shelby, decreed that the General Assembly appoint five justices to administer the county government,

❖

Most of the earliest settlers to stop at the Fourth Chickasaw Bluff came by water, as illustrated by the often-reproduced painting of the Jolly Flat Boatmen*. In addition to settlers who had been present prior to the Chickasaw Cession, others stopped when they heard that West Tennessee would soon be opened to settlement.*

COURTESY OF FIRST TENNESSEE HERITAGE COLLECTION.

❖

Above: General Isaac Shelby was a hero of the Revolutionary War and the first Governor of Kentucky. He and Andrew Jackson negotiated the Chickasaw Treaty of 1818, purchasing Western Kentucky and West Tennessee from the Chickasaws. In 1819, the State Legislature named the first county completely in West Tennessee in Shelby's honor.

COURTESY OF THE LIBRARY OF CONGRESS.

Right: This manuscript is the deed to very early North Carolina land grant in what became Shelby County. The 5000-acre grant on the banks of the north fork of the Looshatchie River was to one Samuel Harris. It adjoined the properties of John M. Alexander and Robert Goodloe, respectively. The grant was probably made before Shelby County was organized, since the name of the county was left blank.

COURTESY OF SHELBY COUNTY ARCHIVES.

made provisions for the organization of a militia unit to be attached to the state's fifth brigade, and ordered the appointment of a solicitor to act as attorney general until one could be appointed for the circuit.

Pursuant to this act, the first meeting of the Shelby County Court of Pleas and Quarterly Sessions convened on May 1, 1820, and, with the appointment of its officials, the new government began functioning immediately. Unlike state and national governments, there was little separation of powers within the county's ruling structure. The magistrates (or justices, or squires) held virtually all legislative, administrative, and judicial authority within the locale. Prior to 1911, except for a brief Reconstruction era experiment, the Shelby County Court of Quarterly Pleas and Sessions controlled all aspects of county government until the E. H. Crump reformers prevailed on the state legislature to restructure same in 1911. From that date until 1974, power was rather ambiguously shared between the County Court and a three-member County Commission. For most of that time, however, the Crump-led political organization made virtually all of the important decisions for governing Shelby County. From 1954 to 1976, without direction from "the machine," the complicated and conflicting divisions of powers made for considerable contention and inefficiency. In 1976, the state legislature and a local referendum restructured county government again, providing for a mayor and a legislative body initially still called the County Court. Soon after restructuring, the name for the new legislature was changed to the Shelby County Commission.

During the early nineteenth century, the county court, or its subordinates, handled all local governmental affairs. Its members (often called squires or magistrates) set the tax rate, appointed all other county officials, including the sheriff and constable, and sat jointly as a court in important cases, while the individual members also held law enforcement and minor judicial authority as justices of the peace. The number of justices fluctuated significantly over the decades, at the will of the state legislature. Their appointments were "during good behavior," meaning most were de facto lifetime appointments. Thus, by the early twentieth century, the sheer number of members had become unwieldy. Moreover, since each of the justices exercised authority county-wide, some used it capriciously and at times corruptly, pinching people for minor infractions and fining them on the spot.

Beginning in 1821, the Shelby County Court began the practice of delegating some of its authority to a "quorum court." Since the legislation creating the county provided that three (of the then five) justices comprised a quorum for the court, the justices soon institutionalized electing three of its

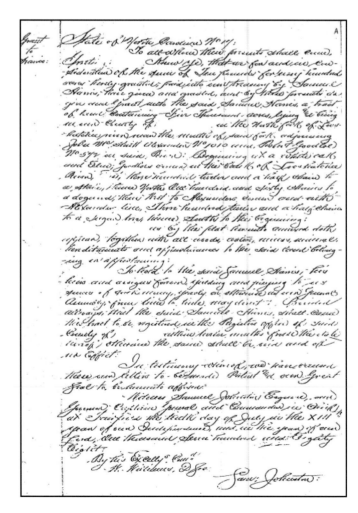

members to act as a sort of executive committee in handling routine county business. Justices not part of the quorum court could take part in its activities if they liked. This arrangement was officially recognized by the state in 1827. In time, the quorum court's functions became almost purely judicial, and the full county court continued to handle legislative and administrative affairs. As the county grew, the legislature established various other courts. This eroded the judicial authority of the county court. Moreover, the Tennessee Constitution of 1834 made local government more democratic by making most of the county offices—heretofore appointed by the court—elective offices.

During the legal and governmental confusion caused by the Civil War and Reconstruction, a county judge replaced the quorum court. Although the latter was restored in 1869, the office of county judge was not abolished until 1875, when the county court's chairman then took over the

judge's remaining functions. Toward the end of Reconstruction in Tennessee, 1868-69, radical Republicans had instituted an appointive, commission-structure of governance for Shelby County. With the return of "home rule" to Tennessee, the Democrats restored the county court system. During the span between 1820 and 1911, municipal governments also encroached on some of the powers and responsibilities of county government.

In 1911, the Crump-led faction of Shelby County Democrats prevailed on the Tennessee General Assembly to restructure their county's government. They patterned their restructured county government after that of the Memphis Commission Government, which the legislature had created only two years earlier. A three-member Shelby County Commission acted as a plural executive. From among themselves they chose their chairman and divided up the duties of administration. The quarterly court, greatly reduced in numbers and more

✧

Early Shelby County courthouses were pretty primitive, with the first one costing only $125.00. After the county seat was returned to Memphis following the Civil War, the impressive Overton Hotel became the home of Memphis and Shelby County governments until around 1910. It stood on the north side of Poplar and west of Main Street, where Ellis Auditorium later stood.

proportionally representative in nature, continued as the legislative branch of county government and controlled appropriations and the tax rate. It, too, elected its chairman, who thereupon had considerably more power than the other members.

The Crump faction had overcome bitter emotional resistance to adopting a commission form of government for Memphis in 1909. Their success made it less difficult to push through the restructuring of Shelby County in 1911, which reduced the power and redistricted the authority of county justices of the peace. The popularity of commission government had been on the rise during the Progressive Era, and influencing it would be much simpler than trying to control fifty or more members of the county court. The inherent contradictions in the new power sharing remained muted through the Crump Era, because the machine generally kept the commission and the court operating in harmony.

Crump outlived many of his key lieutenants, and, toward the end of his life, he had started believing much of his own mythmaking. The 1948 election was a harbinger of change. In that year, Crump's candidates for senator, governor, and president lost statewide. Moreover, the impressively one-sided tallies throughout Shelby County were also eroded. Upon Crump's death in 1954, many of his appointee officials continued to hold office, but they no longer acted in concert nor did they show much of their previous effectiveness. Moreover, younger, post-World War II reformers, many of them veterans of that war against arbitrary rule, wanted their day in the sun.

Some of the postwar reformers challenged the Crump holdovers with a degree of success unknown for nearly half a century. Reform currents in the air would mean a restructured Memphis Municipal Government by 1968 and a similar fate for Shelby County Government by the mid-1970s. Not only did

❖

In the late 1860s, Shelby County erected one of the most modern, innovative, and expensive prisons of its era. It stood at the corner of Front Street and Auction, and its 80 cells could house 350 prisoners. Referred to as an early "glamour slammer," its amenities included steam heating, an exercise yard, bathhouses, a washroom, and a bakery. It cost $281,209.88, which may reflect graft under Reconstruction rule.

disharmony between commission and court impede the effectiveness of county government, but there was a national trend to make county governments more efficient by vesting executive authority in a county mayor or a county manager. A significant number of reformers also wanted to consolidate city and county governments into a "metro system" like Nashville-Davidson in Tennessee and Jacksonville in Florida.

In the immediate post-Crump era, Memphis City Government sometimes seemed badly hobbled. The mayor and four other commissioners were elected at large.

The mayor was charged with administration and finance, but had no more actual political power than any of the other four commissioners. Each of the commissioners had legislative duties when the commission met as a group, but each of them also had the full-time job of managing divisions (such as Fire and Police) of government individually. In the 1955 municipal election, Memphians elected Edmund Orgill as mayor and Henry Loeb to the city commission. However, the voters also reelected three of the Crump organization's men to the commission. This majority assigned Loeb the Department of

✧

Above: By the 1920s, growth meant that the Courthouse no longer could house all of the county's law enforcement needs. In response, the county erected the Shelby County Criminal Courts and Jail Building at 150 Washington. Closed for a number of years after the Criminal Justice Center was completed, the building has been brought up to code and restored. It houses operations of the County Court Clerk and the Shelby County Archives, under the County Registrar.
COURTESY OF SHELBY COUNTY ARCHIVES.

Below: The Shelby County Office Building at 157 Poplar Avenue, just north of the county Criminal Courts Building, is a post World War II expansion. Its architecture shows a sharp departure from the classical elements of the Court House and the Criminal Courts Buildings. It currently is used to convene jury pools and houses administrative offices.
COURTESY OF SHELBY COUNTY ARCHIVES.

Public Services once he was in office. Although Orgill and Loeb agreed on many issues, they were frequently out-voted by the Crump holdovers. Even in 1959, when Loeb became city mayor, he was frustrated at how difficult it was to get things done at city hall. Loeb's successor, former judge William B. Ingram, fared no better, and it seemed to many Memphians that change was sorely needed.

Heeding national trends, a core group of reformers wanted more professionalism in administration and greater citizen influence over legislative processes. They preferred a council-city manager form of government. However, after a four-year hiatus, Henry Loeb was reentering the political arena, and he would have none of it. Of course, Crump loyalists would fight to keep the commission form of government. Thus, Loeb's support for a restructured city charter seemed essential for its passage. Loeb, who had held the mayor's office when it was very weak under the commission system, wanted sweeping mayoral powers. He got his way, and the new city charter fixed absolute power to contract for the city in the hands of the mayor. But Loeb had little chance to set precedents under the new structure. Just weeks after he and the new city council took office, the city's sanitation workers went out on a wildcat strike. Such a strike was illegal under Tennessee law. Perspectives on the strike divided the races

bitterly, especially after the murder of Martin Luther King, Jr.

The changes in Memphis' government were important countywide, because the progressive elements were still hoping and working for consolidation of city and county governments. Ultimately, three referenda were held, and the initiative failed in each instance. On the second effort, a majority of Shelby Countians voted to consolidate. However, a provision of the state constitution required a majority vote in both the major city and in the areas outside that city. In this instance, a majority of residents outside the city voted no. This constitutional wrinkle had been the handiwork of Ellen Davies Rodgers. Mrs. Rodgers, owning a significant plantation near Brunswick, had been an ardent Crump supporter, and she was an equally ardent advocate for rural Shelby Countians. She wanted to ensure that rural interests would not be subordinated to urban needs, and she prevailed.

In an effort to make the city and county governmental systems more compatible and to facilitate consolidation at some point in the future, the reformers made the new county government as parallel to the city government as they could. Commission Chairman Jack Ramsay and his fellow commissioners supported the new structure for county government, as, ultimately, did the county court chairman, Charles W. Baker.

Paralleling the structures of Memphis and Shelby County governments did not achieve consolidation. Several considerations have defeated all further efforts at consolidation well into the twenty-first century. These include, but are not limited to, economics, demographics, and perceptions of the relative effectiveness of the Memphis City Schools

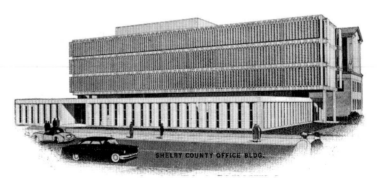

versus the Shelby County Schools. Initially, Memphis' African-American leaders were opposed to consolidation and blanket annexations because those measures would dilute their growing numbers and accompanying political power. Most individuals living outside of Memphis, including those in the county's other municipalities, did not want to be brought under city control because it would mean higher property and sales taxes for them. Finally, with forced busing to achieve racial balances in the city school system, county residents did not want to have their children attend schools that they viewed as markedly inferior and much more dangerous. In an ironic twist, with shifting demographics, African Americans became the majority ethnic group in both city and county. Once consolidation would no longer postpone black control of local governments, black leaders wanted to annex and/or consolidate with outlying areas. Many blacks also wanted consolidation of the two school systems, since county schools consistently got much higher ratings for academic effectiveness.

As of this writing, consolidation of governments and/or school systems has not taken place. However, in efforts to cut costs, many other functions of city and county government have been consolidated or merged. Such agencies include Planning and Development, and aspects of the Criminal Justice system, and the Juvenile Court system,

Left: As chairman of the three-member County Commission, Jack Ramsay led the transition from Crump holdovers to rule by a reform element. He fought for consolidation of city and county governments in the interest of efficiency. When that failed, he lent his support to restructuring county government to parallel that of Memphis' Municipal government. The contention that parallel governments would facilitate consolidation has not yet born fruit.

COURTESY OF SPECIAL COLLECTIONS, UNIVERSITY OF MEMPHIS LIBRARIES.

Below: Henry Loeb campaigned strenuously for the office of mayor of Memphis in 1959 and 1967 and won both times. He insisted on a strong mayor-council structure when the city's government was revamped. Within weeks after his new administration took office under its new charter, the sanitation workers initiated a wildcat strike. James Earl Ray stalked Rev. Martin Luther King, Jr., and killed him when he came to Memphis to support the garbage strike.

COURTESY OF SPECIAL COLLECTIONS, UNIVERSITY OF MEMPHIS LIBRARIES.

✧

Right: In the post-Crump era, Jack Ramsay, Bruce Jordan, and Dan Mitchell ran a coordinated campaign to reform county government. They worked for consolidation and other avenues to build efficiency at the local level. Failing to get consolidated government, they did get voter approval to restructure county government. With a county mayor as chief executive and a commission as the legislative body, the new government also got "home rule."

COURTESY OF SPECIAL COLLECTIONS, UNIVERSITY OF MEMPHIS LIBRARIES.

Below: Ellen Davies Rodgers was a social powerhouse and a political force to be reckoned with. Operating from her large plantation east of Bartlett, she had been a stalwart of the Crump organization. Unlike most other Crump supporters, she did not lose her clout with the machine's demise. She had a state constitutional convention pass a measure that has effectively stopped consolidation so far.

COURTESY OF SPECIAL COLLECTIONS, UNIVERSITY OF MEMPHIS LIBRARIES.

among others. In yet another reversal of trends, however, some of the previously been under taken departmental consolidations

have begun breaking down. For instance, public libraries in the outlying Shelby County cities and towns have withdrawn from the consolidated Memphis/Shelby County library system. Also, the Memphis Police Department has unilaterally withdrawn from some of its consolidated functions working with the Shelby County Sheriff's Department. It remains to be seen whether centrifugal or centripetal forces will prevail.

Until recently, observers and critics have painted the proposed merger of local governments as a near panacea for solving most of the area's problems. In February 2007, however, Tom Jones (former public affairs officer for Shelby County and currently an associate for the syndicated radio program "Smart City") published a feature in *Memphis* magazine challenging that bit of conventional wisdom. He stated flatly that "Merging city and county governments won't fix anything. Other cities figured that out years ago."

ROSTER OF SHELBY COUNTY'S SHERIFFS
1820-2007

NAME	DATES SERVED		
Major Thos. Taylor	May 1-2, 1820	Mike Tate	1916-1918
Col. Samuel R. Brown	1820-1828	(brother of Galen Tate)	
Joseph Graham	1828-1830	Oliver H. Perry, Sr.	1918-1924
John K. Balch	1830-1836	(died in office)	
John Fowler	1836-1842	W. S. Knight	1924-1930
(1st elected directly by the voters)		(filled Perry's term)	
L. P. Hardaway	1842-1846	Col. W. J. Bacon	1930-1936
J. B. Morsley	1846-1852	Guy E. Joyner	1936-1942
W. D. Gilmore	1852-1856	Oliver H. Perry, Jr.	1942-1948
James E. Felts	1856-1858	(son of O. H. Perry, Sr.)	
Robert L. Smith	1858-1860	James E. Thompson	1948-1954
James E. Felts	1860-1864	Edward H. Reeves	1954-1958
P. M. Winters	1864-1868	(died in office)	
A. P. Curry	1868-1870	Dr. J. R. Teabeaut	1958
Marcus J. Wright	1870-1872	(Coroner, acting Sheriff)	
W. J. P. Doyle	1872-1874	M. A. Hinds	1958-1964
C. L. Anderson	1874-1878	William N. Morris	1964-1970
(died of yellow fever)		Roy C. Nixon	1970-1975
E. L. McGowan	1878-1880	(became County Mayor)	
(filled Anderson's term)		James Rout, Jr.	1976
Phil R. Athy	1880-1884	(Coroner, acting Sheriff)	
(died in office)		Billy Ray Schilling	1976
W. D. Cannon	1884-1888	(filled Nixon's term)	
(filled Athy's term)		Eugene Barksdale	1976-1986
A. J. McClendon	1888-1894	Jack Owens	1986-1990
J. A. McCarver	1894-1896	(died in office)	
W. W. Carnes	1896-1898	Otis Higgs	1990
G. W. Blackwell	1898-1904	(filled Owens' term)	
F. L. Monteverde	1904-1910	A. C. Gillis	1990-2002
T. Galen Tate	1910-1914	Mark Luttrell	2002—present
John Reichman	1914-1916		
(write-in Crump candidate)			

Roy C. Nixon (top, left), William N. Morris, Jr. (top, right), and Jim Rout, Jr. (bottom, left) each served as mayors of the new county government. Nixon and Morris had each previously served the six-year-limit as sheriff. Rout had served many years on the County Commission and very briefly as acting sheriff when he was coroner. Former Public Defender A. C. Wharton (bottom, right) was elected Shelby County Mayor in 2002 and reelected in 2006, with strong biracial support.

NIXON, MORRIS, AND ROUT PHOTOS COURTESY OF MEMPHIS & SHELBY COUNTY ROOM, MEMPHIS PUBLIC LIBRARY & INFORMATION CENTER. WHARTON PHOTO COURTESY OF SHELBY COUNTY GOVERNMENT.

Arguing that most discussion of the matter generated more myths than facts, he mustered a few sobering facts himself. Jones's analysis points out that only 35 of America's 3,141 counties have consolidated into "metro governments" with their primary cities. Moreover, only nine of the nation's 100 largest cities have merged their city and county governments. In Tennessee, of twenty referenda to create metro governments since 1958, only three have passed. Nashville/Davidson has been the only major urban center to do so, with the other three largest cities rejecting consolidation in multiple referenda. Although many Nashvillians sang the praises of their consolidation a quarter century ago, some are now much less enthusiastic about having taken that step.

A final irony rests in a commonly held perception that, under the Crump regime, Memphis had had de facto consolidation for most of the early twentieth century. The same group of people, irrespective of whether they held office, made the decisions for both city and county governments. For all of their obvious cronyism and use of intimidation, they did provide relatively inexpensive, honest, and efficient local government services.

✧

Above: This bucolic vista was the site of the Shelby County Poor Farm and Insane Hospital in the early twentieth century. It was displaced in the early 1930s by facilities at the Shelby County Penal Farm further east on Summer Avenue, near Macon Road.

Left: The Ellis Auditorium, built in the 1920s and shown here, provided the Mid-South area's principal venue for major civic and entertainment events. It was located at the northwest cornor of Poplar and Main, on the site once occupied by the Overton Hotel and now housing the Cannon Center for the Preforming Arts.

✧

Right: Shelby County Board of Commissioners, 1982-83. Seated left to right: Mike Tooley, Carolyn H. Gates, Pete Sisson (Chairman), Julian T. Bolton, and Walter Lee Bailey, Jr. Standing: Vasco A. Smith, Jesse H. Turner, Sr., Jim Rout (later Shelby County Mayor), Ed Williams (later Shelby County Historian), Clair D. VanderSchaaf, and Charles R. Perkins.

COURTESY OF MEMPHIS & SHELBY COUNTY ROOM,
MEMPHIS PUBLIC LIBRARY & INFORMATION CENTER.

Below: City and county courts and law enforcement agencies occupied the Criminal Justice Complex in the early 1980s. Of course, law enforcement has been one of county government's major functions since its inception. This building largely brought city and county prisoners and courts under one roof, replacing Memphis Police Central and the County Criminal Courts Building.

COURTESY OF SPECIAL COLLECTIONS,
UNIVERSITY OF MEMPHIS LIBRARIES.

HISTORIC SHELBY COUNTY

28

Left: This aerial view of the Shelby County Penal Farm captures only a fraction of that facility's 5,000 acres. The penal farm was worked by the prisoners and was self-sustaining. It produced vegetables, staples, and milk and dairy products. Later, the farming operations were curtailed, and most of the property diverted to other purposes. Renamed Shelby Farms, it is the largest urban park in the United States, and it houses Agricenter International. The Agricenter has a diversity of missions.

COURTESY OF MEMPHIS & SHELBY COUNTY ROOM, MEMPHIS PUBLIC LIBRARY & INFORMATION CENTER.

Below: The Shelby County Penal Farm produced surpluses of agricultural products and sold them in competition with nearby truck farmers. This image shows prisoners with a cornucopia of produce. Their dairy herds produced high quality milk and cheeses. The prison facility at the penal farm is still operated by the Sheriff's Department.

COURTESY OF MEMPHIS & SHELBY COUNTY ROOM, MEMPHIS PUBLIC LIBRARY & INFORMATION CENTER.

CHAPTER II

Jno. Overton

J. Winchester

Andrew Jackson

CHAPTER III

When the county was established in 1819, the seat was temporarily set at the Fourth Chickasaw Bluff, soon to be the site of Memphis. Overton wanted the county seat to remain in Memphis and suggested that the county be formed in a triangular shape, which would have excluded much of the present county above the Wolf River. His partner, James Winchester, did not like the notion of the odd shape and objected to excluding the fertile lands in the northeast. He also expressed doubts that the legislature would support such an unorthodox configuration. Overton deferred, and the petition had gone to the legislature asking for a county with a roughly square shape. The county later had minor boundary adjustments, with more radical ones sometimes suggested. However, the only major adjustment to take place was the inclusion of a three and one-half mile wide strip of land across the bottom of the county, when an error that had been made in running the state boundary between Tennessee and Mississippi was corrected in the 1830s.

In the early 1820s, settlers streamed into Shelby County, occupying fertile lands and making homes and livelihoods for their families. In addition to the bluff settlement, there were two other settlements in the area that antedate the Chickasaw Cession: Big Creek (near present day Millington) and Egypt (a few miles south of Big Creek). Big Creek and Egypt, however, were sprawling groupings of farms, rather than towns. They were fairly densely populated, and their residents wanted the county seat to be much closer to them than the Memphis site.

Overton seemed to have won the seat for Memphis when he successfully lobbied the legislature to have a special commission decide on the site and have it confirmed by referendum within the county. He also had the legislature dispense with the customary clause requiring that the seat be located within three miles of the county's geographical center. A new act of 1824, however, superseded the one that Overton had maneuvered through passage. It empowered the commission members to place the county seat wherever they wanted it, with no popular election being held to confirm its location. Commission members went with tradition and placed the seat at the virtually uninhabited site of Sanderlin's Bluff, ten miles northeast of Memphis on the north bank of the Wolf River. By 1826, state commissioners laid out the site of the town, a courthouse was built, and the county court moved its sessions to Raleigh. Given the enormous influence of Jackson, Overton, and Winchester, it is a mystery why their interests did not prevail regarding this issue.

Their reasons in jockeying for the county seat were economically sound. Proximity for transacting legal business gave a town a great advantage for commerce and growth. Travel was difficult and isolated farmers generally tried to minimize it. As a matter of convenience, they often conducted their personal business wherever they had to go to pursue legal matters. Accordingly, settlers bought what they needed and sold surplus crops or furs wherever was most convenient. Consequently, for at least a decade, Raleigh was a serious commercial and political rival to Memphis. During those years, the Wolf River was navigable as far upstream as Raleigh, making it a viable entrepot. Later, as the Wolf silted in and river craft became larger and steam driven, and as more roads were cut through the county, Raleigh became much less accessible than Memphis. In the 1840s, Memphis embarked on a growth spurt referred to as the "Boom Era." By the 1860s the growth of Memphis, including its railroads, so outmatched that of Raleigh that the county's political center followed the path of commerce and returned to the Bluff City. Although still not the geographical center of the county, Memphis had become its commercial and population center.

✧

John Overton, James Winchester, and Andrew Jackson were the proprietors of the 5,000-acre Rice grant at the time of the Chickasaw Cession. Overton was the most involved of the partners and worked at improving their land's value by establishing county government. James Winchester ran the survey between West Tennessee and the State of Mississippi and made a significant error in so doing. Andrew Jackson had negotiated the treaty with the Chickasaws and, although he only owned one-eighth of the grant at the time, was criticized for feathering his own nest.

ILLUSTRATIONS COURTESY OF MEMPHIS AND SHELBY ROOM, MEMPHIS PUBLIC LIBRARY AND INFORMATION CENTER.

County government's great functions in the nineteenth century, besides its policing and judicial roles, were its roles in transportation and education. Road building dominated the first half of the century; education later became perhaps the most important function of county administration.

Prior to the Civil War, there is little doubt that the most important administrative function of Shelby County Government was to enhance transportation, both within the county and in connecting local production and consumption with the broader commercial world. This early facilitating mainly consisted of cutting roads, building bridges, authorizing ferries and fords, and dredging navigable watercourses. The early County Quarterly Court minutes are saturated with county government's activities related to these enterprises. Slowly but increasingly, the county's arteries and capillaries of commerce evolved in largely synergistic and symbiotic ways.

When West Tennessee was opened for settlement, there were almost no tracks through the wilderness. There were a few Indian trails that followed previous buffalo trails along the ridgelines and formed natural transportation highways. Of course, rivers like the Mississippi, the Loosahatchie, the Wolf, and even some of the area's smaller streams were also used as routes of transportation. Federal roads were usually the most important, most heavily used, and best maintained. They often followed existing Indian trails and were planned for two major purposes: post roads and military roads. Relatively early, Memphis had three post roads converging on it from the east and the Little Rock Military Road leading west from the Arkansas shore opposite Memphis.

Next in importance were state roads, which were divided into three classes. The first class was a stage road, which was supposed to be bridged, causewayed, mile-marked, and well maintained. The second class of road was to be at least twelve-feet wide, also usable by wagons, with bridges and causeways as needed. Third class roads were mere horse trails, over which only persons on horseback or afoot could be sure of getting through. As additional lands were settled and nearby roads became more frequently used, many were eventually upgraded to the next class. In addition, there were private, toll-charging roadways meant to generate revenues and to add value to nearby lands. Although the state chartered a dozen or so turnpike companies to operate in Shelby County, only four of them ever qualified for state funding, and none of them succeeded financially. Some turnpike corporations seemed to have been created as swindles from the outset.

Within three years of its initial meeting, the Shelby County Court ordered the construction of three major roads to begin. They were to run east along the route of today's Poplar Avenue, north paralleling the Mississippi River to Irvine's Landing, and south toward the Chickasaw settlements of North Mississippi. Planned as second-class roads, road commissioners were to be paid $1.25 per day for locating and marking the roadways and were to furnish estimates on the costs of building bridges. They were also to suggest arrangements for licensing ferries across rivers and creeks. There persists a good bit of confusion regarding early road names and their locations. For example, the main road going eastward along today's Poplar and Poplar Pike corridor was variously known as the Pea Ridge Road, the State Line Road, the Alabama Road, and the Cherokee Trace.

Road making was a serious and expensive undertaking. Because of the levels of precipitation and the quality of the soil and terrain, West Tennessee was more

✧

Methods of road and railroad grading probably did not change much during the nineteenth century. Men and mules working in the Raleigh area about 1910 are removing stumps from the right of way for what would ultimately become Highway 51.

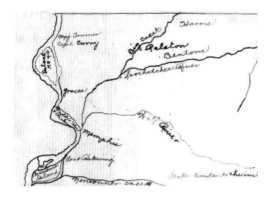

difficult to cut and maintain roads through than most of the rest of the state. Within Shelby County, low lying, swampy land created problems, as did rivers and creeks. A lack of rock for crushing to "macadamize" trail surfaces was a problem, and plank roads did not hold up as long as they did further east. A long debate ran over whether planks or crushed rock were more durable, but West Tennessee used little of either.

Planters and farmers had little use for roads except for a few times each year. Primarily they needed them for sending and receiving their mail and for transporting their harvests (generally cotton) to market. Consequently, they usually resisted using toll roads and helping to finance railroad building. Such roads as they did support were generally cut and maintained by the slaves of nearby property owners and others whose interests were presumably served by such road access. Even the best local roads were often impassable during the spring, but speed of transit was not often a high priority for the planter class.

Despite the numerous difficulties encountered, Shelby County developed an adequate road network. Many of the local roads connected into a state or federal road, a navigable waterway, or a railroad. As Eastern Arkansas drew more settlers and North Mississippi ousted its Indian population and welcomed more pioneers, too, Memphis and Shelby County expanded their trading hinterland. More trade required more roads, which in turn generated more production and trade in a generally expanding and synergistic cycle of growth. However prosaic road cutting and improvements may be, they were absolutely necessary for economic development to take place.

By 1826, Memphis was becoming an incipient trading center. That year, Fayette County planters shipped in 300 bales of cotton across its primitive roads. This $15,000 cargo demonstrated the value of early road building. Consequently, the Shelby County Court had three additional roads built toward Fayette County and one built due north toward Randolph on the Mississippi River. By 1843-44 teamsters were shipping 175,000 bales of cotton to Memphis, some of it coming from distances of up to 150 miles. Oxen drawn wagons traveled in trains of up to 200 vehicles and transported as many as 1,000 bales per train.

Railroads, with their station towns and stops, increasingly transported cotton, the mails, and trade goods to rural consumers. However, much of the growing commerce was marketed through Memphis. Understandably, prior to the Civil War, Tennessee began requiring its incorporated municipalities to maintain public roads within their own corporate limits. Although by the 1850s, Mid-South-area railroads increasingly displaced road borne overland shipments, numerous shorter roads and turnpikes connected the rails and river courses in expanding networks of transit and trade.

As Shelby Countians put in their road networks, primarily for reasons of economy and practicality, those same roads opened routes to churches, schools, country stores, and post offices. Naturally, rural folks gathered in such buildings for socializing, sharing local news and gossip and indulging in cultural pursuits. In the late nineteenth and early twentieth centuries, such socializing and community building was often less homespun and much more sophisticated and refined than one might expect.

Earlier in the nineteenth century, however, living was pretty primitive, as evidenced by an address at the Old Folks of Shelby County festival, September 11, 1872. President W. B. Waldran began his remarks by reiterating that the purposes of the organization of Shelby's Old Folks were

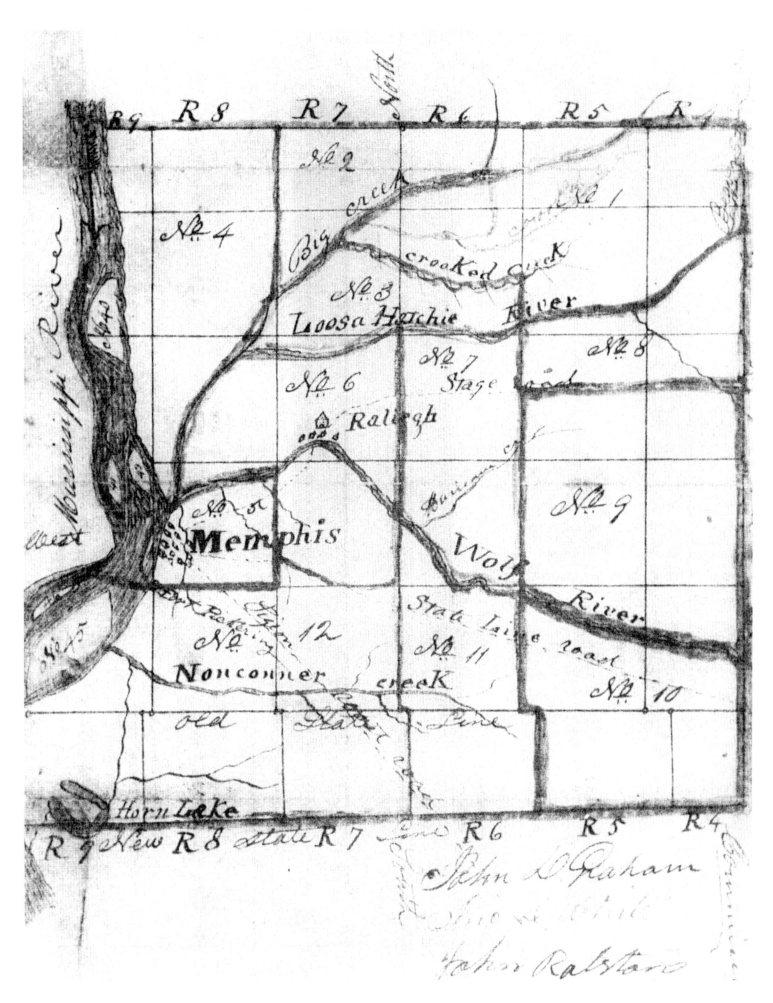

Right: Kirby Farm House is one of Shelby County's most historic properties. It has elements dating from the 1830s and stands facing south to Poplar Pike and the Memphis and Charleston Railroad tracks. The Walter Wills Family has completely restored the house to its appearance near the turn of the twentieth century. The Wills make it available to history and civic groups for their gatherings.

COURTESY OF WALTER D. WILLS, III.

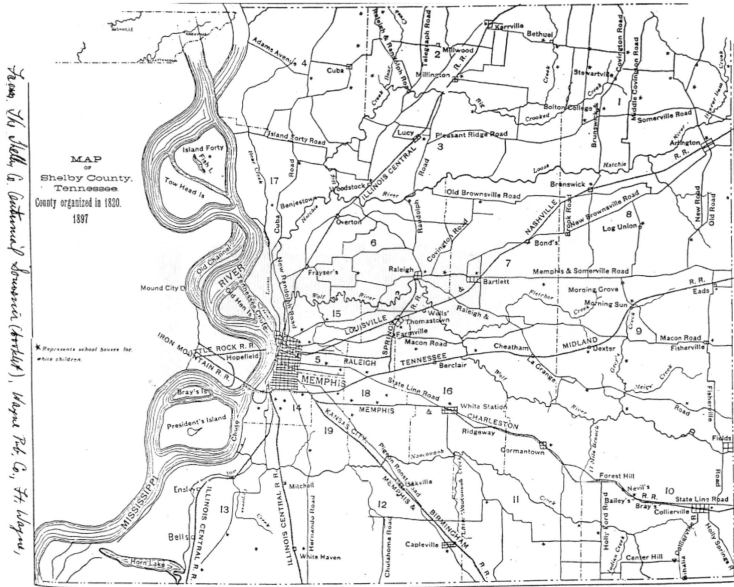

"the promotion of union and brotherhood, the advancement of the welfare of its members, mutual relief, and the collection of historical facts and incidents." He stressed that they never discussed subjects of religious or political nature, and that to qualify for membership, men must have resided in Shelby County for at least twenty years and exhibited sound moral character. Speaking without notes, but apparently having a copy of an early newspaper in hand, he plunged into his brief memoir.

His family had come overland through the wilderness in 1825, and, crossing the Tennessee River, they "saw but little sign of civilization—very few settlers. The whole country was heavily timbered. There were no hostile Indians," but they met with every other obstacle that greeted pioneers coming into Western Tennessee. They settled about ten miles northeast of the village of Memphis [at or near Raleigh], upon government land that had not been sectionized.

He continues,

In 1827 and 1828 the tide of immigration increased, but a very large portion of the new comers were very poor; many of them would have retreated but were not able, and it became with most of them a question of life and death, while they were unable to move away. They had to subdue the forest and bring it into cultivation before they had the promise of bread, and you who think the cutting down of the trees is bringing the land into cultivation should follow a shovel plow, with a jumping coulter, through a rooty, new piece of ground, to know what a virtue patience is. The killing of bear, deer and turkeys saved many a family from suffering; for all their supplies they had to draw on the Chickasaw Bluffs and to reach Memphis, only ten miles distant was no small job. Think for a moment. Surrounded by an unbroken forest, no roads, no bridges, no mills, no schoolhouses, no churches. There was but one wagon road to Memphis and that

✧

Scene at Cotton Gin, Memphis, Tenn.

a poor one, though it was called the Great Alabama and State Line Road [later Poplar/ Poplar Pike]. [Waldran neglects to note that in those earliest days, the Wolf River was easily navigable between Raleigh and Memphis. With settlement, its course became silted and blocked with sandbars and snags].

Memphis was a small town in 1827, the year the first newspaper was started here. What town there was lay well up toward the mouth of the Wolf River. The eleventh number of the first volume of the *Memphis Advocate and Western District Intelligencer* was published March 29, 1827, by Parran & Phoebus. It states: 'A town has been laid off by the owners of lands; they propose to sell the lots on accommodating credits to improvers. William

Lawrence and M. B. Winchester are the Agents.' It Contains Congressional news of the nineteenth Congress, and liberal extracts [what we would term plagiarism] of foreign news from Liverpool and London, which had just been received [via] the steamboat *General Carroll*... Among the advertisements we find the familiar names of Ro. Lawrence, Littleton, Henderson, Anderson B. Carr, Isaac Rawlings, M. B. Winchester, W. D. Ferguson, and F. A. & T. Young. It quoted the prices of cotton in New Orleans, ranging from seven to 14 cents per pound, depending on grade or class.

The town of Raleigh was laid out in 1827, and the road to Somerville through Raleigh, was cut out: soon after which James Brown &

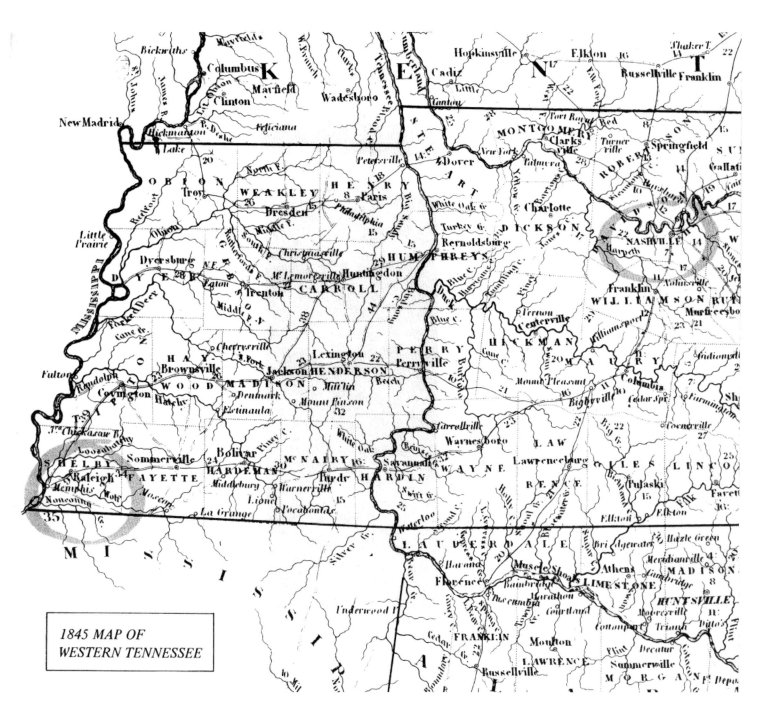

1845 MAP OF
WESTERN TENNESSEE

Co. started a line of four-horse post-coaches. This was a greater epoch in our history than the [1857] opening of the Memphis and Charleston Railroad was. [This contention was probably not universally shared].

In addition to the privations I have enumerated that the early settlers had to contend with, there were many others. Almost every one had the chills and fever; the whole country was infested with mosquitoes, buffalo gnats, and all manner of flies and snakes—all of which have well nigh passed away. I sometimes hear people complain of the few mosquitoes we now have in the spring of the

year, and I assure you that they are a small and very poor sample of what the early settlers had to contend with, and that without mosquito bars.

Now, ladies and gentlemen, from my YOUTHFUL APPEARANCE you must know that forty-seven years ago I was but an unlettered boy, and not competent to keep a record, even if I had had the facilities. It did not occur to us that we were 'making history,' or that anything we did was worth recording. Our common suffering made us 'wondrous kind.' It is refreshing to think of the universal hospitality of those days. Every man's house

✧

The distance across West Tennessee between the Tennessee and Mississippi Rivers is about a hundred miles as the crow flies. Waldran's family making that trek in the 1820s was indeed daring and daunting. This map shows the area in 1845, a generation after the Waldrans made their journey. Often folks came by water, down the Tennessee, Ohio and Mississippi Rivers.

was a free hotel to the full extent of his ability. They 'were careful to entertain strangers.' A man would take his horse from the plow, and ride around to help a newcomer select a home [site?]. They would walk miles to assist each other raise a house or roll logs; they were for years 'a law unto themselves;' they were moral, sober and industrious; there was no fighting or stealing.

Ladies, I would not have you think that all the privations and hardships fell upon the men; not so—the women of that day bore their full share, and the men were as much indebted to the women for success as they were to their own exertions; and there was less repining [low-spirited complaining] among women than among the men; and this we always find the case. The women have more hope than men; they will struggle longer and harder with difficulties than men will; they never abandon

a man or a cause because success is doubtful. Mark with what tenacity she clings to a profligate son or husband; no [matter] how abandoned he may be, she hopes on and works with him while there is breath in his body. This is a virtue a man does not possess in so eminent a degree.

To give you a faint idea of the trials endured by the women in the early history of this country, I will state that I have often seen them walk for miles to church and carry their shoes and stockings in their hands, and sit down on a log just before reaching the church and put them on; and in like manner, after they started home, they would take off and carry their shoes and stockings. This is but one item of the rigid economy it was necessary to practice in that day.

These things may appear to some of you extravagant. I refer you to Bro. Tom Davidson, who rode our circuit in 1826-7, and preached

in our economical [ecumenical?] churches, which consisted of 'brush arbors.' His circuit was about one hundred and fifty miles, along a bridle-path, and often no path, but through the woods, governed by his knowledge of the courses; still I never heard him complaining of hardships, or getting to a house or camp but

what he was welcome. It would interest you to hear him tell of the big camp-meetings. [These may not have been held in Shelby County]. They were confined to no class; old and young adults were subject to the 'jerks' without notice—it usually ran into dancing. I have seen a dozen jerking or dancing at a time at a

Above: Settlers coming into West Tennessee often sent a few of their menfolks over first. These hardies would girdle and clear trees, put in a crop on the land amid the stumps, and build a preliminary shelter. They would go back for wives and children the following spring. When they could, they expanded their land. Often they sold their "improved" land and moved on looking for greener pastures further west.

ILLUSTRATION COURTESY OF THE MEMPHIS PINK PALACE MUSEUM, DAPHNE F. HEWETT, ARTIST.

Left: Among the reasons that Shelby County's pioneers were so mutually supportive was the fact that they made everything nearly from scratch and doing so was extremely labor intensive. Just getting that first cabin assembled required shaping logs with broad axe or adze, hand sawing some of the logs into planks (also used for plank roads and turnpikes), and splitting shake shingles, barrel staves, clapboards, and rails for fencing with froes or wedges.

ILLUSTRATIONS COURTESY OF THE MEMPHIS PINK PALACE MUSEUM, DAPHNE F. HEWETT, ARTIST.

THE BROAD AXE
An essential tool on the frontier was the chisel-edged broad axe used for shaping round logs into square beams. A heavy leather apron was worn for protection.

PIT SAW
Until water or steam-powered sawmills were available on the frontier, all planks for house construction were made by using one or two-man pit saws.

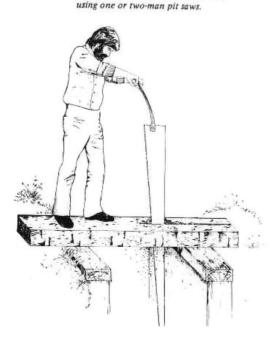

LAYING THE FLOOR
Wooden sills, squared by a broad axe, were laid on top of the stone foundation before installing the floor.

RAISING THE WALLS
A modified mortise and tenon version was common on the West Tennessee frontier where nails or pegs were used. It had no protruding ends and was easily clapboarded later.

✧

Creating that first cabin required an enormous amount of effort. Settlers had to choose a site, place stones for a foundation so the wood would not be directly on the ground, then put in joists and planking. Next, structural logs were notched together in the mortise and tenon fashion. After the structure was completed, openings were cut for door, fireplace, and, perhaps, windows. The logs were chinked and daubed, with a fireplace and chimney of clay-lined wood, initially. Often the initial structure was a single story with a loft above the main room. Generally, cabins were added to multiple times, stone or brick fireplaces and chimneys replaced the sticks, and the logs were clapboarded over. For example, the 1830s Magevney museum home at 198 Adams Avenue is a boarded-over log structure.

FROE, USED FOR MAKING SHINGLES
The froe was a knife-like wedge with a wooden handle used to split shingles, barrel staves and clapboards from a block of wood.

CARPENTER'S ADZE
A surface as flat and smooth as one made with a plane could be produced for "parlor beams" and other exposed surfaces by an adze in the hands of a skilled craftsman.

APPLYING ROOF SHINGLES
Roofs were built with a steep pitch for quick rain runoff and covered with split shingles between one and a half to three feet long.

FINISHING THE DOOR AND CHIMNEY
Door and fireplace openings were cut out of the walls of the cabin.

COMPLETED CABIN
The first chimney was usually built of sticks with a clay lining and replaced with brick or stone as soon as possible.

religious meeting. Young, bashful ladies would lose all self-control, and would jerk and throw themselves so that it would be necessary to hold and guard them; they would jerk forward and backward until sometimes their hair would pop like a carriage whip, and when they began to dance they closed their eyes and uttered not a word.

After Raleigh was laid out and made the county site [seat], the building of it up and opening of the courts was termed and thought to be progress in civilization. But with the sheriff, lawyers, and courts came court cases, drinking saloons, drunken men, fighting and all manner of evil communications; but, notwithstanding all this, Raleigh flourished until the grasping propensity of Memphis seized and moved all the courts; then Raleigh would have gone under but for the timely discovery of the health giving properties of its mineral springs, which have now acquired such a reputation as to promise to make it a wonderful resort—to accommodate which a narrow-gauge railroad is now being built, to connect Raleigh with Memphis.

I will not detain you by relating these trifling incidents, which were so indelibly fixed on my youthful mind. I have rehearsed them today, not so much to interest you as a

reproof to the WHINING and GRUMBLING of this heaven-favored people, who have come upon the stage after the generation has passed away which bore the heat and the burden of the day, and opened up every avenue of useful pursuit.

Having taken a bird's-eye view of this country in its wild or primitive state, and of Memphis in its INFANCY, let us consider some of the drawbacks it had to contend with in its CHILDHOOD, before the railroad era, and when steamboats were too scarce to accommodate the commerce of the Ohio and Mississippi Rivers; when flatboats were an important institution; when produce had to be removed when the water was up, and could not come regularly to market as it does now. For years it was not uncommon to see from fifteen hundred to two thousand of these water crafts laying at the landing at a time, reaching out from the shore four and five deep at certain seasons of the year. The great supply of produce over demand caused prices to rule low, and sometimes the crew would become frightened at the reports of yellow fever at New Orleans and refuse to go further, and cause the captain or owner to sell out for a song and take [the] first steamer for home. I have known of forced sales of flour at two and a half to three dollars per barrel; bulk pork,

✧

If anything, pioneer women generally worked harder than their men. They, too, had to make nearly everything from scratch. They planted and tended the kitchen garden, prepared and cooked the food, carded and spun fibers into thread or yarn, wove the cloth, made the clothes and washed them, etc. Truly, the men worked from sun up to sun down, but "women's work was never done." They also underwent multiple pregnancies, and reared the children who were born every two to three years. They probably needed social interaction more than the men, but usually got much less. Religious services and group activities like quilting bees furnished major exceptions to that generality.

ILLUSTRATIONS COURTESY OF THE MEMPHIS PINK PALACE MUSEUM, DAPHNE F. HEWETT, ARTIST.

two to three cents per pound; corn, ten to twelve cents per bushel; whisky, fourteen to sixteen cents per gallon; lard, two to three cents per pound, and all up-country produce at similar prices. Memphis in that day was much like it is now in one particular—it lacked capital; but very different in another particular;—there was almost universal confidence of man in man; almost anyone could get credit up to the time they began moving to Texas. It was then that my old preceptor (Colonel Titus) decided that it was safer to trust a married man than a single man, because his wheels were locked.

My old friend Norton will tell you we had a large Indian trade, and sold them much on their promise to pay at a certain time, they indicating the time by pointing where the moon would be when they would return, and I never knew one to fail to return at the time indicated; and he would not trade a dime until he had paid his debts. They never disputed accounts. Norton and I spoke the Chickasaw language fluently, and that is the only DEAD LANGUAGE we ever studied. When an Indian finds you can speak his language you can't get him to speak yours.

Up to about 1832 the main current of the Mississippi struck the bluff about the foot of Jackson Street. About that time the bar now known as the Navy Yard, and all below it, began to form, and caused a great eddy. The change of the current of the river carved off Foy's Point on the Arkansas shore, about a half a mile.

Though taxes were very moderate, I remember the people complained of them. They were not able to build wharves, grade streets, or make pavements. We had no public buildings, or banks, or cushioned churches. All the courts were at Raleigh, and we had no police. [Apparently Waldran had relocated to Memphis]. We usually opened stores about daylight and closed them at night, after we had served all of the custom we could get. The town moved along without any marked change until 1832, when it took a fresh start and began to put on city airs.

Waldran then recited markers of progress over the intervening forty years and attempted to project the future for Shelby County over the subsequent half century. He was spot on about the expanding network of Mid-South railroads, about bridging the Mississippi River at Memphis, and Memphis ultimately growing to a city of more than a half-million inhabitants. However, he also envisioned the U.S. annexation of Mexico and a moral regeneration and return to the simple republican virtues of an earlier time. Although he saw reason for concern, as gilded-age values were setting in, he expressed the hope that reform was at hand. He acknowledged landmarks in science and placed his hope in education, which he thought to be getting the reforms that it needed. He said:

But in my day there has been no greater improvement in anything than there has been in the system of education and in the books used. Why, forty years ago the *English Reader* was placed in my hands as the first reader in schools of that day, a book which today requires the talent of our best theologians to comprehend. I committed to memory whole pages without understanding the meaning of a single sentence. We now have teachers educated to teach, and books adapted to all capacities, and as the youthful mind can comprehend, and can mark progress as he ascends the hill of science, study becomes a pleasure; and I predict that if due caution is exercised in the making and selection of books, it will not be long before the old beastly practice of beating an education into a boy will have entirely passed away, and you will hear no more [talk] of compulsory education.

Mr. Waldran was amazingly prescient in his prediction that schooling would greatly improve. Although, as he says, nineteenth-century Shelby County schooling got off to a primitive and uncertain start, by the end of the century that situation was beginning to change. In the twentieth century, Shelby County's school system would become one of its biggest success stories. Formal education had difficulty in gaining acceptance across the South, including Memphis and Shelby County.

Ironically, Frances Wright may well have had the county's first real school at her

✧

Even after the explosive growth in the use of steamboats and railroads, flatboats and rafts remained important methods of shipping products to market. They could be put together during the winter and bulk commodities brought down river with little or no cash expense.

ILLUSTRATION COURTESY OF THE MEMPHIS PINK PALACE MUSEUM, DAPHNE F. HEWETT, ARTIST.

VIEW OF THE NAVY YARD, MEMPHIS, TENNESSEE, FROM THE ARKANSAS SHORE.

❖

The Federal Navy yard at Memphis was built in the mid-1840s at the base of the bluff between Auction and Market Streets. Apparently, dirt was pushed down the bluff face for landfill and any traces of Fort San Fernando were in the rubble so deposited. Later the Pyramid and its parking surfaces were located in about the same area.

COURTESY OF SPECIAL COLLECTIONS, UNIVERSITY OF MEMPHIS LIBRARIES.

Nashoba Plantation in the late 1820s. She had hired an experienced female teacher to come from New Orleans to teach the slaves she was grooming for emancipation and living in freedom. In the 1830s, Irish immigrant Schoolmaster Eugene Magevney was teaching in Memphis and got his start on making a fortune from his fees and by investing in local real estate. Although Magevney gave up teaching to become a prosperous businessman, he maintained his interest and involvement in education. He was a great advocate for establishing "common schools" in the 1840s and 1850s. Tax supported, common schools were begun in Shelby County prior to the Civil War, but they were probably suspended during the conflict.

In the war's aftermath, Mid-South whites greatly resented the fact that northern missionaries were coming in and educating the area's freedmen. During the 1866 rioting near Fort Pickering, white mobs targeted black schools and churches for burning. White Southerners, who placed little value on book learning in and of itself, were often resentful of blacks' education and determined that they should not become more and better educated than whites. Under slavery, even literacy had been prohibited for blacks. With freedom, many of them wanted to taste of that once forbidden fruit.

Although, as Waldran suggests above, there was often not much connection between schooling and true learning until after the Civil War, a start had been made. Perhaps surprisingly, women became the true administrative trailblazers for Shelby County's public education. In 1882, the County Court appointed an apparently dynamic

Mrs. W. H. Horton to serve as county school superintendent. During her tenure, schools became considerably more effective and better supported.

The late nineteenth century was indeed an era of one-room schoolhouses, for in 1886 Shelby County had 148 schools, staffed by just 154 teachers. The major reason for one-room schools was the primitive transportation problem. Schools had to be close enough for students to walk to them

and, even before *Plessy v. Ferguson*, Southern school systems were largely segregated by race. In the 1890s, the redoubtable black crusader Ida B. Wells taught in a county school and commuted to work by train. Wells sued the railroad for denying her the right to sit in the train car of her choosing, and thus began her celebrated civil rights activities.

Mrs. Horton's tenure was followed by a quartet of especially effective, female county school superintendents. Elizabeth Messick, Mabel Williams, Charl O. Williams, and Sue Powers all made very strong contributions to raising the level of education in county schools. Even though Messick and Mabel

✧

Railroads were probably as important to the growth and economic development of nineteenth century Memphis and Shelby County as all other man-made factors combined. The late 1850s brought three major rail lines to Memphis, the most important being the Memphis and Charleston. The locomotive is Civil War era. The Memphis and Charleston Depot and freight yard lasted well into the twentieth century, with the depot falling victim to federally funded urban renewal programs.

Williams were very strong administrators, their tenures were limited by the fact that, for a time, women were forced to resign from the school system when they married. Elizabeth Messick and Mabel Williams both had county schools named in their honor. Messick's was west of Highland, off Spottswood in the Buntyn community. Williams's school was on Polar Pike in Germantown.

Charl O. Williams, Mabel's sister and successor as superintendent, did not leave the position to marry, but she apparently alienated elements of the Crump organization. She left the Shelby County

Miss Wright's neue Ansiedelung.

school system to work for the National Education Association in Washington, D.C. Sue Powers also did not marry. She earned a doctorate and guided the Shelby County School system for nearly three decades, until her retirement in the early 1950s.

Tennessee's state government also contributed to the county's growing educational successes with significant reforms in the early twentieth century. Horse or mule drawn wagonettes provided much better transportation for students and allowed students to be drawn from larger areas. Having more students made having larger, multi-room brick schoolhouses practical. With such facilities, supervision became much better organized and teachers became increasingly professionally trained. The opening of West Tennessee State Normal School east of Memphis in 1912 contributed

strongly to the growing number and to the professionalization of the area's teachers.

✧

Left: In the early twentieth century, Shelby County schools made amazing progress. Among those most responsible for this phenomenon were the Williams sisters from tiny Arlington, in northeast Shelby County. Both served as teachers, as principals, and as superintendents in the county school system. Mabel Williams (Hughes) married and had to leave public education. Her younger sister, Charl, followed in her footsteps as superintendent, but left Shelby County to take an executive post with the National Education Association.
COURTESY OF SHELBY COUNTY ARCHIVES.

Below: Charl O. Williams, second from the right, is the only person identified in this 1922 photograph of the Shelby County Board of Education meeting in the court house. Miss Williams apparently irritated forces in the county political organization, and, rather than become the center of a political wrangle, she resigned and went to Washington. She was a significant figure in Democratic politics and in securing Tennessee's ratification of the Nineteenth Amendment guaranteeing women the right to vote.
COURTESY OF SHELBY COUNTY ARCHIVES

BIRD'S EYE VIEW OF WEST TENNE....... COLLEGE,
MEMPHIS, TENN.

Old Folks' President Waldran's assessment that compulsory education would become unnecessary and fade from the scene was pretty far off the mark. Not all children find school enjoyable, and at some point in the late nineteenth or early twentieth centuries, Tennessee did make school attendance compulsory.

Waldran's powers of prophecy also proved to be dramatically wrong in another area as well. He delivered his oration less than a year before the 1873 yellow fever epidemic, which was followed by even more destructive bouts of the saffron plague in 1878 and '79. Unaware of what the future was soon to bring, he read the names of the members and other good neighbors who had died since the group's last annual banquet. Agreeing with the adage that often the best fruit falls first from the tree, he chose not to "particularize" about the deceased, saying that the memories of the just would not perish. He also remarked that the Old Folks had a tradition that when a man who had faults died, they buried

the memory of those faults with him. Urging his fellows to live their lives so that they could depart them in peace, he brought the meeting to a close.

When the yellow fever did strike, it seems to have hit Memphis much harder than it did the hinterland. Consequently, Memphians who could not get out of the area completely, were forced to stay with kinfolk or friends in the countryside. For many of those who had no other recourse, there were several refugee camps not far from Memphis, which gave many refugees a measure of protection. Of course, there were exceptions. Jefferson Davis, Jr., for example, commuted by train back and forth from Memphis to Buntyn (just west of Highland on Southern Avenue). He was stricken and died within a few days. Fleeing Memphians spread the disease among communities along the major rail and road arteries, but the isolated parts of Shelby County and nearby counties had proportionately much lower rates of disease and death.

✧

Above: Memphis began commercial air service on a two-hundred-acre plot south and east of the city in 1929. Originally, this airport handled only four flights per day.

Left: Mailman Demps Weakly had a delivery route at Raleigh in the early 1900s. Here his son, Travis, gets a ride along Raleigh Millington Road, c. 1910.

CHAPTER III

51

THIRTY YEARS A SLAVE.

From Bondage to Freedom.

THE INSTITUTION OF SLAVERY
AS SEEN ON THE PLANTATION AND
IN THE HOME OF THE PLANTER.

AUTOBIOGRAPHY OF LOUIS HUGHES.

NEGRO UNIVERSITIES PRESS
NEW YORK

CHAPTER IV

MID-SOUTH PLANTATION
LIFE FROM A SLAVE'S PERSPECTIVE

In the mid-1890s, Louis Hughes published a narrative of his thirty years of enslavement. He was born the child of a free white man and a slave woman near Charlottesville, Virginia in 1832. At about the age of eleven, he was told that he was being hired out to work on a canal-boat, but he was actually "sold south," never to see his mother and one of his two brothers again. In a Richmond slave market, a local resident purchased Lou, but rather quickly resold him because he tended to be sickly. At this point, a wealthy Mississippi planter named Edmund McGee, in town to acquire more slaves, bought Louis for $380.00.

Traveling overland on foot and by wagon, Mr. McGee's newly acquired slaves traveled about 20 miles per day and reached Pontotoc, Mississippi (about 65 miles south-southeast of Memphis), on Christmas Eve (1844). This was just in time for 12-year-old Louis to be given to the plantation's mistress, Mrs. Sarah McGee, for Christmas as her new "general utility boy." Throughout his narrative, Hughes generally refers to Mr. McGee as "Boss" and to his wife as "Madam." The husband and wife were first cousins, not a great rarity in the antebellum South.

Hughes gives a detailed description of what Mid-South plantation life on a relatively "grand scale" was like in the mid-1840s. Although not a Shelby County resident until about six years later, Louis's recollection of his new life nearby may provide the best available slave's perspective on the whole area's plantation life. As a house servant in various capacities and at varying locales over a thirty-year period, he had ample opportunity to observe, hear about, and compare the McGee's Pontotoc operation to other such plantations. There was probably not a lot of variation because Hughes himself states that "This establishment will serve as a sample of many of those on the large plantations in the [S]outh."

According to Hughes, he slept on the dining room floor of the big house and had plenty to eat. Initially, his tasks were light: running errands, attending to the dining room, helping with the weaving of cloth, helping churn milk in the dairy house, saddling horses for the whites, and the like. Mr. McGee instructed him in herbal cures for slave illnesses. Lou also accompanied the whites on bird hunting parties in which the riders drove game birds into nets, taking them alive. Later, his tasks became more onerous, and his mistress became a great deal more demanding and cruel.

Lou's description of the "great house" makes it sound not very grand. Its layout seems to have been remarkably akin to that of Davies Manor in northeast Shelby County. (Perhaps the McGee place, too, had once been a dogtrot, single story structure). Although McGee's house was two stories high, it was "built of huge logs, chinked and daubed and whitewashed." Its entry hall was twenty-five feet long and twelve feet wide, with one large room on each side of the hall on each story, and with one large fireplace in each room. It had a dining room running off one of the parlors. The separate kitchen building was about 30 feet from the main building; a dairy house, a smokehouse, the overseer's house, a blacksmith's shop, a cotton gin, and the slave quarters were beyond the kitchen.

The slave cabins were single-room, fourteen-foot square structures of rough-hewn logs. They were daubed with the red clay or mud of the region, but not whitewashed either inside or out. Each cabin had a dirt floor, a shake roof, two windows, a wooden door, and a large crude fireplace. Furnishings included: one bed per family, a plain board table, crude wooden benches, and an iron grease lamp. Construction included very few nails, which were expensive and in short supply.

Not all slave labor was unskilled. Slaves crafted their own crude furniture and most of their agricultural implements. The latter included shovels, hoes, sweeps, cultivators, harrows, and two kinds of plows. Slave artisans also wove dozens of huge oaken baskets each year for carrying the

✦

This portrait of Louis Hughes is from the frontispiece of his memoir, Thirty Years A Slave: From Bondage to Freedom, the Institution of Slavery As Seen on the Plantation and in the Home of the Planter. *Louis spent about eleven of his years in bondage living in Shelby County. His book was originally published in 1897 and a facsimile was reprinted by Negro Universities Press in 1968. Hughes is obviously an older professional man at the time this photograph was taken.*

COURTESY OF SPECIAL COLLECTIONS, UNIVERSITY OF MEMPHIS LIBRARIES.

cotton. Likewise, their handiwork provided much of their own clothing. Female slaves carded wool, spun yarn, and wove cloth, cutting it to size and sewing the clothes for the plantations' blacks. They made about half of the clothes needed on the plantation, and the owner bought the rest, including brogan shoes. The Boss provided each servant with two sets of clothes for summer and two sets for winter. In the winter, female slaves also wore leggings, called pantalets, often made from the legs of discarded men's trousers. Hughes indicated that they had no additional underwear. In addition to the purchase of shoes, McGee would purchase gingham cotton cloth for use in making turbans for the female slaves. House servants often got white folks' hand-me-downs of dress clothes and finer footwear than that for the field workers.

Slave children, up to about the age of seven, were cared for and supervised by an older woman in a double size cabin used as a nursery. The nursing slave mothers took infants in cradles to the cabin and were allowed to leave their tasks three times during the workday to suckle their babies. As soon as the infants seemed old enough, they were weaned onto cow's milk, cabbage pot liquor, and sopping bread. Sometimes this change of diet gave the children colic. Lou thought that the infants' health suffered from a deficiency of nurturing; they did have an inordinately high infant mortality rate.

Field workers began preparing the soil for cotton planting shortly after the first of the year. The seed was usually planted around the first of April, the blooms appeared in early June, and cotton picking began about the middle of August and lasted well into December. In late July, however, there was a great rush to get the "first bale" of cotton to market in Memphis. In addition to the prestige of being first, amid the fanfare, the city's commission merchants (also called "cotton factors" presented the winning planter with a basket of champagne. Planters sometimes divided their field hands into two competing teams, racing to gather in the most cotton. The slaves would choose up sides and strive to outdo each other for the reward of a single cup of sugar for each member of the winning side.

The plantation's gin-house was a large shed similar to a barn but built on square timbers, standing six feet above the ground, with the machinery for running the gin positioned beneath the building. Dry cotton was placed in the loft, from which it was dropped to a man who fed it into the machine. The gin removed the lint and fed it into a separate room, while the seed would drop near the feeder's feet. The lint was carried in large baskets to a place where it was compacted into 250-pound bales for shipment to market.

Other than cotton, Mid-South plantations produced little beyond provisions they raised to help sustain the workforce. Crops included wheat, oats, rye, and especially corn. The hands typically planted the corn about a month before the cotton. Corn was fully tilled before the cotton acreage was ready for cultivation. They cured the leaves from the corn stalks and used them as livestock feed. The stalks themselves were annually plowed back into the soil, to help fertilize it for the next year's crop. Peas were planted between rows of corn and later hulled, dried, and stored. The hands also grew cabbage and yams in large quantities. Slave diets consisted largely of corn bread, bacon or fat meat, cracklings, lard, peas, cabbage, and yams. There were variations between summer and winter staples. Moreover, the master allowed the slaves to imitate the whites in feasting at Christmas time and (ironically) on the Fourth of July. At Christmas, they got special treats, made from wheat flour and sugar. Independence Day, of course,

Above: The interiors of the McGee house and Davies Manor both seem to be somewhat rough hewn and primitive. This photograph of the front parlor shows a couple in period costumes and antique furniture from the nineteenth century. Modifications were made to Davies Manor into the early twentieth century. Restoration of it began in the 1930s.
COURTESY OF DAVIES MANOR ASSOCIATION.

Below: This photograph of a Mid-South log cabin probably dates from late in the nineteenth century. It differs from the cabins that Lou Hughes describes in that it seems bigger, does not have a dirt floor, and has no visible windows. It is possible that it may have been a slave cabin or have been built in the same way.
COURTESY OF THE BLACKWELL COLLECTION.

❖

Above: The large wooden baskets used in the fields for carrying cotton are apparent in this Horace Bradley painting of a nineteenth century harvest. At least one of the cotton pickers in the scene is a woman, and there seems to be a plantation mansion among the trees on the horizon. Such baskets continued to be used on Mid-South plantations well into the twentieth century.

COURTESY OF FIRST TENNESSEE HERITAGE COLLECTION.

Below: The earliest cotton gins had been small, hand cranked machines, but they still revolutionized the uses of cotton and fabrics. Within a few decades, much larger, power-driven gins became fairly common. Big plantations often ginned, compressed, and baled the cotton crops of their neighboring small farmers. Sometimes they marketed those harvests along with their own.

ILLUSTRATION COURTESY OF THE MEMPHIS PINK PALACE MUSEUM, DAPHNE F. HEWETT, ARTIST.

meant barbecued pork, plus sweetened baked goods and dumplings.

Planters generally rotated their crops, especially those grown on poor grounds, but they periodically brought new lands under cultivation, too. To clear forested areas, workers first "girdled" the trees, killing them by cutting through the bark all the way around the trunks. Within a year or two, they burned the smaller trunks and tree branches, as well as the underbrush, which had been "grubbed" out by female workers. Presumably, the clearing gangs saved the larger logs and squared them for future construction.

Slaves were generally not required to work on Sundays and holidays. Lou usually accompanied the family to church on Sundays. Most slaves seemed sincere in their Christian beliefs. They caught up on their own family tasks on Sundays, mainly cleaning, washing, and sewing. They had their own religious services on Sunday evenings. Lou emphasized that the slaves' religious faith gave them the wherewithall to accept and to endure their bondage.

In 1850, McGee purchased a fourteen-acre tract about two miles east-southeast of Memphis, along the Memphis and Charleston railway tracks. Over the span of a year and

a half, twenty-five of his slaves built the grand estate that his Pontotoc plantation had lacked. It was resplendent with a brick mansion stuccoed to look like stone masonry, lavish flower and kitchen gardens, and a four-acre orchard. Because it had a "flag stop" for the trains, it became known as McGee's Station. Lou Hughes was elevated to the position of butler which actually meant more work, although, the tasks were still light. Lou confessed that his rise in status was a source of pride at first. He also noted that the slaves generally took pride in the ostentation of their new home and lorded their prominence over the servants of less affluent slave owners. McGee also moved his planting operations from Pontotoc County to Bolivar County

Early power-driven cotton gin.

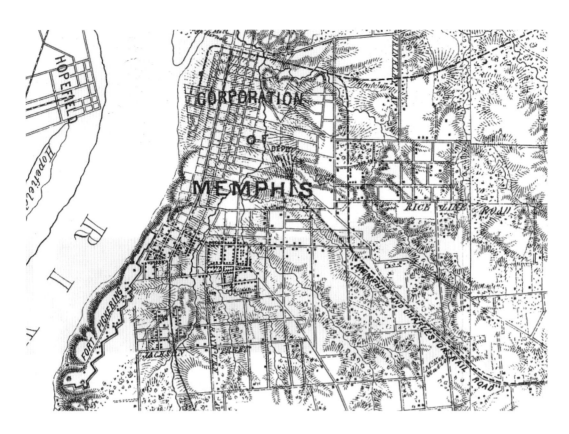

(about 65 miles south-southwest of Memphis) in the much more fertile delta lands abutting the Mississippi River. Hughes refers to two hundred acres for farming, but that figure may well be missing a zero, since he also states that the plantation's slave population was 168 persons. That number of

workers would be far too many for a two-hundred-acre farming operation.

Upon completion of the mansion residence, the McGees held housewarming festivities for relations and close friends. Once the visiting houseguests had departed, Madam McGee resumed her pattern of ranting abuses against

Above: This mid-1860s U. S. Army map of the Memphis area shows the Memphis and Charleston Railroad running southeast on a 45 degree angle before it turns due east and runs off the map. Just above the bend to the east a label reads "McKee's Station," about where Lou Harris places Edmund McGee's opulent residence outside of Memphis. Pronunciation for McKee and McGee can be virtually the same.

COURTESY OF SPECIAL COLLECTIONS, UNIVERSITY OF MEMPHIS LIBRARIES.

Left: The Hunt Phelan House, toward the east end of Beale Street, represents the sort of mansion that Harris describes. It survived, somewhat frozen in time, into the 1990s, when an heir attempted to restore it and make it into a commercially viable museum. Failing to do so, he auctioned off most of the home's contents and has made the property into an upscale bed and breakfast. Hunt Phelan would have been a little more than halfway between Lou's home and the rail depot in Memphis.

COURTESY OF MEMPHIS & SHELBY COUNTY ROOM, MEMPHIS PUBLIC LIBRARY & INFORMATION CENTER.

the servants, including Lou. Berating him for not properly "stoning the steps," she took Lou outside, removed his shirt, and thrashed him. After an initial burst of tears, Lou had an epiphany regarding his ongoing mistreatment by his mistress.

Lou never mentions any temptation to run away until after the housewarming. Perhaps his owner's father, Old Jack (a Scottish immigrant), planted the suggestion in the slave's mind at that time. In Lou's hearing, Jack told his son that he did not trust Lou and could "see running away in his eyes." In the face of renewed abuse, Lou realized how much he wanted to be free. He knew, from hearing his boss read aloud, that Canada was often the destination of runaway slaves. In the face of another threatened whipping, Lou quickly made his way through the woods and through Memphis streets to the riverfront.

He sneaked aboard the northbound steamboat

Statesman, and hid behind some hogsheads (large barrels) of sugar. With no advance preparation, he had to scavenge for food and drink. Three days out of Memphis, the second mate, aware that there was a $500 reward for the safe return of an escaped slave, spotted Hughes. Even so, there was a good bit of sympathy for Lou, and the crew took up a small collection to help him on his way. Lou jumped ship at West Franklin, Indiana. Passing quickly through the village, he was several

miles into the countryside when two horsemen, who had earlier passed him going the other way, returned and caught him as he was eating a meal that he had begged at a farmhouse. The horsemen received a $75.00 reward for their role in his apprehension.

Local authorities processed Lou, jailed him in Louisville, Kentucky, and telegraphed McGee to come reclaim his property. Boss arrived to escort Lou home. Oddly, McGee refused to shackle Lou, bought him new clothes for the trip home, and did not have him flogged following their return. However, not long thereafter, Madam Sarah resumed mistreating Lou regularly.

About three months after his first failed escape, Lou made another bid for freedom. He crept aboard the *John Lirozey* and stowed away beneath a cargo of animal hides. Again, by the third day out, he was famished. Locked in the hold, he cried out for help and was apprehended and put off the boat at Monroe, Kentucky to be held for his master. Thomas Bland, the McGee's slave coachman, was sent to bring Lou back. This time, once home, Lou received a sound beating. Stripped and held in the stocks in the barn, his master whipped him alternately with peach branches and a wooden paddle over a span of two hours, then washed his wounds with salted

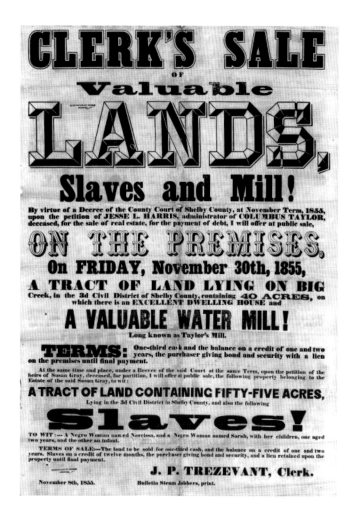

water to intensify the pain and to sterilize Lou's lacerated flesh.

Ironically, the same Thomas Bland who had fetched Lou back from Kentucky also desired to escape from bondage. He persuaded some workmen in the vicinity to teach him to read and write and then attempted to pass this forbidden skill along to Lou. When the master discovered Tom's secret, he beat him severely. A few weeks later, Tom forged a pass that allowed him to hire himself out. He shipped out as a hand on a steamboat headed <u>south</u>! Upon reaching New Orleans, he crewed on an oceangoing steamer to Boston. From there he made his way to Canada and freedom.

It is worth noting here that all three of these efforts to escape from the Memphis area were aboard steamboats. Of course, both Lou and Tom were house servants and may have been better-dressed,

and more knowledgeable and poised while moving among urban whites, than field hands would have been. Even so, there is no reliable evidence of any Underground Railroad stations or activity in Memphis. Once the Civil War was underway, Lou made two further attempts to get free from North Mississippi plantations, butthey were even less successful than his two steamboat misadventures.

Shortly after Lou was returned from his second runaway attempt, Edmund McGee bought two slave sisters through the Memphis slave market of Nathan Bedford Forrest. The young women, Matilda and Mary Ellen, were actually free blacks who had been "sold south" illegally. Within three years, Lou and Matilda married. Surprisingly, perhaps, the ceremony took place in the McGee mansion's parlor with the white family's minister officiating. A year later the union was blessed with twins (oddly, Lou never indicates their sex). This development

seems to have stimulated Madam to initiate a routine of almost continually mistreating Matilda. Unable to stand her situation, Matilda took her two babies, walked to the Memphis slave market of N. B. Forrest, and asked to be resold! Forrest and others wanted to help her, but they could not convince McGee to sell the slave. Shortly after she was returned to McGee's Station, her baby twins died.

Lou's narrative then skips sketchily through the 1860 presidential election and into the onset of the Civil War, with all of its dislocations and privations for Mid-Southerners, black and white. Shortly after the Battle of Shiloh, the Memphis-area McGee family and its slaves were sent to various extended family plantations in north Mississippi. Sandwiched between moving parties of Confederate and Union soldiers, Lou observed a lot of confusion, apprehension, and destruction. Lou's desire to run to the Yankee lines and freedom was nullified by two things: his loyalty to his family and his understanding that any slave caught running away was to be summarily hanged. Lou and his wife did not actually escape until well after Appomattox. Finally, with the help of two Union enlisted men, they did escape to Memphis and then to Cincinnati and points north. Once in the North, Lou, Matilda, and Mary Ellen located first his brother William and then Matilda's mother and another

of her sisters. Ultimately, after a number of different service jobs, Lou settled into a career in nursing.

In a retrospective of his slave experiences, Lou thought it only just to say that his former master was probably a kinder and more humane man than many other slaveholders. Boss fed his slaves well and provided adequate clothing and shelter for them. But Lou faulted him for hiring irresponsible brutes as overseers who abused the field slaves horribly. Of course, Lou had nothing good to say of Boss's wife, Mrs. Sarah McGee. Based on her frequent

and irrational outbursts and her determined cruelty, she seems to have been either demented, chronically sadistic, or both.

Even to one who might be skeptical about possible or even probable embellishments of the Lou Hughes story line and its depictions of nineteenth-century Anglo-American slavery, his narrative still has potentially significant value for Mid-South history scholars. Lou is

highly unlikely to have distorted his descriptions of the more prosaic elements or day-to-day activities of plantation life. Their authenticity would be important to give his accounts their verisimilitude, and such matters have virtually no propagandistic value.

By way of contrast with Louis Hughes's memoir, there is the story of "Uncle" Ned and "Aunt" Rose Kearney, born slaves on the plantation of "Squire" Whit Kearney near Sardis, Mississippi (35 miles due south of Memphis) in the early 1850s. Shortly after eight-year-old Ned began doing regular chores at the "Big House," the Civil War broke out. When "Ole Massa" went to war, he took Ned with him, but sent him back home after just a few days. Ned continued to work at the "Big House" through the Civil War. Whenever Union soldiers were in the vicinity, Ned helped to hide food, livestock, silver, and other valuables in the bottomlands to keep the Yankees from taking them. Far from viewing the Yanks as friends or liberators, Ned said that he considered them the enemy. At war's end, Squire Kearney met with the slaves to tell them that they had been liberated and were free to leave the plantation. He hoped they would stay, and at least some did. Thirteen-year-old Ned, however, wanted to go to Memphis and see the big city for himself. He did so, taking the train. When he got off, he saw men in blue uniforms, and, thinking they were Yankee soldiers, he returned immediately to Sardis. Later, he realized that they were just policemen.

Ned stayed on at the Kearney plantation and fell in love with a woman named Rose, two years younger than he. They married in 1870, following the African or slave custom of jumping over a broom. Shortly thereafter, they moved to Memphis, and both went to work for the Eichberg family, living in a shed in the family's backyard. They worked for various members of the Eichberg's extended family for the next sixty years, moving with the second generation to a 35-acre farm near Berclair, slightly northeast of the city limits in 1921. There, Ned planted apple and pear trees, a strawberry patch, a vegetable garden, and raised corn and cotton. Their livestock included two mules,

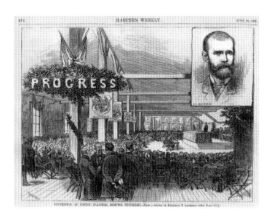

two milk cows, and some hogs. Later they also raised chickens.

In 1923, the Eichberg's took in a very young, very sickly great nephew named John B. McKinney. Ned and Rose Kearney helped rear him from about age three. Over ensuing decades, Ned told John many stories of his plantation past. Again, one must be wary of possible embellishment. Might Ned have told John what he thought a young white might want to hear in the 1930s, Jim Crow-dominated Mid South? Later, Ned and Rose's eldest son Joe told variations on the same stories as late as the 1970s, but his versions had the Union soldiers rather than Whit Kearney telling the slaves of their new freedom. It also has the soldiers scattering the plantation's stored food on the ground that the newly freed blacks might take it. However, Joe was

speaking in a post-Jim Crow, pro-Civil Rights-movement atmosphere.

Certainly Ned and Rose stayed on the plantation for five years following the war, and that was at a time when most of the rural Mid South was economically devastated. Surely that bespeaks some level of racial accommodation. The University of Memphis Library's Special Collections Department has a series of oral history interviews and transcriptions probing Joe Kearney's recollections. It is also a repository for a memoir about the Kearneys by John McKinney.

✥

Top, left: It is difficult to tell whether this Cotton Planters' Convention is Antebellum or later. Either way, Memphis and Shelby County were in the center of the cotton growing and cotton marketing enterprises across the "cotton belt."

COURTESY OF SPECIAL COLLECTIONS, UNIVERSITY OF MEMPHIS LIBRARIES.

Top, right: Joe Kearney, eldest son of Ned and Rose Kearney, conducted oral history interviews in the late 1970s and died in 1984 at age 112. He had told and retold his father's stories so many times over his long life, that he seems to have confused his own past with that of his father. Ned and Rose lived to be centenarians, too, and were celebrated as America's longest married couple before death separated them.

COURTESY OF SPECIAL COLLECTIONS, UNIVERSITY OF MEMPHIS LIBRARIES.

Left: This photograph of Millington's W.E. Polk Family was taken at their Wilkerson Road residence, c. 1890. The blacks are well-dressed and seem to be treated in a familial way.

COURTESY OF THE MILLINGTON STAR.

CHAPTER V

THE CIVIL WAR, RECONSTRUCTION, AND JIM CROW. 1860-1891

Unquestionably, the decade of the 1860s altered daily life in Shelby County more rapidly and more radically than at any other period in the area's history. Secession, Civil War, and Reconstruction changed almost all of life's ground rules for most black and white Shelby Countians. Even the "fever decade" of the 1870s seems to have made a less permanent imprint on the area's character.

The decade of the 1850s had been one of growing political and psychological tensions across the nation. During that time, most Memphians and likely most other Shelby Countians desired to preserve their Union. Memphis had strong commercial ties upriver and was probably less insular in its attitudes than many Southern cities. In the 1860 election, locals voted overwhelmingly for "pro-Union candidates" John Bell and Stephen A. Douglas. They also voted overwhelmingly against secession as deep south states departed the Union. However, when Lincoln called for volunteers to suppress the "rebellion" in South Carolina, the nature of the choices had changed. It was no longer a question of preserving the Union, but, with war imminent, which side to back.

ABy early 1861, "secession meetings were a daily occurrence throughout city and county." (Unless otherwise attributed, this and other actual quotations in this chapter are taken from Douglas W. Cupples, "Memphis Confederates"). In their desire to depart the Union, locals decided earlier and more vehemently than most other Tennesseans. When the state's referendum on whether to secede took place on June 8, 1861, Shelby Countians voted more than 7,000 to 5 in favor of breaking with the Union. Of course, in the increasingly volatile atmosphere of growing secessionist sentiment, many pro-Unionists had left the Mid South. Charles Lufkin's study indicates that between 3,000 and 5,000 residents, mostly foreign born or Northerners, departed via riverboat. Doubtlessly, others left by train or other modes of transport.

On a statewide basis, Tennesseans voted about two-to-one to secede. Once the secession issue was decided, Memphians moved at once to prepare for defense. Soon thereafter, state and Confederate authorities took over defense planning and made Memphis a military depot and ordnance center. The city's manufacturing capabilities, small though they were, turned largely to war production. Foolishly, as it turned out, military planners devoted almost all of the area's defense capability to stopping Union invaders upriver.

Prior to facing the enemy at home, the first bloody battle to affect locals deeply was waged upriver at Belmont, Missouri. Its casualties were high, and Memphis became a crowded hospital center. Soon thereafter came Confederate defeats at Shiloh and Island Number 10. The only force left to protect Memphis then was a small fleet of eight converted ocean going tugboats, "armored" with compressed cotton and locomotive rails. The Union Navy's vastly superior fleet made short work (about 90 minutes, on June 6, 1862) of Confederate naval resistance. Memphis was in Union hands and would stay that way through the war's end. An estimated 10,000 Shelby Countians had watched the conflict from the Bluff top, and the area went briefly into a sort of commercial and psychological paralysis. On land, only a single shot had rung out as the Confederate flag was being replaced with the Stars and Stripes. Who fired that shot and to what purpose was never proved.

The Confederacy had lost the Battle of Shiloh in early April, and Grant's forces were also closing in on Memphis from the east. The bitter fruits of defiance and defeat would last for almost three more years of war and about four years of Reconstruction. "For many, these years would bring privation and hardship unknown since frontier days. For others, it would mean a new

✦

Isham G. Harris was the governor who led Tennessee out of the Union in 1861. In the face of Union victories, he later fled the state and then the country. When he returned, he became a resident of Memphis and returned to political life following Reconstruction. He served in the U. S. Senate from 1877 to 1897, dying in office. He is buried at Historic Elmwood Cemetery.

freedom and new economic opportunities. For almost all, the world that they had known was gone. Their new world was topsy-turvy, and they were strangers in it."

The Memphis area had raised 72 companies of Confederate troops prior to the city falling into Union hands. "Shelby County furnished at least 53 full companies…these [along with later recruits] would doubtlessly aggregate 6,000 men. The voting population [of Shelby County] in 1860 was only about 6,000 men. [of a total county population of about 48,000 people]" Some of those Shelby Countians later fought in the cavalry forces of Nathan Bedford Forrest. Numerous Memphians were forced to move southward both before and after the river battle. Most of those who stayed remained very sympathetic to the Confederate cause. Passive resistance and contemptuous attitudes surfaced quickly in occupied Memphis, and all persons

"disloyal" to the Union were told to reconsider or leave the city. However, pro-Southern "sentiment ran rampant from the city streets to wooded creek bottoms." "Relatives and friends in the surrounding area…gave refuge to numerous Memphians."

At Shiloh, the two-day conflict brought more than 23,000 casualties on the two sides combined. That was a greater level of carnage than the United States had experienced in the Revolutionary War, the War of 1812, and the Mexican War combined. By comparison, combat in Shelby County itself seems almost trivial. After the fall of Memphis, there were no major battles within a 100-mile radius of the city, but that does not mean that the county stayed peaceful or secure.

Union occupation forces immediately drew picket lines around the city, but their control did not extend into the countryside. Despite controlling the city and major roads and

railways in and out, Federal troops were never able to completely shut down Confederate activities further than a gunshot's distance from Union lines. Just beyond those lines, Southern soldiers and partisan groups operated with near impunity. Confederate operatives were familiar with the territory and had the sympathy and support of its civilian inhabitants.

The rural folks of Shelby County found themselves caught in a veritable crossfire, or no man's land. By the time Memphis was captured, a group called "Porter's Partisans" had already burned about 30,000 bales of cotton in Shelby and adjoining counties to keep it from falling into Federal hands. Union troops frequently raided into the countryside, but, short of murdering civilians, they could

Above: Shiloh was the bloodiest battle in the western hemisphere up to that time. This painting shows confusion verging on chaos at the end of the first day's combat. Grant's army made a final stand near the Tennessee River, and Union reinforcements arriving during the night turned the tide of victory against the Confederates the following day.

COURTESY OF SPECIAL COLLECTIONS, UNIVERSITY OF MEMPHIS LIBRARIES.

Below: In 1987, Civil War enthusiasts reenacted the Battle of Shiloh near its very site 125 years after the battle. The event drew a huge turnout of participants and spectators. Reenactors form a sort of cultural cult. For particulars, analysis, and a lot of humor related to this phenomenon, pick up a copy of Confederates in the Attic, *by Tony Horwitz.*

COURTESY OF JOHN E. HARKINS.

not destroy their enemy. Confederates set up networks of scouts, spies, and couriers. They were generally able to obtain military intelligence, money, and supplies from civilian supporters. They also enforced Confederate regulations regarding conscription and desertion, even in areas nominally under Union control.

The Elm Ridge Plantation on the Holly Ford Road, southeast of Memphis, about three miles below Nonconnah Creek, furnishes an excellent example of civilian resistance. Its owners, Andrew Jackson Edmondson and his family, were devout Confederates. Elm Ridge was located in the no-man's land, south of Federal pickets along the Nonconnah Creek and the shifting Confederate lines in Northwest Mississippi, usually along the Coldwater River to the south. The Edmondson home became a communications drop and a rendezvous for Confederate forces. Belle Edmondson, a quick-witted spy for the

Southern cause, recorded some of the home's Confederate visitors in late-December of 1863. She mentions 23 Confederates taking dinner with the family on the 19th, and entered that on "Christmas Eve [their] house was full of Rebels—God bless them." Naturally, almost all such clandestine activities took place after dark. Had the Edmondsons been caught, it is highly likely that their home place would have been burned and that its occupants would have been imprisoned.

General Sherman, himself, had proclaimed that there was "not a garrison in Tennessee where a man can go beyond the sight of his flagstaff without [risking] being shot or captured." In retaliation for guerillas firing on the unarmed steamer *Eugene*, Sherman ordered the burning of the town of Randolph, upriver from Memphis. He followed this order with his General Order #54, commanding that for every boat fired upon from ambush, ten families of Confederate

Nathan Bedford Forrest was probably the most controversial figure on either side during the Civil War and Reconstruction. He has been the subject of a dozen or more biographies and he remains controversial. White Memphians dedicated a downtown park to his memory early in the twentieth century, complete with an equestrian statue. Many Memphis blacks find this memorial objectionable. There is also a Nathan Bedford Forrest Historical Society active in Shelby County.

COURTESY OF SPECIAL COLLECTIONS,
UNIVERSITY OF MEMPHIS LIBRARIES.

sympathizers would be expelled from Memphis. An eight-months pregnant Confederate wife and sympathizer named Elizabeth Avery Meriwether was among those so expelled, although technically she already lived outside the municipal limits. She and her two young sons refugeed South during the winter of 1863, and her third son was delivered at Christmas. In her memoir, *Recollections of Ninety-Two Years*, Mrs. Meriwether recounts these and numerous other civilian and refugee experiences.

While in the Memphis theater of operations, Sherman seems to have been the first Union commander to realize that the war was against a whole people rather than just their armies.

The partisan operations that he encountered played a significant role in his development of a strategy of total warfare against the entire Southern nation. His most dramatic employment of that concept was, of course, the path that his troops later burned from Atlanta to the sea.

As suggested above, Union forces usually held the rail lines, too, and had garrisons or sometimes encampments along them at regular intervals. Confederates raided such posts with some frequency, and such attacks included some pretty fierce fighting. Soon after the fall of Memphis, Confederate cavalry attacked a military supply wagon train headed east along the stage road (current U. S. 64) east of Bartlett. The convoy of 67 wagons, 240 men, and several hundred mules had reached the tiny community of Morning Sun.

The rebels swooped in with a force of about 325 men, hitting the train from the side and rear, but with little effect. Alerted Union troops fired a volley into the charging horsemen, which broke the charge but stampeded their own mules. The Confederates charged several more times, each to no avail. They suffered 13 killed, 12 wounded, and 35 taken prisoner. The Union forces suffered 8 teamsters killed, 3 men wounded, and the wagon master missing. Unionists also suffered the loss of 8 wagons and 31 mules. This action may have been typical of small-scale raids and skirmishes in and near rural Shelby County.

Union garrisons in the towns of Collierville and Germantown were targets of Confederate raids later in the war. In October of 1863, Confederate forces led by General James

Chalmers struck at the railroad depot at Collierville. The building had been fortified as a blockhouse and was surrounded by shallow trenches. A four-hour firefight ensued in which General Sherman and his staff were involved. The Confederates withdrew as a large body of Federal reinforcements advanced to relieve the beleaguered garrison. The Federals lost 14, killed, 42 wounded, and 54 captured. The attackers lost 3 killed and 48 wounded. If Union troops had not arrived when they did, Sherman might have been captured. In an earlier instance, General Grant might have been captured in Collierville at the home of Josiah Deloach, had Deloach not warned him to leave. Although "close only counts in horseshoes, hand grenades, and nuclear fallout," it is interesting to speculate on how differently the war might have gone had Grant and Sherman been removed from participating in it so early in the fighting.

Even as late as April of 1865, rebel partisans attacked a small Union railway fort and garrison fourteen miles east of Memphis at Germantown. As was usually the case, the raid appears to have been inconclusive. Modern Germantown has memorialized the earthworks remains of this place with a small public park named "Fort Germantown."

The most important action fought in Shelby County after the fall of Memphis was doubtlessly General Forrest's raid into Memphis in August 1864. Forrest and his 5,000 troops had been raiding into West Tennessee almost at will. In a fourth concentrated attempt to destroy Forrest's home base, Union forces numbering more than 18,000 were closing in on his position at Oxford, Mississippi. In the face of his nearly hopeless situation, Forrest again took the offensive. Leaving 3,000 men to hold back the advancing Federals, Forrest and the other 2,000 made a dash to threaten the Union's logistical center at Memphis. About three-fourths of his troops invaded Memphis at dawn on the 21st. The attack was a complete surprise, and demonstrates again Confederate effectiveness outside Federal picket lines. Although it failed to capture targeted Union generals, or to release Confederate prisoners held in the infamous Irving Block prison, the raid succeeded in its primary purpose. Union command withdrew its forces from northern Mississippi to safeguard Memphis. Forrest and his highly mobile forces remained a threat until war's end.

Some Shelby County towns recorded no direct military action. Raleigh had only soldiers passing through and residents suffering privation and just surviving "as best they could." At one point, Confederate

✧

Left: Confederate sniper fire, especially at Union vessels on the Mississippi River, brought retaliation against civilians from the Federal occupation forces. For every shot fired at a Union target, Sherman exiled ten pro-Confederate families from Memphis.

ILLUSTRATION COURTESY OF THE MEMPHIS PINK PALACE MUSEUM, DAPHNE F. HEWETT, ARTIST.

Below: Maintaining control of watercourses, roads, and, especially, railroads was vital to the Union war effort. This image shows a locomotive of the era pulling into a depot and the tracks meeting at aptly named Grand Junction about 60 miles due east of Memphis. Of course, the Confederate military did all it could to disrupt Federal logistical routes.

COURTESY OF FIRST TENNESSEE HERITAGE COLLECTION.

❖

Above: Nathan Bedford Forrest's cavalry
raided into Memphis on August 21, 1864,
posing a threat to the Union Army's logistical
center there. Although the raiders failed to
either rescue Confederate POWs from Irving
Block Prison or to capture any of the three
Union generals that they had targeted, they
did cause the Union to pull back the large
force it had sent to take Oxford, Mississippi.
The illustration is from Harpers Weekly.

COURTESY OF SPECIAL COLLECTIONS, UNIVERSITY OF
MEMPHIS LIBRARIES.

Right: General Lewis Wallace had a fairly
high profile, multi-faceted career, with
significant reverses. A major general
following Union success at Fort Donaldson,
he was less fortunate at Shiloh and his
confused actions there nearly lost the battle
for Grant. He was headquartered briefly at
Bartlett (then named Union Depot) and held
mainly administrative posts for the rest of
the war. Although he served in congress, as
territorial governor of New Mexico, and as
U. S. Minister to the Ottoman Empire, he
was also a fairly prolific writer and is best
remembered for his historical novel, Ben
Hur: A Tale of the Christ.

sympathizers ran some pro-Unionist families out of their town. Sherman thereupon required the richest citizens to purchase all of the property of those who had been driven out of the community.

Raleigh's foremost historian, Mrs. Mary Winslow Chapman, included excerpts from the diary of her ancestor Will Goodwin, who joined Forrest's cavalry late in the war at the tender age of sixteen. "When the proper time came, [Will] mounted his horse and rode off to fight for his country... just doing what comes naturally when a man's homeland is invaded by the enemy." Will's record reinforces the mundane "hurry up and wait" aspects of living in the military. It stresses the everyday concerns of getting food and rest, of staying warm and dry, of foraging and regularly moving 30 miles or so per day. He notes that his unit was often well fed and put up by local residents. He recounts his participation in many patrols and skirmishes. He ends his journal in Nashville following his unit's surrender while he is on his way home.

Union General Lew Wallace (author of *Ben Hur*) quartered his troops and established his headquarters briefly in Bartlett. Wallace's men were thought to be less rapacious than many

Union units, but locals' horses, mules, and hay were still commandeered or just plain "taken." In order to survive in such an environment, most locals kept their political opinions to themselves.

Even as the Civil War began liberating blacks, it also began liberating women in a different sense. Shelby County's women

NEW YORK, SEPTEMBER 27, 1862.

BRIGADIER-GENERAL LEWIS WALLACE, COMMANDER OF THE NATIONAL FORCES FOR

worked hard in the service of the Confederacy. Prior to the fall of Memphis, they worked as nurses and in the city's fledgling factories to support the war effort. Their greatest military value, however, may have been in their roles as couriers, informants, and agents of the Southern war effort. Women had much more freedom of movement than had civilian men. They also had clothing that better lent itself to the concealment of contraband goods. Perhaps remarkably, some African-American women also supported the Confederate cause by helping to smuggle contraband.

Shelby County's most noted femme fatales were Belle Edmondson, mentioned above, Loreta Janeta Velazquez, and the Moon sisters, Ginnie and Lottie. All four women got through the war unscathed and either told their own stories or had them told after the war. Given the clandestine nature of their work, there is little, if any, way to verify or refute their claims. The Velazquez story is the most farfetched. By her account, she also disguised herself as a Col. Harry T. Buford, raised a cavalry company, and fought at Bull Run and at Shiloh. Later, in her female persona, she served as a spy and counterspy. Her colorful

Above: The Northern press made much of the fact that Memphians had "defaced" the bust statue of Andrew Jackson that stood in Court Square. Locals had chiseled off the quotation in which Jackson had stated that the Federal Union must and would be preserved. This sculpture was more defaced by the elements than the Confederates. It is now protected inside the Shelby County Courthouse.

Below: Under occupation, the Federal authorities used the Irving Block Building as a prison for military and civilian offenders. Whether justified or not, Memphians thought it to be harsh and unhealthy. Described as "the Bastille of the South," its unsavory reputation has endured. It served as a way station for Ginny McGhee, after she was imprisoned for smuggling.

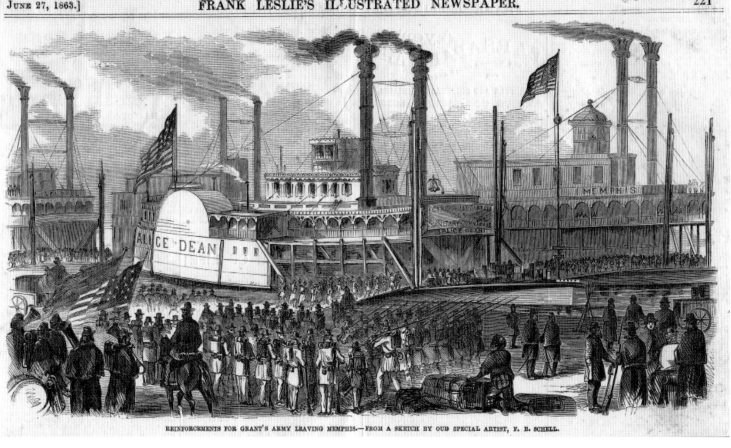

REINFORCEMENTS FOR GRANT'S ARMY LEAVING MEMPHIS.—FROM A SKETCH BY OUR SPECIAL ARTIST, F. B. SCHELL.

✥

Above: Throughout the war, Memphis remained an important transportation hub, via the Mississippi River. Supplies and troops were sent south from the Bluff City to beef up Grant's forces for the siege of Vicksburg. This F. B. Schell sketch provided a glimpse of that action to readers of Frank Leslie's Illustrated Newspaper.

COURTESY OF SPECIAL COLLECTIONS, UNIVERSITY OF MEMPHIS LIBRARIES.

Right: Union forces confiscated a great deal of cotton from pro-Confederate sources and shipped such contraband north. In this sketch, teams of black roustabouts roll cotton bales aboard the steamboat Tatum. Bales and barrels were such popular ways to package commodities in the nineteenth century because they could be easily rolled when on their sides, yet were relatively stable when turned on end. Note the idle dolly in the foreground.

COURTESY OF SPECIAL COLLECTIONS, UNIVERSITY OF MEMPHIS LIBRARIES.

memoir appeared in 1876; she is lost to history from about 1880 until her death in 1897.

Local folklore has it that "the best of all the Confederate spies" was a Memphis woman named Kate Cumberlin, who was noted for smuggling percussion caps south for the CSA. She had disingenuously taken the "ironclad oath" of loyalty to the Union and posed as a wealthy woman working to help blacks and poor whites. She was nearly apprehended on a trip upriver, but escaped capture by the Federal agent who had "found her out." Later the former antagonists are supposed to have married each other.

Not all patriotic Southern women were so fortunate. Sixteen-year-old Ginny McGhee of Collierville was apprehended smuggling contraband gray cloth (for Confederate uniforms) out of Memphis. She was first confined to nearby Irving Block prison. Later, authorities transferred her to a prison in another city, where she died the following winter.

Many civilians, whether guilty or not, were imprisoned or exiled from the city. Many who were guilty got away with their infractions because the city's commercial atmosphere quickly became extraordinarily chaotic and corrupt. According to lawyer John Hallum, who made a fortune brokering deals of various sorts, including

Rolling Cotton on Board the "Tatum."

springing Confederate partisans from prisons, there were few if any consistent ground rules. Deals were broken, betrayals were many, and the ethical atmosphere was Byzantine. Much illicit trade was transacted that a Union general famously remarked that "Memphis has been of more value to the Southern Confederacy since it fell into Federal hands than [the great blockade running center at] Nassau." Cotton, which had sold for as little as $41.50 a bale in 1859, was selling for as much as $360 a bale in 1863. Profiteers and speculators were willing to take great risks.

The Confederacy did not so much lose the war as it lost the ability to keep resisting. Finances were always a major problem for the South. Even at the war's onset, Shelby County government had to issue scrip to help supply, to arm, and equip local soldiers. Once the war was underway, deprivation did horrible things to people. Inflation was quick to surface and extremely disruptive. There were immediate shortages in occupied Memphis.

For example, spools of thread cost $5 each, if they could be had at all. Salt leapt to $100 a barrel. In Memphis, civilians were forced to accept Federal Treasury notes, and merchants were forbidden to pay locals in gold or silver. If caught, they would be arrested and sent north.

In many respects, Southerners had lost the ability to provide for their basic needs because they had been purchasing their necessities from the North for decades. As the war wore on, Southerners accepted many substitutes for things that had long been commonplace. In some areas, conditions bordered on famine. To survive, some people resorted to eating insects and field mice. According to Granville Davis, "Morale gave way in Memphis and in the surrounding region. Desertion became commonplace and conscription laws impossible to enforce."

A failure of morale is understandable. Shelby Countians had made up seven of the ten companies of the 154th Tennessee Regiment. This group fought in many major

✧

Soldiers, understandably despising the standard, alternating military modes of "hurry up and wait," grabbed recreation where they could find it. Artist Henri Lovie here depicts a "gambling establishment in the woods 'outside the [picket] lines,' near Memphis." One wonders if the tent in the background hosted bar, brothel, or both.

so deeply imprinted by the war and all it had destroyed in their lives that they never got over it. Former CSA cavalryman Robert Bruce Bowe epitomizes such reactions. His 1907 grave marker, in the old Edmondson Cemetery almost on the state line between Shelby County and Mississippi, reads in part:

I have [had] no flag or country since 1865, an alien in the land my forefathers [have] defended in war since 1624. Providence, taking side with the strong and oppressive against the weak and just, has caused me to live in doubt the past forty years, and [I] fear I will die so.

Thus, the war's outcome had cost Bowe his faith in God and in his own salvation.

Oddly, perhaps, Mid Southerners in general seem to have been more embittered and resentful about Reconstruction than about their loss of the war itself. In a sense, Reconstruction policies

battles, including Belmont, Shiloh, Perryville, Corinth, and Murphreesboro. They suffered horrendous losses. Out of 1,100 men belonging to the 154th, fewer than one hundred were left alive when the South surrendered. Disease may have been responsible for many more deaths than combat, but dead is dead. Once in military camps, rural recruits were particularly vulnerable to contagious diseases like measles. Even many of those who survived combat physically were often devastated emotionally.

James Baxter Davies of northeastern Shelby County had enlisted in the Confederate Army in March 1862. He fought in a half-dozen major battles, and his health became fragile. After he returned from the war, he was an emotionally broken man. On several occasions, he tried to kill his wife and himself. Ultimately, he slit his own throat with a razor, but somehow survived. Following this act, his wife Pauline successfully sued for divorce and moved away, taking her personal property with her.

When the war finally ended, some Shelby Countians rolled up their sleeves and got on with their lives as best they could. Others were

began in Shelby County with the fall of Memphis, and that political and economic climate from the war extended four years into its aftermath. During the first three years of the war, Memphis' population grew to about 40,000 persons, almost double the total in 1860. Moreover, the make up of its citizenry changed drastically. Pillars of the community refugeed to other areas. Military and medical personnel, Northern merchants, and soon-to-be freedmen more than replaced the area's departed refugees. Crime, vice, opportunism, and corruption all rose dramatically.

For much of the war, both city and county lived under martial law. Early in the occupation, prior to the Emancipation Proclamation, General Sherman refused to return runaway slaves to their owners. In fact, some of the Union's practices for dealing with runaway slaves, which later evolved into policies for the Freedmen's Bureau, had their precedents set in the Memphis military theater.

During the occupation, white Shelby Countians had had little or no legal appeal when those in power misused their authority to maltreat the area's civilians. According to

John Keating, the immediate post-war period was "noted for lawlessness in town and country," with marauders hanging around outside the city. The Freedman's Bureau degenerated into a political arm of the Republicans, who raised the levels of racial divisiveness to their own political ends. The Memphis *Avalanche* referred to the levels of crookedness and exploitation as "a carnival of crime." Favoritism and cronyism were common and obvious in the so-called courts of law.

Because the Tennessee courts of Shelby County shut down during the war, the Union Army established a Civil Commission to "hear suits and complaints instigated by *loyal citizens*,"[emphasis added] without juries. The Commission was composed of Union officers deriving their authority from military power. Since Confederate sympathizers had no real standing before the military tribunals, pro-Unionists had distinct advantages in any litigation before the Commission. Without utilizing the procedures of law courts, the Commission disposed of cases quickly, if often unjustly, at bayonet point.

Both Shelby County citizens and their
government were in horrible financial shape
at war's end. Road building, probably the
most important county function prior to the
war, was simply unaffordable. Some of the
roads were so badly overgrown and otherwise
deteriorated that they were unusable and
temporarily abandoned.

Farms and plantations were also largely all
but destroyed. Even in instances where the
main house had survived, outbuildings and
fences had been used for firewood. Soldiers
and deserters from both sides had
"commandeered" grain and livestock over the
course of the war. The labor supply, black
and white, was greatly diminished by death,
disability, and the Emancipation Proclamation.
Most of the former master class had become
destitute and powerless. Even where families
retained title to their lands, they often
remained "land poor."

In such circumstances, it is hardly surprising
that members of the former master class
resorted to force and intimidation to right
what they saw as a situation gone bad. Toward
the end of the war, many of the regular soldiers
had become irregulars or guerrillas. This sort
of thing had been done from time immemorial,
as demonstrated in Old Testament resistance
to Philistine rule and by tales of bandit heroes
like Robin Hood. Thus, the rise of pooled
resistance via the Ku Klux Klan and kindred
groups should not have come as a surprise. It
would have been more surprising if some sort
of vigilante actions had not taken place. It
should also not be surprising that the former
master class tried to reassert their authority
over their former slaves. The South had spent
decades convincing itself that African
Americans were inherently inferior. Then,
inconsistent Reconstruction policies,
Southerners' refusals to take the "ironclad
oath," and ratification of the Fifteenth
Amendment to the Constitution all contributed
to a complete reversal of roles in the power
structure. It is worth noting that in recent
decades many scholars and the popular culture
have drawn few, if any, distinctions between
the Reconstruction-era Klan and that which
sprang up early in the twentieth century,
inspired Thomas Dixon's novel The Clansman
and the motion picture Birth of a Nation.

No less a figure than C. P. J. Mooney, crusading editor of the *Commercial Appeal* and implacable enemy of the twentieth-century Klan, drew strong distinctions between the two groups. He saw the Reconstruction era Klan as justifiable and relatively benign. His war against the newer Klan in the early 1920s was so effective that it helped kill the Klan's political power in Memphis and won a Pulitzer Prize. Moreover, diaries, letters, and memoirs of white Shelby Countians who lived through Reconstruction almost uniformly support a need for and the efficacy of the earlier Klan. Even Elizabeth Avery Meriwether, who, with husband Minor, had freed their inherited slaves prior to the Civil War, defends the post-war Klan in her autobiography.

Of course, Shelby Countian Nathan Bedford Forrest is almost uniformly condemned for having been the first Grand Wizard of the KKK. Certainly, he at least lent his name to organizing resistance to abuses under post-war, Republican rule. Almost

totally ignored by scholars, however, is a relevant manuscript left by Mary Hannah Gordon, widow of former Confederate General George Washington Gordon. In it, Mrs. Gordon asserts and offers evidence that it was her late husband, rather than General Forrest, who organized and acted as the true head of the Klan. She also maintains that it was Gordon who ordered its dissolution in March of 1869. Given the nature of the organization and the paucity of documentary evidence regarding it, the veracity of Mrs. Gordon's contentions will probably never be proved or disproved. To confuse this issue

✧

The bloody and destructive Memphis race riot of 1866 began with tension between civilians and recently discharged black Union soldiers. Once violence broke out it lasted for three days and resulted in 46 deaths, 75 persons wounded, and four churches, 12 schools, and 91 homes burned. Almost universally the victims were blacks.

ILLUSTRATION FROM *HARPER'S WEEKLY.* COURTESY OF MEMPHIS & SHELBY COUNTY ROOM, MEMPHIS PUBLIC LIBRARY & INFORMATION CENTER.

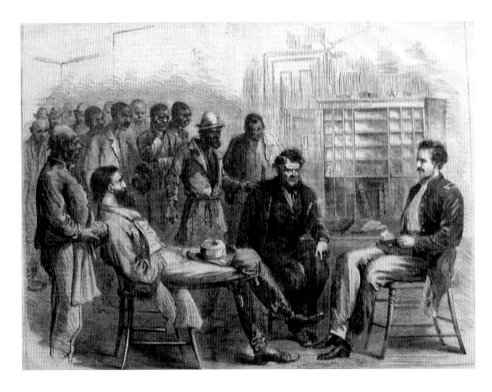

even further, by the mid-1870s Nathan Bedford Forrest emerged as an advocate for racial harmony. He made a speech to that effect at a picnic held by a black fraternal organization.

Irrespective of which Shelby Countian may have led the Klan, the quick dissolution of such a group is truly remarkable. The circumstances thereof were twofold. First, because of changes at the state government level, old guard Democrats returned to power in 1869. Second, there had been serious abuses and atrocities attributed to the Klan, for which it denied any responsibility. Old guard Southerners claimed that non-Klan members were the perpetrators of such foul deeds. History Professor Enoch L. Mitchell, who brought the Gordon manuscript to light in the 1947 issue of the *West Tennessee Historical Society Papers*, examined the available evidence but drew no firm conclusions about true KKK leadership.

As important as Reconstruction and its policies were for white Shelby Countians, they were

certainly even more vital to the wellbeing of local blacks. If the area's defeated whites indeed felt the yoke of "Black Republican rule," it did not last for very long and thus was not as onerous as early twentieth-century historians depicted. Perhaps the race riot of 1866, with its wanton destruction and death dealing, gave blacks an extension of an ascendancy that they may have shared with "carpetbaggers and scalawags" under occupation and until the federal troop strength began to be demobilized. The Memphis riot, one of the three most brutal post-war riots in the South, saw dozens of African-American residents killed and virtually all of their schools and churches destroyed. In the wake of the rioting and the establishment of martial law, many transient blacks either left the Memphis area or returned to the countryside and rural labor. It is impossible to even guess how many of the latter group may have returned to plantations on which they had labored as slaves. They were not, however, immediately deprived of political participation and power.

Under the administration of William G. Brownlow, radical Republicans controlled politics across post-war Tennessee. In 1867, blacks comprised about three-fourths of the

Republican Party's voting strength in Tennessee. About half of Brownlow's votes for governor came from newly enfranchised blacks. Union Leagues organized blacks politically, which gave Republicans a sweep in 1867. The KKK resisted Republican dominance, and the legislature empowered Brownlow "to use unlimited military force against the Klan and to impose stiff penalties for political terrorism." Thus, Brownlow owed much to his black supporters and gave them a good deal of support in return.

Within that context, local blacks made some political gains that lasted into the mid-1870s. Black leaders from Shelby County were important figures at a series of Tennessee Colored Political Conventions in Nashville during the late 1860s and early 1870s. At the 1865 gathering, a U. S. Army sergeant named Henry J. Maxwell gave the keynote speech. He used strong rhetoric, claiming the need for African Americans to make use of the cartridge box, the ballot box, and the jury box to achieve their goals.

At the 1866 Convention, again in Nashville, more moderate blacks tried to emphasize a focus on "Education, Agriculture, Manufacturing and Mining." Nashville's white mayor urged them to avoid politics, making pointed references to race riots in other Southern cities (Memphis and New Orleans). This gambit led to a difference of opinions among the delegates on whether to bow to

intimidation tactics. Memphian Ed Shaw argued that only through voting would black interests be protected. The convention divided between delegates demanding equal rights and those wanting to focus largely on black education and economic improvement. The accommodationists prevailed at first, but after considerable debate, the delegates voted narrowly to unite with the more militant Equal Rights League. Six months later, the Tennessee General Assembly passed a black enfranchisement law. Not long afterward, the legislature removed all obstacles to blacks serving on juries and holding office. In the wake of these actions, the *Memphis Appeal* published a hideously racist rant against such black empowerment.

Taking advantage of this window of opportunity, Shelby County blacks made progress toward political ascendancy. Blacks mustered a heavy turnout in the 1868 election. During this period, the radical state legislature authorized a change in the structure of county government, vesting power in a

✧

Above: Prior to the end of Reconstruction in Tennessee, blacks and traditional southern whites were again finding grounds for reaching an accommodation in their relationships. This sketch shows black nannies caring for white children in one of the Memphis parks.

COURTESY OF SPECIAL COLLECTIONS, UNIVERSITY OF MEMPHIS LIBRARIES.

Below: Tennessee's blacks were eager to vote and lobbied strongly for that privilege. This sketch from Harper's Magazine *shows blacks as voters and poll workers. If blacks ever had anything that approached political ascendancy, it did not last long. In the 1880 election, prominent black politician Ed Shaw was unable to win the sheriff's office, although Shelby County blacks outnumbered whites by about twenty percent.*

ILLUSTRATION FROM HARPER'S WEEKLY, 1867.

board of commissioners. This was viewed as a political machination of Ed Shaw, who served on the commission. It only lasted a few months, however, and then was repealed by a very different legislature.

In February of 1869, Governor Brownlow resigned to take a seat in the U.S. Senate. Tennessee Senate Speaker Dewitt Clinton Senter succeeded him. Once in office, Senter dropped the state's suffrage restrictions against former Confederates, and the following month the KKK was disbanded and dissolved. The election of 1869 saw Acting Governor Senter elected to a full term, and he gave conservative Democrats full control of the General Assembly. A Constitutional Convention was called for January of 1870. Its delegates were made up of 65 Democrats and 10 Republicans. Significantly, there were no black delegates participating. These abrupt changes resulted in the quick dismantling of any pretense of black ascendancy in Tennessee.

Black and white Republicans appealed to the Federal Government to oust the sitting government and impose military reconstruction on Tennessee. Failing to get Federal support, black resistance subsided. Additional Tennessee Colored Conventions were held through 1875, and Nashville hosted the National Colored Convention in 1876.

In Shelby County, black political power had rested upon support from Republicans at the state level, the influence of black religious ministers, coalitions of black fraternal and benevolent mutual aid societies (often referred to as "pole bearers"), and cooperation with local white Republicans.

Ed Shaw became the paramount black political leader in Shelby County. Born in Kentucky in the 1820s, he came to Memphis in the 1850s and operated a saloon and gambling house there after the war. Shaw made his articulate and forceful voice heard on the political scene. He was an advocate of racial equality, racial integration, and full black participation in the political process. When white Republicans appeared to be simply using black voting power in the late 1860s, Shaw ran as an independent against former U. S. General W. J. Smith for Congress and alienated enough black votes to play the spoiler. Thereafter, white Republicans treated their black constituents with more respect. Blacks screened white Republican candidates carefully to ascertain their attitudes and get commitments on the issues. Shaw got elected to the city council in 1873 and served as wharf master in 1874, making him briefly the highest paid public official in Memphis. Blacks built their political strength until 1875, when their coalition broke up. Shaw ran credibly but unsuccessfully for the state senate in 1878 and for Sheriff of Shelby County in 1880.

Roger Hart, in *Redeemers, Bourbons & Populists*, makes the case that Shaw's 1880 contest for sheriff held much symbolic value. Because of the yellow fever epidemics of the 1870s, blacks made up a majority in Shelby County. Whereas whites had outnumbered blacks by 40,000 to 36,000 in 1870, in 1880, blacks outnumbered whites 44,000 to 35,000. Even so, his Democratic opponent won the race by an 8,564 to 5,675 vote tally. Angry

leaders charged that black voters had been intimidated and otherwise cheated. According to Hart, "the defeat of Ed Shaw demonstrated that even with a strong candidate and a clear majority of the voters, black people had little hope for political power when white employers, landowners, public officials, newspapers, [and] ballot-counters united against them." Shaw's prestige remained such that, in April of 1880, he had the honor of escorting former President U. S. Grant on a visit to Beale Street Baptist Church.

Two years later, after breaking with Republican Governor Alvin Hawkins, Shaw was making common cause with the Bourbon Democrats at the state level. In the 1882 and 1884 gubernatorial elections, Shaw campaigned for former Confederate General William B. Bate, who won both times. Thus, Shaw also seems to have become a racial accommodationist. .

As Shaw became less directly involved in politics in the late-1880s, he still practiced law and edited the *Memphis Planet* (newspaper). He died in 1891. As Shaw's political effectiveness waned, so did that of local African Americans. The year Shaw died, enforcement of the Tennessee poll-tax law severely restricted further black participation and effectiveness in the governing process.

After the surrender of the Memphis City Charter in 1880, blacks had little real part in the city's governance because home rule had ceased to exist. The state appointed local members of the white elite to serve in upper and lower chambers of government devoted primarily to administrative ends. Black businessman Limus Wallace did serve on the city council between 1882 and 1890, but local "government" did not have the power to tax or truly legislate until home rule was restored in 1893. In the 1870s and 1880s, blacks had been departing Memphis and returning to the rural hinterland, including outlying Shelby County. It seems probable that in such circumstances, their economic dependence on rural whites would have argued for less militant political participation than had occurred briefly in Memphis. David Tucker, in his seminal *Black Pastors and Leaders*, notes a rural/urban divide in black allegiances. While the black clergy had little success curbing the influence of fraternal societies in Memphis, they had greater influence in the countryside. In any event, as the poll-tax law of 1891 indicates, Jim Crow political skullduggery would further curtail Shelby County blacks' political participation and aspirations. For decades thereafter, blacks retained the legal right to vote, but often could not afford to pay the poll tax. Those who did vote negotiated the best deals they could with various white political factions. In this context, however, their voting power became little more than extensions of white machine politics. The redoubtable E. H. Crump would soon enter Shelby County's evolving political arena and dominate its leadership for nearly half a century.

✧

Above: In a horrible irony, as blacks were assuming more civic responsibilities in Memphis, where they briefly had a successful coalition with Irish and Italian ethnics, they lost political power after the mid-1870s. In this sketch, black militiamen are shown maintaining order after the vast majority of whites had fled the city during the yellow fever epidemic of 1878.
ILLUSTRATION FROM *HARPER'S WEEKLY.*

Below: Most white citizens left Memphis during the yellow fever epidemics of the late1870s. Those who could not leave the area fled to refugee camps outside the city. The relative isolation was partially effective against the disease.

CHAPTER VI

EDWARD HULL CRUMP, JR. AND HIS SHELBY COUNTY POLITICAL ORGANIZATION, 1906-54

There can be no thornier problem in any consideration of Shelby County's history than assessing the roles and impact of Edward Hull Crump Jr. and his political organization on the development of Memphis and Shelby County, (and, to a lesser extent, the state, the region, and the nation). Was his long rule good or bad for Shelby Countians? Was he a benevolent blessing, a baneful boss, or somehow both? Historians and other writers have usually either villainized or lionized Crump, rarely finding much middle ground. Often they seem more driven by their own ideological proclivities than by an open-minded evaluation of the Crump phenomenon in its proper contexts. However, there should be a core of hard facts that can provide for at least a mutual starting point.

Probably the first revision to challenge is the current, nearly universal use of the term "Boss" Crump. The term is pejorative and distorts the entire context in which E. H. Crump and his Shelby County organization operated. Paul R. Coppock, in almost a half-century of reporting and editing Mid-South news and nearly that long chronicling its history, always insisted that it was either "Mr. Crump," or "E. H. Crump." Only outsiders, avowed enemies, and ignorant persons used the sobriquet, "Boss," when addressing him or referring to him publicly. Such distortions do not make for good history.

The oft told, Algeresque tale of Crump coming from humble circumstances in Holly Springs, Mississippi, working his way to dominance in the Shelby County arena, and holding on to power longer than any political boss (lower case!) in American history need not be repeated here. (See pages 114-19 and 134-37 of *Metropolis of the American Nile* for a brief sketch of Crump and the organization). Our emphasis here will lean more toward the organization and its stalwarts in the Shelby County context, than on Crump himself.

Wayne Dowdy, librarian at the Memphis Public Library and author of the most recent book on Crump, has suggested that rather than behaving as a dictator, as has often been charged, Crump generally acted as a sort of chairman of the board, directing his team toward consensus and productivity. Columbia Professor Kenneth T. Jackson, native Memphian and eminent urban scholar, apparently finds nothing to challenge in Dowdy's perspective. E. Denby Brandon, whose M. A. thesis on "Commission Government in Memphis" is one of the finest and most overlooked studies of the organization, also reached a similar conclusion in his 1952 Duke University study. He refers to Crump's role as the "center of responsibility" which coordinated "harmonious teamwork" among his anointed, elected officials. Crump demanded (and got) "both good teamwork and effective and honest administration."

The loyalty, effectiveness, and longevity of Crump's closest lieutenants are almost as remarkable as is the Crump story itself. Judge Lois Bejach, an organization stalwart himself, is quoted as having once said "Crump was the general, Watkins Overton, Tyler McLain, and E. W. Hale were corps commanders and Frank 'Roxie' Rice was the field marshal." Of course, there were numerous other stalwart lieutenants within the organization.

Frank Rice was the earliest and longest serving of Crump's faithful underlings. A native Memphian of Irish and Italian extraction, Rice survived a bout with yellow fever in 1878 and had poor health for much of his adult life. He seems not to have been academically inclined, dropping out of the law program at the University of Virginia. He served as a lieutenant in the Spanish-American War, and had a number of career false starts after returning home.

Early in the twentieth century, he was a minor figure in the organization of machine politico J. J. Williams. In 1907, Rice joined the reform Democrats and managed the Crump campaign for fire

The Shelby County Organization and Their Candidates

✧

Right: This 1930s newspaper clipping of "the Shelby County Organization" includes many of the machine's stalwart supporters and their statewide candidates. Described in the caption as the first string line-up for the big game in the Aug. 4, primary—left to right, these include: Police Commissioner Cliff Davis, County Commission Chairman E. W. Hale, Red Williams, Congressman Walter Chandler, Crump employee Ed Slater, E. H. Crump himself, City Attorney Will Gerber, Senator K. D. McKellar, and Shelby County Sheriff Guy Joyner. Senatorial candidate Tom Stewart, gubernatorial candidate Prentice Cooper, and Public Utilities Commission candidate Pete Hudson were visiting Memphis to get endorsements from the organization and nearly one thousand influential citizens. Mayor Watkins Overton, second from the right is sandwiched between Cooper and Hudson.

COURTESY OF SPECIAL COLLECTIONS,
UNIVERSITY OF MEMPHIS LIBRARIES.

Below: Paul Coppock termed Frank "Roxie" Rice the Crump organization's generalissimo, to describe how important he was to the machine's success. Rice was the group's consummate organizer, strategist, and decision maker until his death. Here he poses beside a fire engine that has been named for him.

COURTESY OF MEMPHIS & SHELBY COUNTY ROOM,
MEMPHIS PUBLIC LIBRARY & INFORMATION CENTER.

Opposite, bottom: Among the public relations activities practiced by the Crump organization were annual Crump's days at the Fair Grounds and on Mississippi Riverboat excursion rides. Here Crump poses with political insiders and several pretty little girls as part of his common touch appeal for personal and political support.

COURTESY OF MEMPHIS & SHELBY COUNTY ROOM,
MEMPHIS PUBLIC LIBRARY & INFORMATION CENTER.

and police commissioner. He and E. H. Crump put together a ticket and program for the Shelby County delegation to have the state legislature restructure city government. Their scheme won passage, and the following year J. J. Williams lost the mayoral race to Crump. Shortly thereafter, Rice was elected county register of deeds. After serving briefly in the state senate and as a state revenue agent, he became Shelby County's back tax collector for many years. Underlings handled the routine business of his office, while Rice managed the organization's affairs from an undesignated office in another part of the courthouse. "He was the top man for hundreds of city and county jobholders, with a street-by-street card index of voters." He funneled campaign money into insuring that, weeks before election day, all "friends" of the organization were registered to vote.

More conspicuously, Rice managed the Shelby delegation to the legislature. Although having only eight members at the time, "Big Shelby" wielded great power in the General Assembly. During the sessions, the delegates met with Rice every morning, even gathering around his bed to receive their instructions when he was ill. Rice also served as political mentor to dozens of young men, and he graded their performances for possible advancement within the organization. Rice

T. G. TATE

IS A CANDIDATE FOR

SHERIFF

of Shelby County

If I am elected Sheriff I will enforce the law, close all dives and roadhouses, and will stand by and support the Attorney General in the enforcement of all laws of the State.

ALLIED PRINTING TRADES UNION LABEL COUNCIL MEMPHIS TENN. 9 **Election August 6, 1908**

❖

Above: T. Galen Tate was at least a Crump ally during the early part of the twentieth century. Later they parted company and the Tates became Crump opponents. Galen apparently lost this race to the incumbent, Frank L. Monteverde, but he won two years later and served 1910 to 1914. Crump himself had intended to run in 1914, but learned after the filing deadline that he could not legally serve as Mayor of Memphis and Shelby County Sheriff at the same time. Although he had surrogate John Reichman elected as a write in candidate, his show of political manipulation in doing so brought him fresh political foes.

persuasion were deemed second to none. He had literally stood shoulder to shoulder with Crump in a politically inspired fistfight when Crump was still on the city council. By 1940, following the deaths of Tyler McLain and Frank Rice, however, there must have been some level of estrangement. Sheriff Guy Joyner and Attorney General Will Gerber became the two key organizational lieutenants, shunting Bryan aside. Then, with no advance warning, the Memphis police raided the Stockyard Hotel's bar. This was owned but not operated by Bryan. This deliberate embarrassment wounded Bryan deeply, but he continued to profess loyalty to the organization until his death in late 1941.

E. W. "Will" Hale, Sr., of Whitehaven and John Frank "Jack" Dudney, Jr., of Collierville served for decades as the organization's elected leaders of the two branches of county government. Hale served on the County Commission for 44 years,

was unabashedly a professional politician and became wealthy at it. A frequent advocate of the underdog, during the Depression he and his office's attorney turned back $250,000 of their fees. He fought against the implementation of a state sales tax, as being too great a burden on the poor. His philosophy was that good government made the best politics, and he did everything that he could to advance the well being of Shelby Countians.

Rice was popular within the organization and without. Critics of the machine never raised any questions regarding his personal integrity. Usually outspoken, he used plain language and unloaded any anger, lest it resurface at a later date. He died in late 1938 and left a vacuum in the organization, which was never totally filled.

Charles M. Bryan, another unusually able and loyal organization insider, supported Crump from the very beginning of his political career. A truly gifted raconteur, orator, and barrister, Bryan was often the organization's legal defender and trouble-shooter. His powers of

chairing it for 32 of those years. Dudney, likewise served on the Quarterly Court for 32 years, chairing it from 1935 to 1954. Both men were pillars of their smaller communities, owning or partnering in country stores and having extensive land holdings in their respective areas. The *Press Scimitar* referred to Hale as the organization's number-two man, following the death of Frank Rice. Dudney predeceased Crump by a few months, and Hale retired not long after Crump's death in 1954. Both men diligently pursued and supported the machine's policies and goals over the decades and contributed significantly to its success.

There were dozens of lesser lights, whether directly involved in politics or not, who supported the Crump organization and benefited therefrom. Space available will not permit even a cursory review of such parties' performances and contributions.

Probably second only to E. H. Crump himself in securing the local organization's power base would be Kenneth D. McKellar. McKellar came to Memphis in the early 1890s, fresh from the University of Alabama law school. Practicing law and growing into politics, he served as a Democratic elector in the 1904 presidential contest and as a delegate to the Democrats' National Convention in 1908. He and Crump belonged to the same reformer camp of young Democrats. In 1911, McKellar was a candidate for the U.S. Senate, which was still chosen by the state legislature. He lost to Nashville's Luke Lea, but later that year he defeated Memphian Thomas Looney for the suddenly vacant Tenth Congressional District seat in the U.S. House of Representatives. Although Crump took no open or active role in that contest, McKellar's margin of victory lay in Shelby County, primarily with Memphis voters. Without at

✧

Left: From the 1930s into the 1960s, Crump Stadium was the major athletic arena in the Mid-South. It hosted major, powerhouse Southeastern Conference football games, the Children's Ball of the Cotton Carnival, Boy Scout Pow-Wow competitions, and "Shower of Stars" gala variety shows to raise funds for St. Jude Children's Hospital. Federal funding helped make it a showplace for its day.

COURTESY OF MEMPHIS & SHELBY COUNTY ROOM,
MEMPHIS PUBLIC LIBRARY & INFORMATION CENTER.

Below: John T. and Anthony P. Walsh were commission merchants and grocers, catering to the needs of their fellow Irish-Americans in North Memphis and rural northwestern Shelby County. Although they got their start in a humble cigar stand, their grocery business became the basis for generating a considerable fortune. John Walsh became actively involved in local politics by the 1890s and was a force to be reckoned with a decade later. Although initially opposed to Crump, the two men later became allies. The figures second and third from the left are probably Anthony and John T., respectively.

COURTESY OF SPECIAL COLLECTIONS,
UNIVERSITY OF MEMPHIS LIBRARIES.

Right: Crump's most checkered political relationship was probably that with Watkins Overton. Overton served as Memphis Mayor from 1928-40 and again from 1949-53. Up to that time, no man had served longer as the city's chief executive. Crump had backed Overton in each of his election victories, but broke with him and became an opponent. Overton ran for mayor again after Crump's death, but reform and change were in the air and Edmund Orgill won the 1955 election.

COURTESY OF SPECIAL COLLECTIONS,
UNIVERSITY OF MEMPHIS LIBRARIES.

Below: Robert A. Tillman is shown here seated at his desk in the Tennessee State Capital during the 1941 session of the General Assembly. He served as General Sessions Court Judge, 1942-45, until he "fell out" with senior members of the Crump Organization, whereupon the legislature dissolved his division of the court. Already a political outcast and having been a victim of arbitrary power, Tillman became an orator on behalf of Gordon Browning and Estes Kefauver in their 1948 campaigns for governor and senator, respectively. Ever a champion of the underdog, Tillman had a private practice and served as an assistant public defender from 1956 until he retired in 1976, often representing the common man, including African Americans.

COURTESY OF MEMPHIS & SHELBY COUNTY ROOM,
MEMPHIS PUBLIC LIBRARY & INFORMATION CENTER.

least Crump's tacit support, this would not have happened.

McKellar became candidate for the Senate again in 1916, but by then the Sixteenth Amendment to the U.S. Constitution required the popular election of senators. McKellar triumphed over a former Tennessee governor and a former senator in the Democratic primary elections and over a former Republican governor in the general election. McKellar also overcame strong challengers in the 1922 and 1928 elections, growing stronger in each contest.

K. D. McKellar was largely responsible for the Federal authorization of the Harahan Bridge across the Mississippi at Memphis and for the damming of the Tennessee River at Muscle Shoals. He became such a powerful advocate of developing the Tennessee River Valley that he was often referred to as "the rich uncle of the TVA." Probably more important than his big ticket items, however, would have been his taking care of the little things. McKellar and his staff gave meticulous constituent services. His correspondence with Tennesseans wanting jobs or some other political assistance ran to about two million pieces. He often worked seven days a week, keeping six secretaries busy taking care of business.

The Crump-McKellar alliance was a long and fruitful one for both individuals and for the organization. Historians have sometimes seen McKellar as being little more than a Crump political puppet. According to Memphis journalist and historian Paul Coppock, however, "In fact McKellar was an ally whose statewide influence and Washington connections were as important to Crump as Crump's votes in Shelby County were to McKellar." Moreover, McKellar was no "Crump appointee." Crump had not given him open support in his House race of 1911 and had been too preoccupied with his own legal problems in 1915-16 to give McKellar direct, meaningful support in his first successful senate race.

McKellar went on to serve six terms in the Senate. With his House service, he served continuously in the American Congress between 1911 and 1953. That meant that he was the longest serving elected congressional official up to that time. Because of his seniority and his role chairing the Senate Appropriations Committee, he exercised a great deal of power and was able to funnel a disproportionate share of Depression-era and military spending dollars into Tennessee, especially Shelby County. He also served as president, pro tem of the Senate in the 1940s, making him acting Vice President and next in line to be president, if something had happened to Harry Truman. Finally, because of his age and failing faculties, by the late 1940s he had difficulty handling

the burdens of his office. Against Crump's advice, McKellar sought a seventh term in the Senate. Even though he still had the Crump organization's support, McKellar lost in the Democratic primary election of 1952 to a youthful, dynamic Albert Gore, Sr. Retired against his will, McKellar died in Memphis in 1957.

Besides having his stalwarts and the support of most Shelby Countians, Crump had a number of serious opponents over the decades. Some such foes the organization pre-empted and absorbed; others it intimidated into quiescence; still others it simply harassed into leaving the area.

The Walsh brothers represent the first group. John T. Walsh and his brother Anthony were first generation Irish Americans. They became prosperous grocers and cotton factors in North Memphis. They also invested in real estate and opened their own bank, which later merged with Union Planters. Their fortune also built the million-dollar, eighteen-story Claridge Hotel at 109 North Main

Street. Courting the votes of his fellow Irish Americans in North Memphis, John T. Walsh took a very active role in local politics. He became a member of the city's lower chamber in 1893, then a Fire and Police Commissioner and Vice-Mayor in 1906. Walsh initially allied with the Malone and the J. J. Williams political factions, but later cast his lot with the Crump-led group. Considered a machine politician by some and a reformer by others, Walsh supported Crump's organization for the duration. His son Tony worked in Crump's insurance business before becoming City Finance Commissioner on the Crump ticket in 1927.

Other local political figures eventually chafed at the Crump organization's control. Crump never exercised full control of city hall during the late teens and the early and mid-twenties, although he had initially supported each of his successors as mayor between 1916 and 1927. Even after the 1927 election, Mayors Watkins Overton, Walter Chandler, and Jim Pleasants all sought to

✧

The Crump team attended the 1940 National Democratic Party's Nominating Convention. A former Whitehaven boy had become owner of a posh restaurant in Chicago, and he gave a dinner for Tennessee delegates when they attended the convention. Recognizable bigwigs from left to right include: Will Gerber, Kenneth McKellar, Guy Joyner, E. H. Crump, Prentice Cooper, Walter Chandler, Will Hale, John Vesey, and Mr. Isbel (the restaurant owner).

pursue independent courses but found themselves purged from office. Cliff Davis was apparently sent to Washington to serve in Congress because he enjoyed too much personal popularity on the local scene. Others like Major Tom Allen of the Light Gas and Water Division and Col. Roane Waring of the Memphis Street Railway Company never had an open break with Crump, but found some of their projects frustrated by the organization as cautionary reminders of who ran things in Shelby County.

Perhaps the most peculiar of the organizations' purges was that of Robert A. Tillman. A linotype operator,

Tillman worked his way through law school. He held several offices in the local Typographical Union and served as its delegate to the National Federation of Labor. Because of his strong position with organized labor, Crump's organization picked him to serve in the Shelby County delegation to Tennessee's General Assembly. He served from 1937 through 1941, and was the delegation's floor leader for the 1941 session. In 1938, he was made an Assistant Public Defender and then was appointed Public Defender from 1939 to 1941. In 1942, he was elected as the machine's candidate for the newly created Division IV of General Sessions Court. However, when Tillman refused to conduct his court to please some of the organization's bigwigs, they wanted him ousted from office. But, because of his personal popularity and oratorical skills, the machine did not want to run a candidate against him. Consequently, at the behest of the Shelby delegation, he was removed from the bench via a Private Act of the Tennessee Legislature. In March 1945, the state simply dissolved his division of general sessions court.

In the 1948 elections, which challenged the extent of the Shelby County organization's power in the races for governor, senator, and president, Tillman "took the stump" on behalf of the opposition and may well have helped Gordon Browning and Estes Kefauver win their statewide races. Crump candidates still won Shelby County by two-to-one margins, but that margin was not enough to decide the statewide elections' outcomes. After Crump's death, Tillman returned to work in the Public Defender's office until his retirement in 1976. In retirement, he related his experiences to younger generations and retained an inordinate level of suspicion about the ongoing machinations of Crump's supporters.

After having lost the unquestioning loyalty of a number of organization anointed, elected officials, the group's leaders came up with a simple remedy. If a candidate

wanted the machine's endorsement, he had to make a total commitment to being a team player. The way to insure this, as reported by Bob Tillman and others, was that in the run up to selecting the machine's candidate for a given office, the presumptive candidate would be cajoled into signing an undated letter of resignation. If he later turned on "his friends," they then dated the resignation and turned it in to the appropriate official. Unless the departing official wanted to admit that he had been "bought off" before the election, he had no recourse but to depart with as much good grace as he could muster.

Most conspicuous of the men that the organization ruined and ran out of town were prominent African-American leaders Robert R. Church, Jr., and Dr. J. B. Martin. Both men had once been allies of the organization or "brown screws in the Crump machine," as their fellow politico George W. Lee described himself and other blacks who collaborated with Crump. Once the Democrats seemed firmly ensconced as the ruling national party,

✧

Grocery magnate Clarence Saunders was an early Crump opponent in statewide races. He backed candidates not endorsed by the organization and did innovative campaigning, like dropping leaflets from airplanes at political rallies. Saunders made a huge fortune quickly by innovating the self-service grocery market. He also lost his fortune quickly when he lost control of the Piggly Wiggly chain. He ceased to be much of a political factor after the 1920s.

Shelby County by a margin of 59,874 to 825. A mere two years later, Crump's new candidate, Prentice Cooper, defeated Gordon Browning by a margin of 56,302 to 9,214. Even so, controlling one fifth of a state's votes does not confer dictatorial power. It may be sufficient to sustain an arbiter or a king-maker, but it does not make one a king. Crump did not get everything he wanted. He apparently wanted to be appointed U.S. Senator, but was passed over. He also seemed to want having the Memphis-Arkansas Bridge named for him, but had to settle for lesser plums like having Crump Boulevard and Crump Stadium honor his name.

Throughout its long hold on power, the Crump organization did have a small number of conspicuous critics and opponents with staying power. *Commercial Appeal* Editor C.P.J. Mooney in the nineteen-teens and twenties, and *Press Scimitar* Editor Edward Meeman from 1931 until Crump's death in 1954, were probably the organization's most effective and persistent foes. Others included prominent

however, such black men's Republican connections had no further value to the organization. Regulatory and policing functions of local government were used to harass such men until they fled the area.

There are dozens of harassment stories in local folklore, and there is likely some truth at the heart of most of them. Even when there was no provable basis to such tales, they suggested an intimidation factor that reinforced widespread, pro-Crump solidarity. Although often aware of such a fear factor, most local citizens liked the results of Crump's system and supported him politically. They defended their way of doing things and thought they could fire Crump and his plebiscite government any time that they chose.

There is little doubt that Crump's machine had virtually uncontested power across Shelby County. The most dramatic proof of that fact was demonstrated in the 1936 and the 1938 Tennessee gubernatorial elections. In 1936, Crump's candidate, Gordon Browning, beat his primary election opponent, Burgin Dossett, in

attorney Lucius Burch, local eccentric Tom Collier, and grocery tycoon Clarence Saunders of Piggly Wiggly fame. Until the post-war election of 1948, however, such opponents provided little beyond nuisance levels of annoyance for the organization.

The 1948 primary election ended the myth of Crump invincibility in statewide elections. Although opponents did not prevail in Shelby County, Crump's foes won the three major statewide Democratic Party primary races and won in the general election as well. Internationalist East Tennessean Estes Kefauver took the Senate seat; old nemesis Gordon Browning reclaimed the governor's office; and civil-rights oriented President Harry Truman carried Tennessee against Strom Thurmond's "Dixiecrats."

In the wake of Crump's defeat in the 1948 election, the victors asked for and pushed through a number of reforms to end practices they deemed "dangerous to a free society." The measures that they called for were: 1) inauguration of an effective civil service program for all city and county employees, to protect their livelihoods and paths of advancement, 2) enactment of a "Little Hatch Act" to outlaw requiring public employees to engage in political activity and to prohibit them from engaging in politics other than as private citizens, 3) passing an adequate permanent voter registration law, 4) adopting and using voting machines in all city and county elections, and 5) undertaking studies to make a gradual transition to a non-political city management plan.

The group's statement of goals in the *Commercial Appeal* (August 7, 1948) finished with the following healing statement:

> Our county and city officials and employees are, for the most part, honest, efficient, and well-trained. There seems to us no need for any immediate wholesale governmental reform, but the suggestions enumerated above are, in our opinion, absolutely necessary to remove the pall of fear and apprehension, which hangs over many citizens in this community.

Although the state passed the measures recommended by the Kefauver committee in 1949, Crump's candidate, Frank Clement, won the gubernatorial race in 1952 and ushered in an eighteen-year period during which either Clement or his former Secretary of Agriculture, Buford Ellington, alternated as governor. Voting machines, civil service, ending the poll tax, and the state's Little Hatch Act, had not greatly limited the effectiveness and influence of the Crump organization within Shelby County or across the State of Tennessee.

Although Crump and his cronies never liked for the Shelby County organization to be called "the Machine," it was a machine in the sense that it was complex, and its parts worked smoothly together toward the same ends. It reached into virtually every social, civic, and ethnic group in the local communities. Generally speaking, one could not be elected to office in the VFW or the local garden clubs without "the organization's" approval.

For all of the reasons illustrated above, Crump's popular image became more iconic than reflective of the genuine man. In fact, Wayne Dowdy suggests that in his later years, Crump started to believe the myths he had helped create. Toward the end, as American mores and values evolved, he became something of a parody of himself. Despite this factor, however, Professor Kenneth Jackson has ranked the Crump organization among the three most important political machines in American History.

"Mistah" Crump, near the end of his long reign.

COURTESY OF MEMPHIS & SHELBY COUNTY ROOM, MEMPHIS PUBLIC LIBRARY & INFORMATION CENTER.

CHAPTER VII

SHELBY COUNTY AND THE WIDER WORLD: "WORLD CLASS," IN THE NATIONAL SPOTLIGHT, AND DISTINCTLY OURS—A POTPOURRI OF THE INTERESTING AND THE INCIDENTAL

Over nearly two centuries, Shelby County and its citizenry have had numerous points of notability, distinction, and, sometimes, notoriety. Perhaps as symbolic of such characteristics as anything in local history has been the Overton Park-Interstate 40 highway controversy. In the wake of the Federal Highway Act of 1956, planning and construction went forward for the area's Interstate highways, with limited access expressways through and around Memphis. Interstate 40, connecting Wilmington, NC, with Barstow, CA, was to run east-west through Memphis, connecting locally with Interstate 55, running north-south. I-40's east-west corridor was slated to go through the north section of Memphis's Overton Park, the city's premier, large, nature park, comprised of about 300 acres. Part of Overton Park is climax growth forest, and the park also houses the city's zoological and botanical gardens. As planned, the I-40 expressway could have had a negative impact on the zoo, the park, neighboring Southwestern College campus, and adjoining Hein Park residential enclave. As early as 1958, there was a rising crescendo of citizen protests to "save the park." In a decades long legal and propaganda battle, those wanting the park left untouched ultimately prevailed. Thus, the nation's 3,000-odd mile I-40 highway is interrupted by a 3.6-mile gap in mid-town Memphis. A stubborn group of Shelby County citizens had prevailed over government authorities at the city, county, state, and federal levels. They simply ran out the clock, or rather the calendar. Memphis municipal government had to yield to park preservationists or lose many millions of dollars of greatly needed federal funding. The city took the money.

The advent of federal superhighways and post-World War II prosperity also ignited a major revolution in Memphis-area demographic patterns. As has been amply demonstrated by preeminent urban historian and Memphis native Kenneth T. Jackson, governments at local, state, and federal levels have effectively subsidized their own cities' extinctions by building super-highways and other arteries of infrastructure into their surrounding hinterlands. In so doing, they have sponsored an explosion of annexations, suburbs, exurbs, and superburbs that have sapped their cities' vitality and Balkanized communities based on factors of socioeconomic class and ethnicity, including race. For Memphis, this has given rise to bedroom communities characterized by low density, relative racial homogeneity, greater affluence, lower crime rates, higher status, and, especially, better public schools. Within Shelby County, this has meant the blossoming of what had been small rural communities into thriving satellite cities with populations of about 40,000 citizens each. Bartlett, Collierville, and Germantown have been the most conspicuous beneficiaries of these trends within Shelby County. Nearby, non-Shelby County communities like Southhaven, and Olive Branch, Mississippi, furnish prime examples of similarly rampant expansions across county and state boundaries. Although middle class African Americans are fleeing the inner city, too, and largely for the same reasons as whites, the suburban growth trend has contributed significantly to racial self-segregation and to continuing racial tensions.

Largely because of higher black birth rates and greater rates of out migration by Memphis and Shelby County whites, African Americans have become majorities within both Memphis and Shelby County. Blacks are overwhelmingly Democrat in their political affiliation, and whites are almost equally committed to the Republican Party. Numbers have converted into political power and in 1991, former-Memphis City School Superintendent Willie Herenton became the first black to be elected Mayor of Memphis. Dr. Herenton has subsequently been reelected four times. Although his administration and his attitude have become increasingly less

Street railroads began operating in Memphis after the Civil War. They were initially either horse or mule drawn and certainly not rapid mass transit. Such enterprises were not efficient and were quickly replaced by electric trolleys in the early 1890s. Within that decade, a good bit of Memphis residential development moved east, and, in 1899, the city's annexations quadrupled its area. This was the beginning of residential and commercial sprawl that has continued and intensified over the decades since then.

popular with voters, he won reelection again with a plurality in the fall of 2007.

Likewise, in 2002, voters elected popular former public defender A. C. Wharton as Shelby County's first black mayor. The Wharton Administration's popularity has continued to grow among voters, because of his low-key, modest personality and because he has kept his bailiwick squeaky clean amid an atmosphere of rampant local political corruption. The Memphis City Council has had a black majority for over a decade. The Shelby County Commission is nearly evenly divided by race, with one white Democrat providing the swing vote on many measures.

Early in the twenty-first century, Federal Bureau of Investigation "sting operations" have implicated a disproportionate number of Shelby County political figures in influence peddling and other corrupt practices.

Members of the Memphis School Board, the Memphis City Council, the Shelby County Commission, and senators and representatives to the Tennessee General Assembly, as well as county administrative employees, have been indicted and/or persuaded to resign in the face of malfeasance charges.

Corruption in county government is hardly new, however. Cronyism, including illegal favors for its friends, went largely ignored by voters under the Crump machine's rule. Even after reform elements came to power, there were several convictions for political corruption. Post-Crump sheriffs seemed to be particularly vulnerable to temptation, with unsavory practices like maintaining slush funds and coercing deputies to work for sheriffs' reelections being part of the office's unethical legacy. Colorful, maverick Sheriff Jack Owens, facing a federal investigative probe, committed suicide at a gasoline station. Current Sheriff Mark Luttrell seems to be popular with voters of both races and ethically beyond reproach.

The most infamous local corruption case has probably been that of the Shelby County Juvenile Court's complicity in a baby-selling scandal. This story became a 1990s motion picture staring Mary Tyler Moore. Tennessee Children's Home administrator Georgia Tann and Juvenile Court Judge Camille Kelley apparently pressured unwed mothers to give up their babies and then gave preference to affluent couples willing to pay to adopt quickly and with minimal red tape.

Even more dramatic than the Tennessee Children's Home scandal was an earlier series of court actions and murders known as the Bolton-Dickens Feud. Between 1857 and 1871, partners of the slave and cotton trading company of Bolton and Dickens fell out over more than $100,000 in debts accrued in defending Isaac (Ike) Bolton against murder charges arising out of controversy related to an illegal sale of a free black. Ike and Wade Bolton insisted that their company must pay Ike's legal and attendant expenses. Dickens insisted that this was cheating him and refused, but the courts

found in favor of the Boltons. Although Ike and Wash Bolton died before the Civil War ended, Wade Bolton survived, and the litigation dragged on.

In early 1869, two attempts were made on Tom Dickens' life. In the second effort, two gunmen from Alabama invaded Dickens' house, where they killed two bystanders and wounded Dickins and another bystander. Later, one of the assailants was killed while

Left: Young Dr. Willie W. Herenton became the first African American to serve as Memphis City School's Superintendent and the first black to be elected Mayor of Memphis. In 1991, Herenton defeated popular incumbent Richard C. Hackett by a mere 142 votes in a volatile, racially charged atmosphere. Herenton had the support of the African-American Ford machine in his 1991 victory, but scant Ford support thereafter. He has been reelected four times, with little organized white opposition, making him the longest serving chief executive in the city's history. In 2007 he won an unprecedented fifth term, although his popularity has diminished considerably and he has begun projecting considerable reverse racism.

COURTESY OF MEMPHIS & SHELBY COUNTY ROOM, MEMPHIS PUBLIC LIBRARY& INFORMATION CENTER.

Below: Sheriff Gene Barksdale (right) and his then chief deputy A. C. Gillis (left) are shown here welcoming increased African-American participation in the Sheriff's Department. Barksdale was defeated for reelection by Jack Owens in 1986. Near the end of his term, Owens committed suicide amid rumors of a pending indictment. Gillis won the 1990 election and served as sheriff until 2002, giving him the longest tenure as sheriff in Shelby County's history. Gillis chose not to run again in 2002. Both Barksdale and Gillis left office with their reputations somewhat sullied.

COURTESY OF SPECIAL COLLECTIONS, UNIVERSITY OF MEMPHIS LIBRARIES.

✧

The Tennessee Children's Home baby-selling scandal was one of the most conspicuous instances of official misconduct in Shelby County's history. Collusion between Georgia Tann (on the right in the lower photograph) of the home and Juvenile Court Judge Camille Kelly (center in the above photograph) gave both women income far beyond their salaries. In part, because adoption records are sealed, it took a long time for the facts of this case to surface.

resisting arrest on the streets of Memphis. The other, although wounded, escaped. Shortly thereafter, Tom Dickens and his son Samuel encountered Wade Bolton at Court Square. Tom drew a pistol and, without warning, shot Wade. Bolton died some days later, after having refused to allow a probe to remove the bullet. Tom Dickens was later cleared of all charges, and the feud had apparently ended. Within two years, however, Tom Dickens was bushwhacked and killed, while riding alone on a road north of Memphis. One week later, Tom's son Samuel was killed in the same manner and at the same place. All told, at least eight people died in this savage blood feud and whoever perpetrated the two final murderers was [were] never identified.

Not all aspects of Shelby County's relations with the law are so tawdry. In fact, Shelby Countians have contributed to very positive aspects of our legal and political heritages. Frances Wright, well known locally for her utopian experiment to free slaves, won an important, precedent-setting case in the Circuit Court of Shelby County allowing her to retain legal control of her Nashoba property, rather than have it fall into the hands of her estranged and greedy husband. Later, prior to America's entry into World War I, a young

Shelby County delegate to the General Assembly named Lois, although Bejach was a man] D. Bejach authored a statute which gave Tennessee's married women the right to retain and control their own property. Previously, brides' property had passed automatically to control of their husbands as soon as they were legally married. This fundamental legislative act is still known statewide as "the Bejach Law."

Shelby Countians also contributed mightily to the civic wellbeing of our nation's women via the Tennessee Legislature's ratification of the 19th Amendment to the U.S. Constitution. Shelby County lobbyists and the Shelby delegation to the General Assembly were both crucial to their state's ratification of woman's suffrage at the state and national levels. Pro-suffragist forces managed to pass a Tennessee female enfranchisement act in 1919, and Tennessee became the 36th and decisive state in ratifying the 19th Amendment a year later. Crump's Shelby County organization gave unstinting support to both efforts; with stalwarts Kenneth McKellar, Hubert Fisher, Joseph Hanover, and Charl O. Williams fighting in the forefront of those battles.

Addressing another need for equal protection under the law, Tennessee became the nation's second state to provide public defenders for accused indigents. Memphis

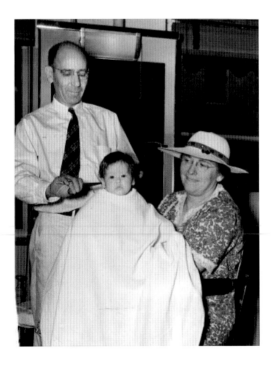

attorney and later judge Samuel O. Bates crafted the legislation to establish the Shelby County Public Defender's Office and provide legal representation for those who could not afford to engage counsel. Later, at the national level, native Memphian and Supreme Court Justice Abe Fortas was a key figure in the court's *Miranda v. Arizona Decision*, ensuring that all parties arrested for committing crimes are "read their rights" protecting them from self-incrimination and guaranteeing them legal representation. President Lyndon Johnson later nominated Justice Fortas to succeed Earl Warren as Chief Justice, but Fortas withdrew his name when details of his financial dealings drew sharp criticism, and he seemed unlikely to be confirmed. A year later, he resigned from the court and returned to private practice. One must wonder how a Fortas-led Supreme Court might have affected America's constitutional history.

The murder of Rev. Martin Luther King is arguably among the very most notable and most consequential crimes in American History. The pursuit, capture, and extradition of James Earl Ray provided extraordinary dramatic follow-up to the assassination that revolutionized the nation's race relations. Scheduled for trial in Shelby County Criminal Court, Ray copped a plea, received a life sentence, and a potential "trial of the century" never happened. This circumstance and Ray's later retraction of his confession have inspired a plethora of conspiracy theories. Local law enforcement agents and attorneys close to the investigation, however, have remained confident that Ray was indeed King's murderer.

According to Earl Warren, the most important case to come before the Supreme Court while he was Chief Justice was the 1962 case of *Baker v. Carr*. The suit was filed in the name of Shelby County Court Chairman Charles W. Baker against Tennessee's Secretary of State and was effectively argued by former Memphis Mayor Walter Chandler. The Baker decision established the "one person, one vote" doctrine and required that Tennessee election districts must be equal in population. In blatant violation of its own constitution's decennial redistricting requirement, Tennessee

Top: Lois Bejach, framer of "the Bejach law" was a Shelby County attorney, state legislator, and long serving judge. Prior to the First World War, young Bejach authored the Tennessee statute which allowed women to retain control of their property after they married. This was a major step in Tennessee women's march toward legal equality.

COURTESY OF SPECIAL COLLECTIONS, UNIVERSITY OF MEMPHIS LIBRARIES.

Middle: Joseph Hanover is generally credited with being the Shelby County attorney most responsible for Tennessee granting women the vote within the state in 1919 and becoming the swing state in ratifying the 19th Amendment to the United States Constitution the following year. The Tennessee Legislature passed ratification by the margin of a single vote. That vote guaranteed votes for millions of American women thereafter.

COURTESY OF SPECIAL COLLECTIONS, UNIVERSITY OF MEMPHIS LIBRARIES.

Bottom: Abe Fortas held the highest judicial post of any Shelby County legal figure. Lyndon Johnson appointed him to the U.S. Supreme Court and later nominated him for Chief Justice to succeed Earl Warren. When it seemed that Fortas would not be confirmed, Johnson withdrew his nomination. Allegations of financial misconduct influenced Fortas to return to private practice a year later.

COURTESY OF SPECIAL COLLECTIONS, UNIVERSITY OF MEMPHIS LIBRARIES.

had not reapportioned its districts since 1901, thus ignoring the state's vast demographic changes over a 61-year span. The court's Baker decision ended long-standing discrimination under which representation within Tennessee was heavily skewed to favor rural as opposed to urban interests. Within about five years of this decision, a majority of America's states had reapportioned their districts based on this and subsequent precedents.

In the realm of pure politics, Memphian Ed McAteer has been called a "king maker" in U.S. presidential politics. Many insiders consider his role to have been key to coordinating and energizing religious conservatives to support Ronald Reagan in the 1980 primary and general elections. His "Religious Roundtable," along with Rev. Jerry Faldwell's "Moral Majority," was instrumental in enabling Ronald Reagan to triumph over incumbent and fundamentalist President Jimmy Carter. McAteer's groups supported Reagan again in the 1984 election and George H. W. Bush in 1988, contributing to those Republican victories.

Curiously, the same Ed McAteer, who had the ear and enjoyed the thanks and praise of presidents, retained his grassroots orientation toward politics. In his final years, he acted as emcee for a local, monthly Dutch Treat Luncheon, a conservative political forum.

In the field of history education, two former Shelby Countians have each made a major impact at the international level. Kenneth T. Jackson of Columbia University is arguably the greatest of America's historians in the field of urban and suburban life. His 1985 *Crabgrass Frontier* remains the definitive work on America's suburban revolution. Margot Stern Strom is cofounder and executive director of *Facing History and Ourselves*, a rapidly growing, international movement devoted to teaching history at the primary and secondary levels through the prisms of group hatreds and social justice. *Facing History* has trained thousands of history teachers to place their subject in the ethical context of America's highest ideals.

Shelby County has numerous additional points and personalities of distinction. It can claim two giants of Civil War history, Nathan Bedford Forrest as participant and Shelby Foote as the war's premier chronicler. Forrest had become wealthy as a slave and livestock trader. He rose from the rank of private to that of lieutenant general during the Civil War. Robert E. Lee later described

Forrest as the war's best general on either side. Forrest's legacy provides a major bone of contention between local blacks and whites, since some scholars blame Forrest for a "massacre" of black troops at Fort Pillow and for later heading the Ku Klux Klan during Tennessee's Reconstruction. The issue of whether Forrest should continue to be honored locally has provided fodder for racial tensions.

Shelby Foote, a novelist turned historian, wrote the most critically acclaimed and best selling, multi-volume history of the Civil War. He referred to Forrest as one of two authentic geniuses during the Civil War, the other being Abraham Lincoln. Foote, perhaps reflecting his own cultural roots, was much less critical of Forrest than Ivy League dons. In the 1990s, Foote became a bit of an icon himself as consultant and commentator for the highly acclaimed Ken Burns, PBS *Civil War* television series.

Peter Taylor, perhaps the greatest of America's late twentieth century's short story writers, lived part of his early life in Memphis and captured parts of the area's cultural ethos in his short story, "The Old Forest," and his short novel, *Summons to Memphis*. John Grisham, one of the nation's most popular novelists has also been a sometime Shelby Countian and set his first best-selling thriller, *The Firm*, in Memphis. *The Firm* and several other Grisham novels have been made into blockbuster motion pictures. The Shelby County poet to achieve the greatest fame and acclaim is probably Judge Walter Malone, whose "Opportunity" is a paean to optimism and is standard fare in many American Literature anthologies. His work is celebrated on a plaque in Court Square, Memphis.

Shelby Countians have made numerous other significant contributions to entertainment, the arts, and athletics. Of course the local giant among giants is rock icon Elvis Presley. Graceland, his former residence, is one of the two or three most visited museum homes in the nation. Shelby County's other national and international music luminaries include W. C. Handy, Father of the Blues; B. B. King, probably the world's

✧

Top: Shelby County Court Chairman Charles W. Baker was the official plaintiff in the 1962 lawsuit of Baker v. Carr, in which the U.S. Supreme Court ruled that unequal representation in state legislatures violated the principle of "one man, one vote."

COURTESY OF MEMPHIS & SHELBY COUNTY ROOM, MEMPHIS PUBLIC LIBRARY & INFORMATION CENTER.

Middle: Former Memphis Mayor and Shelby County Congressman Walter Chandler argued the Baker v. Carr case before the Supreme Court. Earl Warren is quoted as having said that this was the most important case to come before the court during his tenure as chief justice. Walter Chandler's son Wyeth later served as Memphis mayor for ten years and then several terms as circuit court judge.

COURTESY OF SPECIAL COLLECTIONS, UNIVERSITY OF MEMPHIS LIBRARIES.

Bottom: Mississippi Delta-born novelist Shelby Foote is, oddly enough, better known as a historian than for his works of fiction. Recruited to provide a formulaic popular history of the Civil War for a multivolume American history series, Foote became so enmeshed in his project that he dropped his commissioned book and spent two decades writing his highly regarded, three-volume history of that conflict. Foote became a national celebrity, at least among the literati, as a result of his stint as commentator on a very popular and highly acclaimed PBS series on the Civil War.

COURTESY OF MEMPHIS & SHELBY COUNTY ROOM, MEMPHIS PUBLIC LIBRARY & INFORMATION CENTER.

Right: Elvis Presley treated his Hollywood chum Nick Adams to a motorcycle ride at the Mid-South Fair in 1956. Presley sometimes rented the Fair Grounds after hours, to give private parties for his friends. He remains easily the personality most closely associated with Memphis and Shelby County, even thirty years after his death. His cult status and his place in American music entitle him to still be called "the King."

PHOTOGRAPH BY ROBERT W. DYE.

Below: Second only to Elvis among local music luminaries is the fame of W. C. Handy, usually called "the Father of the Blues." Although Delta-area cultural aficionados consider Handy more of a popularizer than a pure blues artist, his fame and his music endure. Unlike many of the later blues artists, Handy was a trained, formal musician. Handy is seated on the right, with his famous trumpet in his hand. There is a statue of him on Beale in a park named in his honor.

COURTESY OF MEMPHIS & SHELBY COUNTY ROOM,
MEMPHIS PUBLIC LIBRARY & INFORMATION CENTER.

foremost blues guitarist; Isaac Hayes, "the Black Moses of Soul Music," international operatic diva Callen Esperian; and, most recently, pop idol Justin Timberlake.

In the area of athletics, locals can claim Anthony "Amp" Elmore, world heavyweight and super heavyweight kick-boxing champion with five different titles; world class golfing great Cary Middlecoff; and star baseball catcher and premier broadcast "color commentator" Tim McCarver. *Memphis* magazine designated McCarver the Memphis area's most distinguished athlete in its end-of-the-twentieth-century issue.

Finally, the Memphis area has had at least its share of just plain eccentrics, the most conspicuous of whom is Robert "Prince Mongo" Hodges. A former haberdasher and restaurateur, Mongo often dresses like witchdoctor from a B-grade movie and, with a straight face, claims to be from the planet Zambodia. He has occasionally run for political office and has been a magnet for thousands of protest votes. Usually his political activism has provided little beyond comic relief. In the 1991 Memphis mayoral race, however, his 3,000-vote tally proved serious indeed. It sapped off enough votes in predominantly white precincts to allow a 142-vote margin of victory for black challenger Willie Herenton over white incumbent Dick Hackett.

Paradoxically, despite many unique factors of Mid-South culture and many peculiarities within that context, Memphis and Shelby

County are increasingly becoming "Anywhere USA." The entire nation is undergoing a vast homogenization of its traditional subcultures, even as Asian and Hispanic newcomers provide additional cultural spice and leavening. Probably the most important factor contributing to this sameness evolution is the mass media, especially television. Whether for information or entertainment, lowest common denominator tone and values emerge to claim market shares. Much of it is simply shallow escapism as in such very well crafted, often cloned series like the *Law and Order* and the *CSI*. Perhaps the popular and oxymoronic "reality shows" and other faux competitions like *American Idol* and *Dancing with the Stars* are even worse. Probably at the bottom of the heap are the sleazy situation comedies that make promiscuous and non-traditional life styles seem mundane, clever, and desirable. Such cultural contaminants are not part of a left wing conspiracy, but rather spring from market forces and economies of scale. Irrespective, they are destroying what once passed for gentility in our society.

The print media are nearly as bad as the small screen in the destruction of our regionalism and our parochialism. Memphis daily newspapers have not been "home owned" since prior to World War II, but for decades they were still generally operated by local, by birth or orientation, editors and journalists. The afternoon delivery *Memphis Press-Scimitar*, which ran the most in-depth local news content, ceased publication in 1983. The morning daily, *The Commercial Appeal*, has morphed so many times in recent years that it is difficult to know what it seeks to be, other than profitable. It uses human-interest features from anywhere USA, experiments with different formats, and continues to lose readership. The major "alternative newspaper," the weekly and free *Memphis Flyer*, has taken up a good bit of the slack in providing local news and opinions, but its leftist slant is hardly a good

fit with the area's traditional mores. Suburban newspapers are generally weeklies and limited to social and civic events of their particular townships.

Corporate culture also significantly influences local culture. The trend toward consolidation has meant increasing out-of-region ownership and management of once purely local businesses. We all have cultural baggage, and imported business executives certainly bring somewhat divergent views and values with them. They tend to share such perspectives with their employees and with their associates in local civic and cultural endeavors. Some such leaders apparently see themselves as cultural missionaries to the Mid South, wanting to alter the society that they claim to find so charming. Others might be construed as opportunistic, twenty-first-century carpetbaggers, eager to make the money and run. Their attitudes and values are a very far cry from those prevalent with Front Street business leaders for the century before World War II.

Emerging suburbs are built amazingly alike across regions of the U.S. They often have similar architecture, "big box" chain stores, regional and national chain restaurants, more uniform products, and ever fewer

✧

As the photograph above indicates, Robert "Prince Mongo" Hodges has often enjoyed being outrageous. His notoriety has helped him be the focus of protest votes, playing the role of spoiler in the Memphis mayoral election of 1991. Claiming to have come from the Planet Zambodia, the prince showed unusual taste in what he considered "art."

COURTESY OF SPECIAL COLLECTIONS,
UNIVERSITY OF MEMPHIS LIBRARIES.

✧

Above: Memphian Kemmons Wilson gave American a major boost in its post-World War II trend toward standardization and homogenization of our culture. Wilson came up with a set of hostelry basics that made his Holiday Inn chain of motels the largest and most imitated in the world. Wilson became a very wealthy man, and travelers got much better lodgings and related services as a result. Many other economies of scale have severely diluted the regional distinctiveness of much of early twenty-first-century America.

PHOTOGRAPH BY ROBERT W. DYE.

Right: This post-World War II, Berclair subdivision of tract homes demonstrates another early example of economies of scale leading to standardization and architectural sterility. Only the clothes hanging on lines and the cars in the driveways indicate that these are even human habitations. Over the decades, homeowners have added to and otherwise customized such homes, but such subdivisions at this stage could easily be described as "Anywhere U.S.A." The trend continues in upscale housing and in commercial and office center developments.

PHOTOGRAPH BY ROBERT W. DYE.

brands. The term "Mc Mansions" is as universally recognized as the overbuilt, pretentious, and characterless homes it represents. Suburban "Mc Malls" seem equally soulless and repellant. Eighty percent of America's restaurant meals are now served by chain businesses. Something in us must long for a return to the older, simpler ways. Otherwise, why would Cracker Barrel restaurants have become such a popular substitute for disappearing, old-time country stores?

There also seem to be increasingly lock-step ideas and ideologies promoted in our schools and universities. The inviolable rigidity of Jim Crow bigotry of a century ago has been replaced by a certainly less heinous but equally rigid code of political correctness. Americans, including Shelby Countians, seem to be becoming increasingly generic in patterns of thought and speech.

An increasing social and cultural sterility is often reflected in inept local public policy. Paving Memphis's Main Street as a pedestrian mall, has been a disaster. The 1990s shiny new Pyramid arena lasted less than fifteen years before being rendered obsolete by FedEx Forum. The quasi-public (meaning that politicians don't want to take any hits) Riverfront Development Corporation seeks to replace the remaining green space of the Public Promenade with high rise commercial buildings. The Libertyland theme park, which opened to great fanfare for the nation's bicentennial, has gone broke and is having its assets auctioned off.

The Mid-South Fair itself, a venerable 150-year-old institution may also be in danger of dying. The fair was a vehicle via which rural and urban dwellers and lifestyles came together in Shelby County. Much of the fair's emphasis has become trendy and tawdry, and some proponents seem to favor ditching its agricultural elements altogether and catering to whatever is current in the carnival trade.

Some politicians and other opportunists want to turn the Fairgrounds' acreage on East Parkway to other purposes and are looking at other areas' big development projects for inspiration. Former Shelby County Mayor Jim Rout has taken the fair's helm, and the fair has been promised the use of the fairgrounds through 2008. Promoters at Millington, in north Shelby County and others at Tunica, Mississippi, are currently wooing the fair. Although there have been suggestions for relocating the fair at the Agricenter International, on the eastern perimeter of Memphis, no formal proposals have been made for doing so. Among these possibilities, perhaps the Mid-South Fair will survive and will refocus on its agricultural heritage.

Similar to the fair, Cotton Carnival was another venerable institution that brought our region's rural and urban interests together. Founded early in the Great Depression as "the party with a purpose," Carnival replaced the long defunct local Mardi Gras and celebrated and promoted the area's cotton industry. Although dominated by the area's "high society," Carnival was also for the masses. Even city and county grade schools had their faux royalty. There were children's and adult parades down Main Street and a Midway carnival along the riverfront. The children's' balls at Crump Stadium cut across class lines, but secret societies' memberships and their raucous parties were by invitation only. The latter did include elites from the hinterland.

In the late twentieth century, however, Cotton Carnival missed an opportunity to partner with the incipient Memphis in May International Festival and help showcase Memphis in a much broader context. Ultimately, MIM activities crowded Carnival out of the month of May. Carnival also abandoned its focus on cotton and became briefly the Great River Carnival. Later still, it became simply "Carnival Memphis," and changed its purpose to celebrating a different local industry each year. Perhaps it has had to adapt in order to survive.

Front Street's cotton and commission merchants were for many decades the city's power brokers and their acceptance a key to

attaining social status. More than that, however, Front Street was where town and countryside came together commercially and otherwise. In the twenty-first century's commercial atmosphere of instantaneous communication and computer analyses, there is no longer any need for a cotton exchange or for cotton classers. Most of the major cotton merchants no longer have their offices along historic "Cotton Row" (Front Street) and one rarely sees a bail or a "snake" of cotton in the area. Local cotton merchants recently bankrolled a small, high-tech Cotton Museum in the former trading room of the Cotton Exchange Building. It is doing a good job of telling the story of cotton and of its phenomenal impact on the world's economy and culture. Despite its excellence, the museum seems to be struggling to become financially self-sustaining.

✧

The distinctive, Arabesque Shelby County Building at the Fair Grounds was for many years the scene of small school and "pick up" basketball games. It was used for various exhibits during the fair and for flea markets at other times of year. Severely damaged by a fire during a weekend flea market, the tower probably could have been salvaged and the building restored. Local officials did not wait to assess the situation. Claiming that the structure represented a danger, they removed it. It turned out to be very difficult to demolish, and obviously was in no danger of collapsing.

*Above: Each fall, at least since World War II,
several hundred thousand people have
attended the Mid-South Fair at the Memphis
Fairgrounds. They have crowded in for the
games, the rides, the food, the products
booths and demonstrations, talent and
beauty contests, and the various competitions
in agricultural production.*

COURTESY OF THE MID-SOUTH FAIR.

*Below: Sharing information and showing off
one's agricultural prowess had initially been
at the heart of the Mid-South Fair. Here
rural folks and urbanites came together and
kept at least traces of their symbiotic
relationship from years gone by. In events as
prosaic as livestock and poultry competitions,
farmers found their efforts recognized
and rewarded.*

COURTESY OF THE MID-SOUTH FAIR.

Of course, not all of these generic
changes are bad things. Memphis and Shelby
County have recently become vastly more
sophisticated than they were just a few
decades ago. In areas of food, language,
customs, and levels of education there is
vastly more variety and opportunity. There
is more social and economic mobility, and
the region's traditional racial bigotry is at
least muted, if not receding completely. In
fact, reverse racism may currently be
generating more problems than traditional
redneck "bubbaism."

Moreover, the "good old days" were not
always all that good. There are far fewer
rural indigents, and they no longer live at
subsistence levels and in virtual debt peonage
as sharecroppers. Local people generally
know more about nutrition, exercise, and
health habits than ever before. Grocery
products, although not necessarily more
nutritious, are better preserved, relatively
cheaper, and much safer than at earlier times.
Health care, despite its explosive costs, is
infinitely more effective and more widely
available than at any time in the past. The list

of life's material improvements could go on and on.

With so much material wellbeing, why do we so long for a return to an Arcadian simplicity of lifestyle? Is it possible to have the best of both worlds? The answer is probably "NO!" In most practical senses, we really can't have it both ways. But, through the uses of history and historical imagination, we can retrieve and, in a sense, relive our yesteryears. That is, if only we can find them. There, indeed, is the rub.

What is to be done? How can its citizenry stop Shelby County from losing its cultural baby with the bath water? Can even the few remaining pockets of rural culture in Shelby County be preserved over the long haul? The answer is, probably not. Given the irresistible power of profit motive and economies of scale, the twin encroachments of rampant redevelopment of farmland to residential and commercial purposes will in all likelihood prevail. Probably the best we can hope for is to preserve, promote, publish, publicize, commemorate, celebrate, and re-create our history as best we can, through the plethora of institutions already striving to do these things. Even then it will be a struggle.

Between 1987 and 1992 Memphis had an International Heritage Commission. Run completely by volunteers, this organization received only printing services, postage, and exhibit space to celebrate the diverse cultures of fifty-five distinct, organized ethnic groups. With the change of administrations in 1992, the commission lost the minimal support that it had gotten from city hall and disbanded. Less than a decade later, the Memphis Irish Society, active for more than sixty years and representing the county's second largest

ethnic group (about 150,000 people), ceased to function.

To reduce the possibility of such a profound cultural losses happening again and again, those who know and appreciate local history must proselytize for its preservation. They must know about, use, and support government agencies and nonprofit groups dedicated to our area's heritage. Governmental agencies include the Tennessee Historical Commission, the Shelby County Historical Commission, and the Memphis Landmarks Commission. Historical and preservation groups are too numerous for complete inclusion here but they include: the Tennessee Historical Society, the West Tennessee Historical Society, the Association for the Preservation of Tennessee Antiquities, Memphis Heritage, Inc., Descendants of Early Settlers of Shelby and Adjoining Counties, the Tennessee Heritage Trust, and the Tennessee Genealogical Society.

Archival and manuscripts repositories collect and preserve our documents, icons, rare books, maps, etc. For Shelby County history, these include the Tennessee State Library and Archives, Special Collections at the University of Memphis Libraries, the Rhodes Institute for Regional Studies, the Shelby County Archives, and the Memphis and Shelby County Room of the Memphis Public Library.

✧

Above: The lovely young women in this swimsuit competition of a beauty contest may well have been vying to be named "Fairest of the Fair." Country folks and city folks alike participated in various competitions and got to know a little more about each other's subcultures. The audience's expressions are sometimes as interesting as the images of the photographer's intended subjects.
COURTESY OF THE MID-SOUTH FAIR.

Below: Cotton Carnival carriage. This horse-drawn vehicle in a Main Street parade illustrates the glamour projected by Cotton Carnival. Lovely ladies, lavish parties, barge landings for "royalty," and lively parades have all been part of the magic and mystique of Carnival. In recent years, however, this tradition has moved from its agrarian roots to a more urban and business orientation.
COURTESY OF MEMPHIS & SHELBY COUNTY ROOM, MEMPHIS PUBLIC LIBRARY & INFORMATION CENTER.

Memphis and Shelby County have numerous public and private museums and museum homes. Major ones include the Memphis Museum System, with its Pink Palace, Magevney House, Mallory-Neeley House, etc. Also of importance, but less directly tied to the Shelby County locale are: the Mississippi River Museum on Mud Island, the National Civil Rights Museum, the National Ornamental Metals Museum, and the Children's Museum of Memphis. More local in orientation are: the Davies Manor Museum Home, Graceland, Woodruff-Fontaine Home (APTA), Chucalissa Indian Village, W. C. Handy Museum and Gallery, Memphis Rock and Soul Museum, Soulsville, and the Memphis Cotton Museum.

Local history desperately needs broad-based support. Where was the outrage when *The Commercial Appeal* dropped its popular "Past Times" local history column a few years back? Why was there not more support for *Old Shelby County* magazine, over the five years of its publication? Why does the West Tennessee Historical Society, the umbrella heritage organization for Memphis and Shelby County, have fewer than 400 members out of its area's population of nearly a million and a half souls? Why are books on local history such hard sells in the Memphis area? Generally speaking, the answer to each of these questions is "ignorance and apathy."

We can and we must do much more, if we are to preserve Shelby County's history and its traditional culture. We certainly don't want to wait another 120 years to have an updated history of "Big Shelby" published. Locate and read books about Shelby County's wonderful history. Paul Coppock's magnificent six-volume set of books on the Mid South are still available in local bookstores and through the West Tennessee Historical Society. Back issues of the West Tennessee Historical

Society's annual journal (*Papers*) are still available in printed volumes through the society and on line through the Shelby County Register's website.

Opportunities for preserving and promoting Shelby County's heritage abound! Dear readers, it is up to you to take advantage of them.

EPILOGUE

The makeup of this book turned out to be considerably different from what I had initially outlined for its contents. Honest and earnest historical research and writing are often that way. The available evidence frequently dictates what will be included and how that information will be treated. Clio, the Muse of History, can be a very demanding mistress. Via her dictates, I found myself including a great deal of information on early Shelby County from the Old Folks' *Record*, much of it verbatim. Doing so, especially using some of the mildly archaic language from frontiersmen like J. J. Rawlings and W. B. Waldran, conveys a tone and tenor of the times better than any modern description could do.

My greatest regret is that I could not make space to give even passing attention to Shelby County's history of law enforcement, its health and human services agencies, its historic rural communities, and many well-known and dynamic personalities. Doing so simply was not possible, given available word constraints.

I have laboriously collected and categorized a great deal of information that I have been unable to use in this book. It seems almost unimaginable that, if I continue to enjoy reasonably good health and lucidity over the next few years, I will do other than try to convert the bulk of that research into a scholarly and much more detailed account of Shelby County's past. At the very least, I will try to use this research in series of future articles for *The West Tennessee Historical Society Papers* and in my column for *The Best Times*. Optimally, a comprehensive, multi-volume history of Shelby County should result.

✧

The Shelby County Flag contains the County Seal in gold on a green field, surrounded by a gold border. The motto is "Agriculture and Commerce," illustrated by the products above and the riverboat below. The color green suggests agriculture and the gold suggests prosperity from commerce.

COURTESY OF SHELBY COUNTY GOVERNMENT.

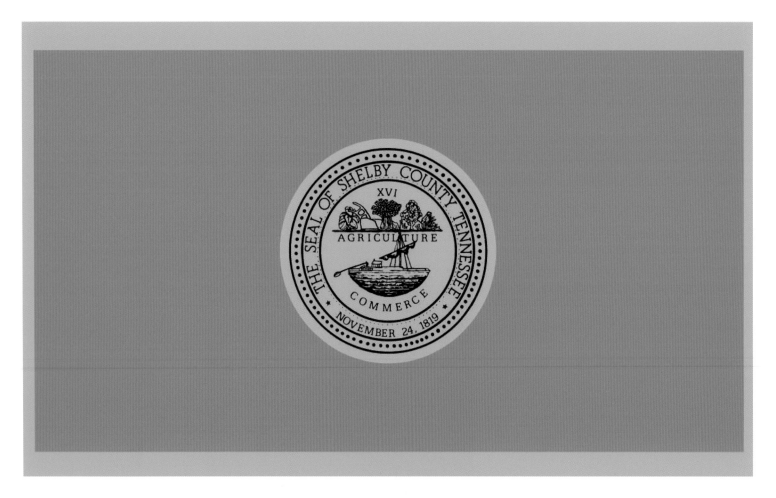

BIBLIOGRAPHY

Please Note: The alphabetical listing below includes books, articles, theses and dissertations, and a few unpublished manuscripts. It is not segregated into formats, but intermixed. In general, the works entered here either pertain mostly to Shelby County, to Shelby County and Memphis, or to Memphis but also impacting significantly on Shelby County. Works that seem to be overwhelmingly about Memphis have often not been included. Little effort has been made to include individual family histories, individual church histories, or published records, or other primary sources. Such information is available online at the **Tennessee Genealogical Society's web site**, at www.wdbj.net/bibliography/index.

To further limit the length of this bibliography, an effort has been made to minimize the duplication of information from multiple sources. In instances where a thesis or dissertation has had chapters excerpted and published as journal articles, the longer work is generally cited. In cases in which several articles were published prior to a book by the same author on the same topic being published, the book is cited. If a dissertation is also later published as a book, usually the book is cited. When a title or subtitle adequately explains the entry's contents, usually no annotation follows. The **West Tennessee Historical Society Papers** and the **Tennessee Historical Quarterly** are abbreviated **WTHS Papers** and **THQ**, respectively. The **WTHS Papers** are now available on line through the Shelby County Register's website. None of the theses or dissertations is indexed. Most are available at local research libraries. Researchers should also consult the newspaper clipping files at Memphis Public Library and the Memphis *Press Scimitar* (newspaper) files at the Special Collections Department at the University of Memphis.

Austin, Linda Tollett. "Babies for Sale: The Tennessee Children's Home Adoption Scandal." Dissertation, Memphis State University, 1992. This is a scholarly treatment of one of Shelby County's most infamous scandals. The Juvenile Court was involved in the operation.

Baker, Thomas H. "The Early Newspapers of Memphis, Tennessee, 1827-1860," *WTHS Papers.* XVII, 1956, 20-46. Good information about early life in Memphis and Shelby County.

Bancroft, Frederic. *Slave Trading in the Old South.* New York: Frederick Ungar Publishing Co., 1959. This classic work, originally published in 1931, debunks the contentions that there had been relatively little commercial slave trading in the old South, that slave traders were treated as social outcasts, and that the institution itself had been relatively benign. This study remains the standard work on its topic and has been republished at least through a 1996 edition. It depicts the southern slave trade in general and also in specific areas, including the Memphis markets.

Beifuss, Joan Turner. *At the River I Stand: Memphis, the 1968 Strike, and Martin Luther King.* Memphis: B & W Books, 1985. Beifuss's award-winning book summarizes the contents of the University of Memphis Sanitation Strike Collection. It explains the most volatile and far reaching event in Memphis history, within its context. 370 pages, indexed.

Bejach, Lois D. "The Seven Cities Absorbed by Memphis." *WTHS Papers.* 8 (1954) 95-104. This represents an older interpretation of Memphis's annexations.

_____."The Taxing District of Shelby County." *WTHS Papers* 4 (1950) 5-27. This study is largely revised, expanded, and superceded by Lynette B. Wrenn's *Crisis and Commission Government.* See below.

Berkeley, Kathleen C. "Ethnicity and Its Implications for Southern Urban History: The Saga of Memphis, Tennessee, 1850-1880." *THQ* 50 (Winter 1991) 193-202.

Biles, Roger. *Memphis in the Great Depression.* Knoxville: University of Tennessee Press, 1986. A scholarly work with emphasis on the Crump regime.

Black, Roy W. Sr. "The Genesis of County Organization in the Western District of North Carolina and in the State of Tennessee." *WTHS Papers* 2, (1948)) 95-118.

Blankenbeckler, Diane, compiler and editor. *Short Histories of African American Schools in Shelby County, TN.* Memphis: Memphis Landmarks Commission, no date. This information is taken directly from the Shelby County School Board minutes, other sources, and first-person interviews. Quotations are taken directly from oral histories. It has a good deal of information on the county's operation of its schools, including white schools.

Blankenship, Gary R. "*The Commercial Appeal's* Attack on the Ku Klux Klan, 1921-1925." *WTHS Papers* 31 (1977) 44-58. Recounts the rise and fall of the Klan's political power in Memphis and Shelby County, and C. P. J. Mooney and his newspaper's roles in that story.

Boddie, John Bennett. *Historical Southern Families.* 5 Volumes. Red Wood City, CA: Pacific Coast Publishers, 1960. Has good information on the Overton family of Tennessee.

Bond, Beverly G. and Janann Sherman. *Memphis in Black and White* in *The Making of America Series.* Charleston: Arcadia Publishing, 2003. This well illustrated book gives more emphasis to black-white relations than any work previously published. 160 pages, indexed.

Boom, Aaron M. "Early Fairs in Shelby County." *WTHS Papers* 10 (1956) 38-52.

Bordelon, John. "'Rebels to the Core:' Memphians under William T. Sherman." *The Rhodes Journal of Regional Studies.* 2 (2005) 6-36. Demonstrates that Sherman's concept of total warfare began with his experiences in the Memphis area in late 1862.

Bowman, David. *Memphis and the Politics of Development.* LaGrange, TN: LaGrange Books, 1998. Critique of land developers' control of local political decision making.

Brandon, E. Denby, Jr. "The Background and Operation of the Commission System [of Municipal Government] in Memphis, Tennessee." Duke University MA thesis, 1952.

Burch, Lucius. *Lucius: Writings of Luicus Burch,* compiled by Cissy Caldwell Akers, Shirley Caldwell-Patterson, Bill Coble, and John Noel. Nashville: Cold Tree Press, 2003. For a man who never held office, Burch was probably the most influential Shelby Countian of the twentieth century.

Burrow, Rachael Herring Kennon. *Arlington: A Short Historical Writing of the Town.* Memphis: E. H. Clarke and Brother, 1962. This book is not as modest as the title suggests.

Bussell, Alan. "The Memphis Press Scimitar and E. H. Crump: 1932-1948." University of Wisconsin M. A. thesis, 1959. Details the Meeman-Crump political antagonism.

Capers, Gerald. *Biography of a River Town: Memphis, Its Heroic Age,* second edition. New Orleans: by the author, 1966. Caper's book is the standard history of nineteenth-century Memphis and was a major milestone in the establishing of academically sound municipal histories. It does not devote a lot of attention to the county outside of Memphis and is somewhat weak on the last two decades of the nineteenth century.

Cargill, Bernice Taylor and Brenda Bethea Connelly, editors. *Settlers of Shelby County, Tennessee and Adjoining Counties.* Memphis: Descendants of Early Settlers of Shelby County, Tennessee, 1989. This book is mainly sketches of the club members' ancestors.

Carriere, Marius, Jr. "Dr. Samuel Bond and the Crystal Palace Medal." *WTHS Papers* 41 (1987) 1-3. Cotton grown in northeast Shelby County won the medal at the 1851 World Exposition in London for best in its class.

_____. "Blacks in Pre-Civil War Memphis." *THQ* 48 (Spring 1989) 3-14.

Cartright, Joseph H. *The Triumph of Jim Crow: Tennessee Race Relations in the 1880s.*
Knoxville: University of Tennessee Press, 1976. Title explains.

Chamberlain, Shirley Sigler. *History of Cuba, Tennessee, with Family Accounts and Genealogy.* Millington, Tennessee: by the author, 1984. This is a three hundred-page book devoted to the history of a defunct town in northwestern Shelby County. About half of the book covers Mrs. Chamberlain's relatives. It contains valuable information and is indexed.

Chandler, Walter. "The Courthouses of Shelby County." *WTHS Papers* 7 (1953) 72-8.

Chapman, Mary Winslow. *I Remember Raleigh.* Memphis: Riverside Press, 1977.

Church, Roberta, and Ronald Walter. *Nineteenth Century Memphis Families of Color, 1850-1900.* edited by Charles W. Crawford. Memphis: Murdock Printing, 1987.

Coleman, Leslie H. "The Baptists in Shelby County to 1900." *WTHS Papers,* 15 (1961) 8-39.

_____. "The Baptists in Shelby County, 1903-1950." *WTHS Papers,* 16, (1962) 70-103. The Baptists have long been the most powerful religious influence in Shelby County.

Contemporary Club. *Collierville: A Place Called Home.* Collierville: Contemporary Club, 1999. This is a beautifully photographed book depicting Collierville's most historic structures.

Coppock, Paul R. *Memphis Memoirs.* Memphis: Memphis State University Press, 1980.

_____. *Memphis Sketches.* Memphis; Friends of Memphis and Shelby County Libraries, 1976.

_____. *Paul R. Coppock's Mid South.* Four Volumes. Edited by Helen M. Coppock and Charles W. Crawford. Memphis: West Tennessee Historical Society and the Paul R. Coppock Publication Trust, 1985-1994. Except for the *West Tennessee Historical Society Papers,* Paul Coppock's six volumes are the broadest and richest sources for Mid-South history. They are particularly strong on both political and social history. Paul's vignettes include all of his local-history newspaper columns. All volumes are indexed.

Crawford, Charles W. *The Appeal of Memphis: A Retrospective of 15 Decades* Memphis: *The Commercial Appeal,* April 21, 1991. This retrospective is a decade-by-decade summary of Memphis-area events that appeared in the newspaper's sesquicentennial supplement.

Crosby, Molly Caldwell. *The American Plague: The Untold Story of Yellow Fever, the Epidemic That Shaped Our History.* New York: Berkley Books, 2006. Places the catastrophic Memphis and Shelby County outbreaks in their temporal, medical, and geographical contexts. Indexed.

Cupples, Douglas W. "Memphis Confederates: The Civil War and Its Aftermath." University of Memphis dissertation, 1995.

Davies-Rodgers, Ellen. *Along the Old Stage-Coach Road: Morning Sun and Brunswick, Shelby County, Tennessee.* Brunswick, Tennessee: The Plantation Press, 1990.

_____. *The Holy Innocents: The Story of a Historic Church and Parish.* Memphis: The Plantation Press, 1965. Has a good bit of history of Arlington, Tennessee in it.

_____. *The Romance of the Episcopal Church in West Tennessee, 1832-1964.* Memphis: The Plantation Press, 1964.

_____. *Turns Again Home: Life on an Old Tennessee Plantation, Trespassed by Progress.* Brunswick, Tennessee: The Plantation Press, 1992. Davies-Rodgers' books are self-published and contain a lot of repetition and much self-promotion.

Davis, Granville. "An Uncertain Confederate Trumpet: A Study in the Erosion of [Confederate] Morale." *WTHS Papers* 38 (1984) 19-50. This covers the Mid-South area.

Davis, James D. *The History of the City of Memphis.* Memphis: Hite, Crumpton & Kelley, 1973. Reprint facsimile edition, edited by James E. Roper Memphis: West Tennessee Historical Society, 1972. Frequently cited as Memphis' earliest history, the original book is rife with fiction and errors. Professor Roper's commentary in the reprint edition is much more valuable and often more interesting than Davis' text.

DeClue, Stephanie. "Poetic Justice: The Life and Works of Walter Malone." *WTHS Papers,* 53 (1999) 49-60. A sketch of Shelby County's best known poet and his best known works.

Dougan, John. "Binding the Free: Apprentice Indentures in Shelby County, Tennessee, 1829-1858," unpublished manuscript, 1994. Has narrative and a list of indentures.

Dowdy, G. Wayne. *Mayor Crump Don't Like It: Machine Politics in Memphis.* Jackson: University Press of Mississippi, 2006. This is the most recent book-length treatment of E. H. Crump, political leader in Memphis and Shelby County. It incorporates the contents of several articles previously published in the *WTHS Papers* and other journals. Dowdy is the curator of the Crump Collection of manuscripts at the Memphis Public library and has had access to documents not available to earlier researchers.

Downing, Marvin. "John Christmas McLemore: 19th Century Land Speculator." *THQ* 42 (Fall 1983) 254-65. McLemore was a major land speculator and developer in Shelby County.

Durham, Walter T. *Volunteer Forty-Niners: Tennesseans and the California Gold Rush.* Nashville: Vanderbilt University Press, 1997.

_____. *A Directory of Tennessee Agencies, Governmental and Non-Governmental, Bringing State and Local History to the Public.* Nashville: Tennessee Department of Library and Archives, 2004. This much needed directory is now available on line.

Dye, Robert W. *Shelby County,* in the *Images of America Series.* Charleston: Arcadia Publishing, 2005. This soft cover picture book has very crisp images across a broad range of Shelby County communities and vistas. The cut lines convey strong descriptions and contexts to complement the photographs. 128 pages, not indexed.

Frank, Edwin G. "The Meriwethers of Memphis and St. Louis." University of Memphis M. A. thesis. This family is an extremely important element in Memphis history.

Frayser, Leigh. "A Demographic Analysis of Memphis and Shelby County." MA thesis, Memphis State University, 1972

Garrett, Kenneth. "Captain Garrett's Diaries," Chapter X (pages 254-371) of Ellen Davies Rodgers' *The Holy Innocents, The Story of a Historic Church and County Parish.* Memphis: The Plantation Press, 1965. Garrett's journal has enormously useful information about daily life in and near the northeast Shelby County town of Arlington, Tennessee, spanning the years between 1892 and 1909.

Getz, John B. "History of the Court of General Sessions, Shelby County, Tennessee." *WTHS Papers,* 50 (1996) 179-94. This has a good overview of this court system and a listing of the judges, including their tenures and brief biographical sketches.

_____ and Joe Walk, compilers and editors. *History of the District Attorney General's Office and the Public Defender's Office of Shelby County Tennessee.* Memphis: John B. Getz, 2003. In addition to the institutions, this book contains tables of those holding the respective offices, biographical sketches such office holders, and detailed information on all of the courthouses and jails in Shelby County history. Not indexed.

_____. "The Shelby County Public Defender's Office." *WTHS Papers,* 56 (2002) 122-27. This article has important information about the Martin Luther King murder case against James Earl Ray. It also contains a sketch of former Judge Robert A. Tillman, a former Crump insider, who became one of the organization's most persistent and effective opponents.

_____. "The Wrights: Profile of a Tennessee Family Prominent in the Legal Profession." Unpublished manuscript dealing mainly with the careers of Judge Archibald Wright and his son Luke E. Wright. It lauds the careers of the two men.

Goodspeed's History of Hamilton, Knox and Shelby Counties. Nashville: C.

and R. Elder, Booksellers, 1974. This is a reprint of portions of the 1887 edition published by Goodspeed Brothers, Nashville. Goodspeed's is the only attempt at a "comprehensive" history of Shelby County, but it covers less than seventy years, all from the nineteenth century. It has standard information on the founding of the county and the early history of county government, drawn mainly and uncritically from the Shelby County Court minutes. It is considered to be conceptually anemic, unscholarly, and often inaccurate. The Shelby County "sketch" is in pages 795-1063, with the reprint edition keeping the original pagination. Probably the most valuable aspect of the Goodspeed treatment is its large body of biographical and genealogical sketches of late nineteenth century Shelby Countians. Even those, however, are not very substantial and not necessarily accurate. Not indexed.

Graham, Gene. *One Man one Vote: Baker v. Carr and the American Levellers.* Boston: Little Brown, 1972. In terms of democratizing the United States, this case is sometimes ranked at the top level of Supreme Court decisions.

Grant, H. Roger. "Memphis and the Interurban Era." *THQ* 46 (Spring 1987) 43-8.

Gray, Maria Sabina (Bogardus). *A Genealogical History of the Ancestors and Descendants of General Robert Bogardus.* Boston: Privately Printed, 1927. Has good information on the Snowden Family of Shelby County.

Green, Laurie B. *Battling the Plantation Mentality: Memphis and the Black Freedom Struggle.* Chapel Hill: University of North Carolina Press, 2007. An exhaustive examination of race relations in Memphis during the twentieth century. 432 pages. Indexed.

Greene, Maude. "Folklore of Shelby County, Tennessee." MA thesis, George Peabody College, 1940. Undocumented good stories and results of early oral history interviews.

Hall, Russell S. *Germantown.* in the *Images of America Series.* Charleston: Arcadia Publishing, 2003. This beautifully illustrated, 128-page book focuses on the things that made Germantown a community. That is shared experiences, schools, churches, businesses, etc.

Hall, Sir Peter. *Cities in Civilization.* New York: Pantheon Books, 1998. Hall ranks Memphis among the world's cities that have had a profound impact on civilization and culture.

Hallum, John. *Diary of an Old Lawyer, or Scenes Behind the Curtain.* Nashville: Southwestern Publishing House, 1895. Sketchily indexed. This book seems to be a memoir rather than an actual diary. It is written in flowery language and difficult to use. It depicts how byzantine the illegal trading was in Memphis and Shelby County during the Civil War. Later researchers have been skeptical of Hallum's work.

Harkins, John E., editor. " The Creation of Shelby County." *WTHS Papers,* 37 (1983) 96-102. Based on information supplied by Annice Bolton, Harkins places the legal measures involved in creating Shelby County in historical context. Mrs. Bolton's discovery corrects widespread misinformation about the petition for creating the county.

_____. *Metropolis of the American Nile: An Illustrated History of Memphis and Shelby County.* Memphis: Guild Bindery Press, second edition, 1991. Although designed as a "coffee table book" and almost twenty five years after its initial publication, this book is still probably the best summary of Memphis history. It contains minimal county history.

_____. MUS *Century Book: Memphis University School, 1893-1993, An Illustrated History.* Little Rock: August House, Inc., 2003. This book contains a good bit of social history and information about the families of the locale's power elite through the twentieth century.

_____ and Georgia S. Harkins. "*San Fernando de las Barrancas*: An Essay Review." *WTHS Papers,* 50 (1996) 195-99. Gives a thorough review of writings in English on the Spanish fort which occupied the Memphis area in the mid-1790s.

Hart, Roger L. *Redeemers, Bourbons & Populists: Tennessee 1870-96.* Baton Rouge: Louisiana State University Press, 1975. This book examines Tennessee's transition from Reconstruction to a single party, Jim Crow-dominated state.

Honey, Michael K. *Southern Labor and Black Civil Rights: Organizing Memphis Workers.* Urbana, Ill.: University of Illinois Press, 1993. A somewhat leftist perspective on the unionization of Memphis area industrial workers.

Hooper, Ernest Walter. "Memphis Tennessee: Federal Occupation and Reconstruction, 1862-1870." University of North Carolina dissertation, 1957.

Hughes, Louis. *Thirty Years a Slave: From Bondage to Freedom, The institution of Slavery as Seen on the Plantation and in the Home of the Planter.* This autobiography was first published in 1897. It was reprinted, New York: Negro Universities Press, 1969. Not indexed. It provides the basis for chapter four of *Historic Shelby County.* It is also available in an electronic edition, Chapel Hill: University of North Carolina, 1997.

Hunt, Ruth Wyckoff, editor. *Raleigh Sesquicentennial Scrapbook.* Memphis: Centennial Press, 1973. Contents are photo copies of news clippings, with commentary provided by Hunt.

Hutton, Marilyn J. "The Election of 1896 in the Tenth Congressional District of Tennessee." Dissertation, Memphis State University, 1978. This has a surprisingly strong amount of general information on Shelby County politics in the mid-1890s.

Jackson, Kenneth T. *The Crabgrass Frontier: The Suburbanization of the United States.* New York: Oxford University Press, 1985. Jackson is a native Memphian and probably the nation's foremost urban historian over recent decades. This book appears to be definitive work on its topic. It details national trends that also usually apply to Memphis and Shelby County. Indexed.

Jenkins, Ernestine. "The Voice of Memphis: WDIA, Nat D. Williams, and Black Radio Culture in the Early Civil Rights Era." *THQ,* 65-3 (Fall, 2006) 254-67. This is a brief version of the rise of America's first "all black" radio station.

Keating, John M. *History of the City of Memphis and Shelby County.,* two volumes. Volume two completed by O. F. Vedder. Syracuse: D. Mason & Co., 1888. Very valuable information, but largely undigested. Repeats some earlier myths. Not indexed or documented.

Kemper, Jackson. "An Early Visit to Memphis." edited by Kemper Durand, *WTHS Papers* 37 (1983) 88-95. Episcopal Bishop Jackson Kemper's observations of Memphis in 1838, when it was still a fairly small town.

Key, V. O., Jr. *Southern Politics in State and Nation.* New York: Alfred A. Knopf, 1949. Key's treatment of Tennessee politics, while still valuable, has been significantly revised in the last half-century.

Langsdon, Phillip. *Tennessee: A Political History.* Franklin, Tennessee: Hillsboro Press, 2000. This effort is encyclopedic in scope and has many biographical sketches of principals in making Tennessee's political history. It presents the sweep of the Volunteer State's politics in all its Byzantine complexity and ruthlessness. Indexed.

Lanier, Robert A. *The History of the Memphis & Shelby County Bar.* Memphis: The Memphis & Shelby County Bar Association, 1981. This is a 92-page summary of legal history in Shelby. It is documented and indexed.

LaPointe, Patricia M. *From Saddlebags to Science: A Century of Health Care in Memphis, 1830-1930.* Memphis: The Health Science Museum Foundation of the Memphis and Shelby County Medical Society Auxiliary, 1984. Scholarly treatment of this topic, includes illnesses and treatments in rural areas surrounding Memphis.

Laws, Forrest. "The Railroad Comes to Tennessee: The Building of the La Grange and Memphis." *WTHS Papers,* 30 (1976), 24-42.

Lee, David D. *Tennessee in Turmoil: Politics in the Volunteer State, 1920-1932.* Memphis: Memphis State University Press, 1979. Does an excellent job of putting the Crump regime and Shelby County's role in their statewide historical context for the era covered.

LeForge, Judy Bussell. "State Colored Conventions of Tennessee,

1865-66." *THQ*, 65:3 (Fall 2006) 230-53. Covers Black efforts to secure full liberty and equality in the wake of the Civil War. Provides state-wide context for the political and racial struggles in Memphis.

Lewis, Selma S. "Social Religion and the Memphis Sanitation Strike." Memphis State University dissertation, 1976. Lewis stresses the roles of AFSCME and religious activist ministers, noting that there was no controversy in the black religious community regarding black ministers' support for the strike.

_____. *A Biblical People in the Bible Belt: The Jewish Community of Memphis, Tennessee, 1840s-1960s*. Macon, Georgia: Mercer University Press, 1998.

Lindberg, Thomas, Jonathan Lindberg, and Daniel E. Johnson. *The Power of One: The Ed McAteer Story*. Privately printed, 2004. This lionizing of McAteer is more of an edited compilation than a true biography. Not indexed.

Long, Alice S. "'My Dear Manly Son:' The Death of Jefferson Davis, Jr., at Buntyn Station, Tennessee, 1878." *WTHS Papers*, 49 (1995) 1-22.

Long, John Mark. "Memphis Mayors, 1827-66: A Collective Study." *WTHS Papers*, 52 (1998) 105-33.

Lowe, Shirley Williams, editor. *Welcome to Rosemark: A History of Our Town*. Rosemark: Compiled and published by Rosemark's Tennessee Homecoming '86 Publications Committee, 1986. This is a combination scrapbook and photograph album, with clusters of community and family histories.

Lufkin, Charles L. "The Northern Exodus from Memphis During the Secession Crisis." *WTHS Papers* 42 (1988) 6-29. Documents that 3,000 to 5,000 persons left the Mid South for points north as the crises deepened and pro-Union sentiments were silenced.

Magness, Perre. *Good Abode: Nineteenth Century Architecture in Memphis and Shelby County, Tennessee*. Memphis: The Junior League of Memphis, Inc. 1983. Photographs by Murray Riss. Includes all major nineteenth century buildings still standing at the time of publication.

_____. *Past Times, Stories of Early Memphis*. Memphis: Parkway Press, 1994. These vignettes are republications from her sixteen years of popular columns appearing in *The Commercial Appeal*.

Majors, William R. "A Reexamination of V. O. Key's *Southern Politics in State and Nation*: The Case of Tennessee." *East Tennessee Historical Society Publications* 49 (1977) 117-136. Majors reevaluates the influence of the Crump machine on Tennessee politics and the Crump-McKellar relationship.

Mallory, Laula G. "The Three Lives of Raleigh." *WTHS Papers* 13 (1959) 78-94. Depicts Raleigh as county seat, spa resort, and Memphis suburb.

Malone, James H. *The Chickasaw Nation: A Short Sketch of a Noble People*. Louisville: J. P. Morton and Co., 1922. The classic early treatment.

Marszalek, John F. *Sherman: A Soldier's Passion for Order*. New York: Free Press, 1993. A biography that focuses in part on Sherman's role in occupying the Memphis area.

Masler, Marilyn. "Art and Artists in Antebellum Memphis." *THQ* 57 (Winter 1998) 218-35.

Matthews, James S. "Sequent Occupancy in Memphis, Tennessee, 1819-1860," *WTHS Papers* 11 (1957) 112-34. Provides demographic information on Memphis and vicinity to 1860.

McIlwaine. Shields. *Memphis, Down in Dixie*. New York: E. P. Dutton and Company, Inc. 1948. McIlwaine repeats many myths and errors from earlier sources and reputedly relied very heavily on the research of his students at Southwestern, now Rhodes, College. Unfortunately, his errors have influenced later scholarship.

McGraw, Brother Joel William, FSC, Reverend Milton J. Guthrie, and Mrs. Josephine King. *Between the Rivers: The Catholic Heritage of West Tennessee*. Memphis: Catholic Diocese of Memphis, 1996. This is a compendium of information on the churches, schools, organizations, and institutions in West Tennessee between 1836 and 1996. 473 pages, not indexed.

Meeks, Ann McDonald, "Whitehaven and Levi: The Evolution of Rural Communities in Southwest Shelby County, 1819-1970." MA thesis, Memphis State University, 1984. This study and a subsequent *WTHS Papers'* article limiting the scope to 1819-1860 are both excellent on the life and times aspects of the period covered.

Meeman, Edward J. *The Editorial We: A Posthumous Autobiography*, edited by Edwin Howard. Memphis: Memphis State University Press, 1976. Ed Meeman was editor of the *Memphis Press Scimitar* and E. H. Crump's most persistent and effective critic.

Melton, Gloria Brown. "Blacks in Memphis, Tennessee, 1920-1955: A Historical Study." Washington State University dissertation, 1982.

Memphis Magazine. April, 1976—the Memphis Public Library maintains a comprehensive index to this and several defunct popular local magazines like the *Delta Review* and *Mid South* (the *Commercial Appeal*'s Sunday supplement magazine).

Meriwether, Elizabeth Avery. *Recollections of 92 years, 1824-1916*. Nashville: Tennessee Historical Commission, 1958. This memoir is a highly literate, standard work. It reflects the author's observations of social and political life in the Memphis area prior to her family relocating in St. Louis during a yellow fever epidemic. It also reflects her dramatic life and her staunchly pro-Confederate perspectives.

Miller, William D. *Memphis During the Progressive era, 1900-1917*. Memphis: Memphis State University Press, 1957. Focuses on Crump as a force for reform politics.

_____. *Mr. Crump of Memphis*. Baton Rouge: Louisiana State University Press, 1964. In both of these volumes, Miller has been accused of being too soft on the Crump regime. His biography of Crump was authorized by the Crump family, and his access to the Crump papers was limited. These papers are now available at Memphis Public Library.

Moran, Nathan K. "Organizing Jackson's Purchase, Land Law and Its Impact on West Tennessee." *WTHS Papers* 49 (1995) 192-208. Shows how North Carolina and Tennessee laws, practices, and land grant policies affected patterns of settlement and aspects of county administration in West Tennessee.

Morris, Celia. *Fanny Wright: Rebel in America*. Chicago: University of Illinois Press, 1992. This is the fullest biographical treatment of the founder of Nashoba. 337 pages. It is scholarly, thorough, and indexed.

Nash, Charles H. "The Human Continuum of Shelby County, Tennessee." *WTHS Papers*, XIV, 1960, 5-31. An archeological study of the area.

Norman, Helen Watkins. "Elvis is Only the Beginning: Institute Fellows Find Plenty to Savor, Research in Memphis and the Mid-South." *Rhodes; The Magazine of Rhodes College* (Spring 2004) 12-27. This article gives an overview of the early stages of the Rhodes Institute for Regional Studies, which provides a forum for community involvement and for intensive, high quality undergraduate research into the history, culture, and economics in the Memphis area.

Norris, John "Park Field—World War I Pilot Training School." *WTHS Papers* 31 (1977) 59-76. This airfield later became Millington Naval Air Station for World War II, and it lasted through the Cold War. There is still a naval support facility at the Millington locale.

Nunn, Stephen. "Shelby County Government: A Brief History, 1820-1977." Unpublished paper produced by the Public Affairs Office of Shelby County Government, August 1977. Nunn gives a brief overview of Shelby County Government as it transitioned into its mayor-commission structure in the mid-1970s.

Old Folks of Shelby County. *The Old Folks' [Historical] Record*. Memphis: R. C. Hite, 1875. This is a bound volume of a monthly magazine published in 1874-75. It is a compendium of addresses, editorials, history articles, obituaries, advice, poetry, witticisms, etc. 586 pages, not indexed.

Old Shelby County Magazine: History, Humor, and Folkways of West Tennessee. Edited by Cathy Marcinko and Lydia Spencer. This magazine has numerous excellent articles on local history and folklore. Unfortunately, it discontinued publication after five years. Not documented, not indexed.

Ornelas-Struve, Carol M., Fredrick Lee Coulter, and Joan Hassell. *Memphis, 1800-1900*, three volumes, edited by Joan Hassell. A Memphis Pink Palace Museum Book: New York: Nancy Powers & Company, Publishers, Inc., 1982. Created to accompany the museum's nineteenth century "Boom Era" exhibit, illustrated with images from the exhibit. Neither indexed nor documented. Very strong on social history and line drawings.

Osteen, Faye Ellis. *Millington, The First Hundred Years.* Southhaven, Mississippi: The King's Press, 2002.

Pohlmann, Marcus D. and Michael P. Kirby. *Racial Politics at the Crossroads: Memphis Elects Dr. W. W. Herenton.* Knoxville: University of Tennessee Press, 1996. The authors attempt to explain the racial political divide in Memphis and Shelby County.

Pope, Dean. "The Senator from Tennessee." *WTHS Papers* 22 (1968) 102-22. Excerpt from the author's senior thesis at Princeton on Kenneth D. McKellar. This article focuses mainly on McKellar's roles in Washington.

Prescott, Grace Elizabeth. "The Woman's Suffrage Movement in Memphis: Its Place in the State, Sectional, and National Movements." *WTHS Papers* 18 (1964) 87-106.

Rea, John C. "The Normal Depot of the Southern Railway." WTHS Papers 38 (1984) 99-104.

_____. "The Street Railways of Memphis," unpublished manuscript available in local research libraries. This comprehensive treatment is very valuable for showing how the trolley lines affected suburban expansion and for attention to interurban lines. Contains endnotes, but no bibliography and is not indexed.

Ringel, Judy G. *Children of Israel: The Story of Temple Israel, Memphis, Tennessee, 1854-2004.* Memphis: Temple Israel Books, 2004.

Roberts. W. C. "The History of Education in Shelby County, Tennessee." MA thesis, Louisiana State University, 1934. Quality is low by current academic standards.

Robinson, Clayton R. "The Impact of the City on Rural Immigrants to Memphis, 1880-1940." University of Minnesota dissertation, 1967.

Robinson, James Trey. "Fort Assumption: The First Recorded History of White Man's Activity on the Present Site of Memphis." *WTHS Papers* 5 (1951), 62-78.

Rodgers, Ellen Davies, See Davies-Rodgers, Ellen. Mrs. Rodgers hyphenated her maiden and married names on books she authored.

Roitman, Joel M. "Race Relations in Memphis, Tennessee, 1880-1905." MA thesis, Memphis State University, 1964.

Roper, James E. *The Founding of Memphis, 1818-1820.* Memphis: The Memphis Sesquicentennial, Inc., 1970. Detailed and documented information on early Memphis and Shelby County.

_____. "The Revolutionary War on the Fourth Chickasaw Bluff." *WTHS Papers*, 19 (1975) 5-24.

Russell, Clarene Pinkston. *Collierville, Tennessee, Her People and Neighbors.* Collierville: The Town of Collierville and the Collierville Chamber of Commerce. 1994. This 535-page, hard cover book is an exhaustive treatment of Collierville and much of southeast Shelby County. It is extensively documented, illustrated, and indexed.

Sampson, Sheree. "Reclaiming a Historic Landscape: Frances Wright's Nashoba Plantation in Germantown, Tennessee." *THQ* 59 (Winter 2000) 290-303.

Schaffer, Suzanne, compiler. *A History of Fisherville and a History of the Fisherville Civic Club.* Memphis: published by the author, 1981. Has illustrations of the Crump machine's influence in the 1920s and '30s.

Shelby County Code Commission. *A Compilation of the Acts of the General Assembly of the State of Tennessee Relating to Shelby County, Containing Certain Acts, Private Acts and Public Acts for the years 1819 through 1955.* Memphis: S. C. Toof & Co., 1960.

Shelby County Sheriff's Department. *Yearbook, 1976.* Edited by Frank and Gennie Myers. Memphis, Walsworth Publishing, 1976. This is a book of largely uncaptioned photographs with very little text. Its tabular information is useful.

Shelden, Randall G. "A History of the Shelby County Industrial and Training School." *THQ* 51 (Summer 1992) 96-106.

_____. "Origins of Juvenile Court in Memphis, Tennessee: 1900-1910," *Tennessee Historical Quarterly.* 52:1 (Spring 1993) 34-43.

Shelton, Henry Clay, III. "The New Guard, Shelby County, Tennessee Party Politics, 1952-1970," BA thesis, Wesleyan University, 1972. Shelton's thesis describes the process of white Republicans' rise to power in the aftermath of the Crump regime.

Sigafoos, Robert A. *Cotton Row to Beale Street: a Business History of Memphis.* Memphis: Memphis State University Press, 1979. This standard work more thoroughly integrates the histories of Memphis and Shelby County than any other study to date. It is also fact-filled, and gracefully written. It is probably the most useful single volume available on Shelby County history, inclusive of Memphis. Indexed.

Smith, Jonathan Kennon Thompson. *Bartlett: A Beautiful Tennessee City.* Jackson, Tennessee: Published by the author, 2001. This is a 133 page, well-documented, indexed, and illustrated history of Shelby County's second largest city.

Stathis, John C. "The Establishment of the West Tennessee State Normal School, 1909-1914." *WTHS Papers* 10 (1956) 78-99.

Stone, Thomas R. *Politics of Change: The Restructure and Administration of Shelby County Government, 1974-1994.* Memphis: Shelby County Mayor's Office, 1996.

Sweeney, James R. The "Trials' of Shelby County: 'Judge Lynch' Presiding" *THQ* 63 (Summer 2004) 103-130. Brutality involved in a 1917 rape and murder case.

Tennessee Historical Commission. *Biographical Directory of the Tennessee General Assembly,* Volumes I-VI, 1796-1991. Produced by various editors and agencies over a span of years.

Tilly, Bette B. "Social and Economic Life in West Tennessee Before the Civil War." Memphis State University dissertation, 1974.

Tollison, Grady. "Andrew J. Kellar, Memphis Republican." *WTHS Papers* 16 (1962) 29-55. Kellar was an instrumental, perhaps a crucial, figure in negotiating the compromise that settled the disputed 1876 presidential election and gave Rutherford Hayes the office.

Tracy, Sterling. "The Immigrant Population of Memphis." *WTHS Papers* 4 (1950) 72-82. This article focuses on the mid-nineteenth century.

Trundle, Andrew. "Doctrine, Demographics, and the Decline of the Southern Baptist Convention in Shelby County, Tennessee." *The Rhodes Journal of Regional Studies* 2 (2005) 66-97. Examines Shelby County's religious demographics in a "white flight" context.

Tucker, David M. *Black Pastors and Leaders: Memphis, 1819-1972.* Memphis: Memphis State University Press, 1975. This is a scholarly work on a topic not treated until it appeared.

_____. *Memphis Since Crump: Bossism, Blacks, and Civic Reformers, 1948-68.* Knoxville: University of Tennessee Press, 1980. Strong political analysis of the Crump regime and its aftermath. Faults the Crump regime for its methods and the local citizens for their ongoing support of the machine. Almost half of the text deals with the Crump era, and the rest cuts off about 1968 with the Loeb regime.

Walk, Joe. *Chronological Listings of Selected Local Officials, Government Buildings, African-American Officials, [and] Policemen (Over Varying Periods).* Memphis: Published by the author, 1996.

_____. *Law Enforcement Line of Duty Deaths in Memphis and Shelby County: Collierville Police Department, Germantown Police Department, Memphis Police Department, Shelby County Sheriff's Department, Tennessee Highway Patrol, United States Marshals Service, [and] United States Secret Service.* Memphis: Published by the author, 1996, revised 2000.

_____. *Memphis and Shelby County Government Buildings: County Courthouses, Jails and Workhouses: The Early Years: 1820-1880.*

Memphis: Published by the author, 1996, revised 2000.

Walker, Randolph Meade. "The Role of Black Clergy in Memphis During the Crump Era." *WTHS Papers* 33 (1979) 29-47.

Warshauer, Matthew. "Andrew Jackson: Chivalric Slave Master." *THQ,* 65:3 (Fall 2006) 202-229. Author gives a detailed and thoughtful analysis of plantation slavery at Jackson's Hermitage, capturing the dual relationships within the slavery system.

Waschka, Ronald W. "Early Railroad Development at Memphis," *WTHS Papers,* 46 (1992) 1-12.

_____. "Road Building in and Near Memphis." *WTHS Papers,* 47 (1993) 50-64.

Wax, Jonathan I. "Program of Progress: The Recent Change in the Form of Government of Memphis." *WTHS Papers* 23 (1969) 81-109; and 24 (1970) 43-66. Shelby County patterned its restructuring after that of Memphis. Many of the same reformers were involved in both movements and most wanted consolidated metro government.

Wells, Ida B. *The Memphis Diary of Ida B. Wells.* Edited by Miriam DeCosta Willis. Boston: Beacon Press, 1995. Commentary on the local racial scene in the late nineteenth century.

West, Carroll Van, editor. *The Tennessee Encyclopedia of History & Culture.* Nashville: Tennessee Historical Society, 1998. This collaborative work helps to fill a long-time need for a comprehensive reference source on Tennessee history and culture. It seems to be noticeably lighter on its coverage of West Tennessee than it is on the other two grand divisions of the state and seems to have a disproportionate number of entries on West Tennessee topics written by persons from outside of West Tennessee and/or by persons not involved in researching and writing West Tennessee history. The book is comprehensively indexed.

Williams, Edward F, III. *Early Memphis and Its River Rivals.* Memphis: Historical Hiking Trails, 1968.

Williams, Samuel Cole. *Beginnings of West Tennessee, in the Land of the Chickasaws: 1541-1841.* Johnson City, Tennessee: The Watauga Press, 1930.

Williams, Thelma Sigler. *The Early History of Millington, Tennessee.* Millington: City of Millington, 1975. This is an eighteen-page booklet based primarily on Mr. and Mrs. Williams' 1930's interviews with many of the town's early settlers.

Witherington, Albert Sidney, III. *The History of Germantown: Utopia on the Ridge.* Germantown: Published by the author, 1997. A scrapbook-format publication.

Wojak, Joe. "The Factors of Urban Development: Cotton Brokers and Merchants in Antebellum Memphis, 1850-1860." *WTHS Papers* 50 (1996) 70-88. This is a study of the impact of cotton "factors" on urban economic and physical development.

Worley, Millie. "Reconsidering the Role of the Irish in the Memphis Race Riot of 1866." *The Rhodes Journal of Regional Studies.* 1 (2004) 38-70. Worley effectively refutes most of the existing scholarship that blames the Memphis Irish community for four days of racial violence. Makes extensive use of primary sources.

Wrenn, Lynette Boney. *Cinderella of the New South: A History of the Cottonseed Industry, 1855-1955.* Knoxville: Univeristy of Tennessee Press, 1995. Shows the impact of the cottonseed by-products on the Mid South's economy.

_____. *Crisis and Commission Government in Memphis.* Knoxville: University of Tennessee Press. 1998. A clear and thorough reexamination of the taxing district of Shelby County during the post-yellow fever thirteen years when Memphis did not have home rule and experimented with a commission structure of local government.

Wright, Sharon D. *Race, Power, and Political Emergence in Memphis.* New York: Garland Publishing, Inc., 2000. Focuses on the 1991 mayoral election. Indexed.

Wynn, Linda T., Editor. *Journey to Our Past: A Guide to African-American Markers in Tennessee.* [Nashville]: Tennessee Historical Commission, 1999. This booklet contains the texts and locations of African-American theme historical markers erected by the Tennessee Historical Commission. It also contains a valuable, 43-page historical sketch of African Americans in Tennessee. It is indexed alphabetically, topically, and by location. Almost one-third of the markers included are located in Shelby County.

Yellin, Carol Lynn and Janann Sherman. *The Perfect 36: Tennessee Delivers Woman Suffrage.* edited by Ilene Jones-Cornwell. Oak Ridge, Tennessee: Iris Press, 1998. A veritable encyclopedia of Tennessee's ratification of the Nineteenth Amendment to the U.S. Constitution, including Shelby Countians roles in the state legislative process.

Yellin, Emily. *A History of the Mid-South Fair.* Memphis: Guild Bindery Press, 1995. This illustrated history of one of Shelby County's oldest institutions shows connections between rural and urban Shelby Countians over many decades.

Young, J. P. "Happenings in the Whitehaven Community, Shelby County, Tennessee, Fifty or More Years Ago." *Tennessee Historical Magazine* 7 (July, 1916) 96-103.

_____. editor. *Standard History of Memphis, Tennessee.* Knoxville: H. W. Crew, 1912.

Beginning in 1890 electrified street railways dynamically changed urban demographics and recreational patterns. This Poplar Avenue trolley shows well-dressed citizens, perhaps enroute to an Overton Park outing. The city of Memphis has continued to expand for more than a centery since then. It is also surrounded by thribving suberban communities.

SHARING THE HERITAGE

historic profiles of businesses, organizations, and families that have contributed to the development and economic base of Memphis and Shelby County

✦

Looking north along Front Street at Union Avenue, c. 1905. The architecture and the business being conducted along the east (right) side of Front look more like the set for a Western movie than the business heart of a metropolitan Southern city. On the west side of the street, the castellated, Richardsonian Romanesque architecture and the deep rust colored sandstone of the Cossitt Library ought to conflict visually with the Neo-classical lines and muted color of the Federal Post Office and Customs house. Yet, their radically different styles somehow worked well together, and both inspired civic and aesthetic pride. Sadly, both buildings were expanded and had their most distinctive architectural features ripped off in the process. Although both are still there in 2007, by the late twentieth century both landmarks had become unrecognizable.

COURTESY OF THE W. PATRICK MCCARVER COLLECTION.

SPECIAL THANKS TO

Commercial Appeal

Fidelity Mortgage &
Funding Inc.

Grady W. Jones Company

Hampton Inn & Suites at
Beale Street

RESIDENCE INN BY MARRIOTT MEMPHIS DOWNTOWN

The building housing the Memphis Residence Inn by Marriott has been a part of the city's architectural landscape since 1930. It opened as the William Len, heralded by the local newspaper as a grand hotel with 250 rooms, 250 baths and "an artificially-cooled lobby and barbershop."

Grady Manning, president of Southwest Hotels, Inc., named the hotel in honor of his father-in-law, William Len Seaman. In the early twentieth century, Seaman, formerly of Savannah, Tennessee became one of the wealthiest and best-known citizens of Arkansas.

The hotel closed in 1970 and then reopened in the early 1980s when an investment firm converted the buildings' 250 rooms into 89 apartments. The Hertz Investment Group bought the building in 1994 and held it until 2000, when it donated the property to Neve Yerushalayim, a college for women based in Israel.

Memphis-based Wright Investment Properties bought the building from the nonprofit organization with the intention of turning it into an extended-stay property. The company spent ten months converting the twelve-story property to its present status.

The conversion went quickly, thanks to the fact that the building had been completely renovated in the 1980s when it was adapted for use as an apartment building. The conversion left what Larry Wright, president of Wright Investments Properties, termed the "perfect footprint" for his hotel venture.

The building's footprint and size of the rooms fit the Residence Inn room size perfectly, making for an easy transition from an apartment building to an extended-stay hotel. Although the latest renovation maintained the same configuration of rooms, the division of a large rooftop apartment allowed an additional unit. The extended-stay property is the only property of its kind poplar I-240 area. The extended-stay concept allows guest to enjoy the amenities of a fine hotel without sacrificing a full kitchen with stove, oven, microwave, and refrigerator.

Each room is outfitted with high-speed Internet access, while the lobby and common areas provide wireless Internet access. Guests receive a complimentary hot breakfast and are invited to a daily social hour in the late afternoon.

Modern amenities have not erased the historical details that helped the hotel earn a spot on the National Register of Historic Places. Extensive effort went into keeping the building true to its history and character while adding all the modern comforts that modern travelers have come to expect.

The art deco details throughout the building are especially apparent in the hotel's lobby, which, like other renowned hotels, is the building's most architecturally significant space. The ironwork around the lobby's staircases and mezzanine reflects the art deco design of the hotel's original logo, a theme carried throughout the lobby and common areas in the hotel's intricate inlaid woodwork.

Longtime Memphis Mayor "Boss Crump" had his hair cut in the mezzanine barbershop of the Williams Len on a regular basis. The chef's daily luncheon special in the hotel restaurant cost a mere seventy-five cents.

The vertical marble columns, the ornate elevator doors, and the light fixtures were preserved from the original building. Gilded mirrors and modernist furnishings heighten the period look throughout the hotel.

It is attention to detail that makes the building special. The hotel's beds are all feather beds and are triple sheeted. The hotel ranks in the top ninety-five percent in bed comfort when compared with other hotels. Beds are presented with four fluffy, oversize pillows, calling attention to the fact that every guest can look forward to a good night's sleep.

The goal is to make guests feel so comfortable that they will want to stay awhile. Some tenants stay more than a year, making the inn their downtown Memphis office. Rates for suites vary according to the length of stay as well as room size, making it affordable to any visitor staying more than the minimum five nights. The hotel does a significant amount of business with large corporate clients.

Guests have at their disposal two meeting rooms that will accommodate as many as fifty people, with catering available as needed. Along with Internet access in both rooms and common areas, fax and copy machines are located off the lobby.

The Memphis Residence Inn by Marriott stands as an ideal example of how an older, historically significant building can be preserved, renovated and used as a modern place of business without sacrificing the building's history and culture. Come see why the Memphis Residence Inn is a favorite among corporate and leisure travelers.

ALBERT COOK PLUMBING COMPANY

"Dependable Service at Reasonable Prices" has been the slogan of Albert Cook Plumbing Company since the family owned-and-operated business began in 1955.

Albert "Ace" Cook, his wife Eleanora (known as "Cookie") and their three young sons started the operation out of their home with only one truck.

The business prospered and, in 1957, Albert Cook Plumbing moved to a storefront building at 1013 East Parkway, South, across from the old Fairground's Merry-Go-Round, now known as Libertyland.

As business continued to grow, the firm moved to a larger location at 2101 Central Avenue in 1964. The building, built in the 1930s, formerly housed the Bluff City Lumber Company and when customers visit the showroom, they can still see the old flooring, which displays samples of the different kinds of wood used for homes in the area seventy years ago.

An Albert Cook Plumbing radio spot during this era used a jingle with the words, "King of the Kitchen and Prince of the Bath." The popular jingle prompted customers to call the business and ask for Prince Albert, an apt name for a prince of a fellow.

As the company grew larger, so did the Cook family. With four sons and a daughter, Eleanora retired to become a stay-at-home mom. A permanent bookkeeper, Ann Kirk Bugbee, was hired and still works for the company today. "Miss Ann," as she is fondly known, has been the engine and motivation at Albert Cook Plumbing for nearly fifty years and is a large part of the top management team. With Miss Ann's semi-retirement, Fleta Young, who has been with the company eighteen years, and Beth Dooley, who has been with the company five years, handle the day-to-day office tasks.

In the late 1960s through the 1970s, Albert Cook Plumbing was considered one of—if not the—largest plumbing company in the southeastern United States, with more than a 100 employees, in excess of 40 trucks, 2 backhoe rigs, and 25 percent of the local work. A lot of plumbers got their experience at Albert Cook, and many went on to open their own businesses or become plumbing inspectors.

Albert Cook Plumbing has been affiliated with national, state, and local Home Builders Associations and plumbing, heating-cooling associations since the 1960s. Albert served on the local Plumbing Advisory Board from 1962

The children of Albert and Eleanora Cook: Perry, Wayne, Patricia, Bobby, and Gary with their spouses: Sally, Diane, Eddie, Karen and Lori, c. 1990.

to 1965. Both Albert and his son, Bobby, have served as presidents of the local Association of Plumbing, Heating, Cooling Contractors: Albert from 1969 to 1970 and Bobby from 1979 to 1980. Bobby's other associations and community projects include: Home Builders Association Liaison Council for several years, a Life Spike Award for Home Builders Association membership recruitment, and the Memphis Press-Scimitar Goodfellows Christmas Collection Booth for underprivileged children through the local plumbing association. Bobby also served on Delta Faucets National Advisory Board from 1986 to 1987, and was chairman of the Shelby County Plumbing Licensing Board from 1984 to 1992.

Albert's brother-in-law, the late Lee Bobbitt, was very instrumental in helping the company grow by being very tenacious in his supervisory work and scheduling for more than thirty years. Lee was well respected by plumbers, builders, and the Cook family for his work habits, ethics, and the Christian principles he displayed daily.

Albert's oldest son, Barry Wayne, is the firm's current "Mr. Lee," and displays many of Lee's traits and Christian ideals.

Albert's youngest son, Gary, is a very capable plumber and heads up the multifamily arm of Cook Plumbing. When not working in the trenches of a big new apartment building, Gary is a very competent riding supervisor and manager.

Paul E. "Eddie" Nelius is married to Albert's only daughter, Patricia. Without question, Eddie is the best repair plumber in the Tri-State area. In his spare time, Eddie fills the roll of advisor to the other plumbers when unusual circumstances or mysteries occur. He is also an excellent estimator.

Albert Cook Plumbing is still operated by family today, including Barry Wayne, Robert R. "Bobby," Gary M. Cook, and Paul E. "Eddie" Nelius. Numerous relatives have worked for the company over the years, including brothers, grandsons, nephews and in-laws. Although incorporated in 1974, the business is still operated by family only.

The company currently works in Shelby, Tipton, and Fayette Counties in Tennessee and in DeSoto and Marshall Counties in Mississippi.

Albert Cook Plumbing Company has installed plumbing in approximately 30,000 new homes and 60,000 apartments in the Memphis area in its 51 years of continuous operation.

BOYLE INVESTMENT COMPANY

Boyle Investment Company has had a profound impact on Memphis for nearly seventy-five years although, in reality, the company roots reach all the way back to the city's founding. Boyle family ancestor, John Overton, founded Memphis in 1819 in partnership with Andrew Jackson.

In the early 1900s, Edward Boyle developed stately Belvedere Boulevard. The 1960s saw development of River Oaks and Farmington. In the early 1970s, Boyle paved the way for the city's growth eastward with one of Memphis' first office parks, Ridgeway Center, which today offers more than two million square feet of space. In the 1980s, Boyle began development of Humphreys Center, which has become East Memphis' bustling medical/office center. The 1990s saw the development of even more ambitious projects like Schilling Farms, a 443-acre mixed-use community in Collierville. With the new century, Boyle continues to accelerate its activity in Memphis while developing a new thrust into Nashville.

Three brothers formed Boyle Investment Company in 1933: Bayard Boyle, Sr., Snowden Boyle, and Charles Boyle. "My father and his two brothers focused their efforts initially on buying land and developing residential subdivisions and shopping centers," says Bayard Boyle, Jr., Chairman of the Board. "My father had a remarkable ability

to identify and acquire properties in areas that would soon become major growth corridors.

"Today, we still stick with those same principles of careful research and planning, whether it's a residential subdivision, a shopping center, or an office building we're developing," he adds.

The firm's President, Henry Morgan, notes that Boyle focuses much of its resources in the office and retail sectors of the real estate market. "Over the past several decades, we have developed numerous high-profile projects, including the regional headquarters for the U.S. Postal Service, Marsh Center and the Morgan Keegan Building at Ridgeway Center, the headquarters facility for Baptist Memorial Health Care Corporation, the Village Shops of Forest Hill, Preston Shepard Place power center in Plano, Texas, Thomas & Betts World Headquarters at Southwind, and the headquarters building for Helena Chemical Company at Schilling Farms," he says.

The Boyle name became synonymous with fine residential neighborhoods with the development of Belvedere in midtown Memphis a century ago. In the decades since, Boyle Investment Company has developed such outstanding neighborhoods as Pleasant Acres in East Memphis, River Oaks, Farmington, The Garden of River Oaks, The Cloisters of River Oaks, Blue Heron, and two exclusive golf course neighborhoods in Southwind: The Gardens of Southwind and Golf Walk.

Boyle has never been content to rest on its accomplishments, and the company continues to make news with announcements, openings, and groundbreakings for new projects.

In the retail sector, Boyle has been involved recently with the development of

❖

Above: Belvedere Boulevard.

Below: Boyle's Gallina Centro shopping center located at the common border between Germantown and Collierville.

Gallina Centro, a premier community center at the common border between Germantown and Collierville.

In the residential arena, Boyle has developed Braystone Park, a 100-acre family-oriented residential community in Collierville, and Wickliffe, which offers estate-sized lots in the heart of the high-value area of North Raleigh-LaGrange Road.

In the office sector, one of the most notable accomplishments is the fact that Ridgeway Center continues to boom as the epicenter of the East Memphis office market. Another exciting development is a one-of-a-kind mixed-use community on the Berry property in Franklin, Tennessee.

According to Bayard Boyle, one of the firm's greatest assets is a "deep bench" of experts—longtime employees who have been with the company for years. "We have a number of executives in key positions who have been with the company for more than twenty-five years," he notes. "Their expertise and long-term involvement with the company have been a great plus for us."

Henry Morgan adds, "We've built a strong company because the family, from the beginning, has been committed to developing for long-term value. We operate on the belief that properties are long-term investments that should be carefully planned, built, and maintained."

Paul Boyle, Henry Morgan, Jr., and Bayard Morgan represent the third generation of the Boyle family in the company. Vice President Paul

Boyle points out that while Boyle will continue to be an active player in Memphis real estate and development, it is also turning its attention to the Nashville market. Meridian Cool Springs, a forty-acre project in Franklin, Tennessee, will offer a unique mix of office, retail, restaurant, and hotel uses, including a 175,000 square foot headquarters building currently under construction for Community Health Systems. "We're excited about the company's future, and we remain dedicated to maintaining a long-term vision that delivers enduring value for our partners and tenants," Boyle concludes.

Boyle Investment Company is located at 5900 Poplar Avenue in Memphis, Tennessee and on the Internet at www.boyle.com.

✧

Above: Morgan Keegan building in Ridgeway Center.

Below: Rendering of Belvedere Boulevard from a 1907 edition of The Commercial Appeal *newspaper.*

The plan for Belvedere was published in the Commercial Appeal *on April 7, 1907, and deemed "too visionary to ever be realized." Note the fountains in the circles and the trees planted along the sidewalk. (Photo courtesy of the Memphis Room)*

LIFEBLOOD

Every three minutes, someone in Shelby Country receives a lifesaving blood transfusion—blood given by Lifeblood's volunteer donors. As the leading provider of blood and blood products to hospitals in a fourteen-county area, Lifeblood ensures that patients always have the blood they need for life.

Today, the Memphis community hosts the second largest medical district in the country (per capita), a Level 1 Trauma Center, and one of the largest treatment centers for those with sickle cell disease. There is a constant need for blood donors.

Lifeblood's mission to serve this community's blood needs was set in motion in the late 1930s, when the fourth blood bank in the United States was founded at John Gaston Hospital. For years, blood banks existed only in hospitals. There were no donor lists—it was the responsibility of the patients' families to find donors for their loved ones. Dr. Lemuel Diggs, a leading hematologist, led the efforts to establish a safe and secure blood supply for the community.

In late 1949, Dr. Merlin Trumbull, Director of Pathology at Baptist Hospital, visited and studied community blood banks throughout the country. After his research, he proposed a similar community blood center be created in Memphis. The proposal was rejected on the grounds that it would be more expensive to operate than the then existing system of hospital-drawn paid donors.

In August 1950, Dr. Diggs suggested that Memphis and the Mid-South would benefit from a nonprofit community blood center. In 1954 another proposal to establish a blood center in Memphis was rejected for the same reason, as in 1949—it was too costly. Finally, all of these proposals led to a successful venture. In 1962 the Committee on Blood Bank Operation of the Memphis and Shelby County Medical Society approved a Blood Assurance Program that supplemented—rather than replaced—then-existing hospital-based donor collection program.

The Community Blood Plan of Memphis, Inc. was chartered February 19, 1963 as a not-for-profit corporation. The original objectives were to reduce dependence on paid donors, establish a pre-deposit blood assurance program, work toward a more even flow of donations, and develop a roster of donors with rare blood types.

In 1974 the first Community Blood Plan Donor Center opened its doors at 1715 Union Avenue, just a mile and a half east of the Medical Center. It began operations with four employees and two donor chairs. During the entire year of 1974, only 1,335 donations were accepted at the donor center, with about 600 donors on mobiles.

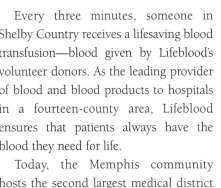

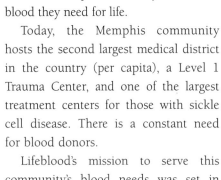

✧

Above: Lifeblood has served the Mid-South since 1963.

Below: Fred Jones, founder of the Southern Heritage Classic, hosts blood donation events to encourage his friends to give blood.

In July 1974, Dr. Eric Muirhead received a federal grant of $183,000 to establish an identifiable non-hospital based facility for the Community Blood Plan. The expansion of a true regional blood center became a reality in January 1975, when the board of directors changed the name to Mid-South Regional Blood Center. Nearly 7,000 donors were accepted in 1975; 14,600 in 1976; 17,300 in 1977 and almost 20,000 in 1978.

Groundbreaking took place at 1040 Madison Avenue on February 15, 1978. By 1979 the Mid-South Regional Blood Center had 45 employees, collected more than 25,000 units of blood and provided more than 40,000 transfusable products to the community.

In 1984, a new logo, "Lifeblood," was adopted to easily identify the blood center to more than 600,000 eligible blood donors in Shelby County while clearly distinguishing it from other facilities collecting blood in the area.

Today, patients in our community hospitals require more than 100,000 units of blood and blood products each year. About 33,000 Lifeblood volunteer donors provide about sixty percent of what is needed. The remaining must be imported from other volunteer community blood centers throughout the country. Depending on other communities to care for patients in our local hospitals puts patients' care at risk, especially during times of the year when blood centers across the country are experiencing blood shortages. Lifeblood's goal is to eliminate the dependence on other volunteer blood centers to fulfill the needs of our community.

You can be a part of saving lives in your community. To learn more about donating to Lifeblood, call 1-888-lifeblood or visit www.lifeblood.org. With your help, we can ensure that all patients have the blood they need for life.

✧

Above: Many area corporations, like First Tennessee, support Lifeblood by financial gifts and employee donation programs.

Below: Students at the University of Memphis donate on campus at the AutoZone Lifeblood Donor Center.

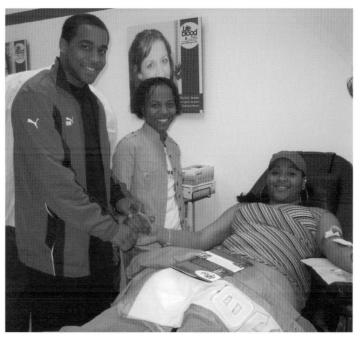

MEMPHIS CITY SCHOOLS

The Memphis public school system has come a long way in the past two centuries. What began as schools held in people's homes have become the nation's twenty-first largest school system and the second largest employer in Memphis.

From 1826, the year the Memphis school system was chartered, until 1848, all Memphis schools were privately offered by well-to-do citizens. In the early 1800s, education was scarce for lower- to middle-class white children and nonexistent for black children. That began to change, however, with the opening of the first free school in 1848, named Third and Overton for its location. In that year, a system of free schools was adopted in the city largely through the influence of J.W.A. Pettit, often referred to as the father of the free school system of Memphis.

Through Pettit's influence, Memphis began assigning city treasury funds to schools, with a first year budget of $20,000. Pettit, the first superintendent, was not paid. Then, in 1852, when there were thirteen schools, the treasury imposed a city school tax rate, followed by a county school tax rate in 1854. Creation of the tax rates allowed children who formerly could not afford school tuition to receive a public education, but it would be more than a decade before public education was extended to black citizens.

In 1868, the City of Memphis began supporting public schools for black students, and in 1891, the first class graduated from a black public high school. The oldest school

still in use by the Memphis City Schools is Cummings Elementary, which was erected at 1037 Cummings in 1902 for white students and still operates in the same location. The oldest school still in use that was originally for the education of black students is Klondike Elementary School, which was built in 1902 at 1250 Vollintine.

Prior to January 24, 1973, segregation was practiced in most Memphis City Schools. However, in that year, court-ordered busing was instituted to help integrate the schools. The order caused much controversy, and many white parents withdrew their children from the Memphis City Schools system in favor of private schools. In January of that year alone, 7,532 students withdrew from the public schools.

Over time, school integration was accepted, and, through a series of annexations by the City of Memphis, Memphis City Schools now operates 187 schools (not including charter schools) across the City of Memphis under the direction of Dr. Carol R. Johnson, who became the district's eleventh superintendent in October of 2003. The creation of ten charter schools over the last several years brings the total number of schools that are part of Memphis City Schools to 197. About eighty percent of the district's students are black, and more than sixty percent come from low-income families. In 2005-06, the district's English-As-A-Second Language (ESL) office was serving more than 5,000 students with 64 different nationalities.

✧

Below: A school in the Binghampton community in the 1920s.

Memphis City Schools operates on a $834 million budget and has 16,000 employees and 118,000 students.

In recent years, the Memphis City Schools system has made exemplary progress in raising educational standards. In 2005, for the first time since the stricter state accountability standards were implemented under the federal No Child Left Behind legislation, the school district made Adequate Yearly Progress (AYP) and moved into an improving category. In 2006, the State Department of Education declared Memphis City Schools to be in good standing.

Under the leadership of Superintendent Johnson, the district has implemented a number of initiatives to improve and accelerate student academic achievement. Among them are a district-wide literacy campaign, a strengthened focus on mathematics, the Secondary Course Recovery Program providing a second chance for at-risk high school students to make up needed coursework, increased student participation in the arts, and a variety of professional development programs for the district's teachers. The district's plan for improved learning by students incorporates programs to improve school leadership and teaching, and the district has succeeded in being selected for highly competitive national programs and grants to achieve that goal, such as its selection for the "New Leaders, New Schools" program, the New Teacher Project, the Harvard University Business School Project, and Teach for America. Through a partnership with the University of Memphis College of Education, the University's Leadership Fellows Program also helps the district achieve its goal of strengthening school leadership by providing intensive training and mentoring to select candidates for urban school leadership in the district.

The district has recently been recognized for a number of its efforts, including being one of only thirty-one school districts named in 2006 to the American Music Conference list of the "Best 100 Communities for Music Education in America," being singled out by the National Middle School Association as a model for its national campaign for policy reforms, being one of six school districts in the nation to receive a $16 million federal "Striving Readers Grant" to improve middle school literacy, and having a school in both 2004-05 and in 2005-06 selected as a national No Child Left Behind-Blue Ribbon School.

Today, Memphis City Schools is a diverse, urban school district committed to student achievement and educational reform that works. Memphis City Schools has built strong community relationships, state-of-the-art learning facilities and some of the best schools in the state and nation.

✧

Above: A new school was built and opened in the Binghampton community in 2006, named for Dr. William Herbert Brewster.

Below: Early literacy is a focus in Memphis City Schools.

HALLE INVESTMENT COMPANY

Since the arrival of the three Halle brothers in the early 1850s, the family has been prominently identified with the progress of Memphis. Having left their home in Altona, the Danish suburb of Hamburg, Germany, where the von Halle family had lived since the 1680s, the sons of David Philip von Halle were anxious to come to the bluffs of Memphis and establish themselves in the business and civic affairs of the River City.

The family quickly assimilated in the young city and became identified with the merchandising business in the Front Street and Main Street districts. The Halle brothers established their businesses and partnerships by investing in properties in the years prior to the Civil War. The youngest brother established the Oak Hall clothing company in 1859.

The city was to go through turbulent times following the reconstruction of the South after the Civil War as well as suffering the devastating effects of the yellow fever epidemic of the 1870s. Many families perished or left the area never to return. The Halle family remained and continued to establish other businesses. The Halle-On-Main and Phil A. Halle clothing companies joined Oak Hall in the downtown area and became, for many decades, known as leaders in the merchant history of the area and were identified with the carriage trade of the Mid-South.

Members of the Halle family during the past 150 years have served on numerous boards, commissions, and civic organizations. Their involvement has included serving in both appointed and elected capacities, as well as holding positions on various bank and business boards. Members of the family have been instrumental in the founding of various charities, including the citywide celebration known as the Cotton Carnival, which has benefited Memphis and the Mid-South for over seventy-five years.

Halle Investment Company began developing and investing in property as an owner and in various partnerships. David Philip Halle, Jr., a seventh-generation Memphian, has been involved with the development of more than 1,800 residential lots, commercial and office areas, and other investments centered primarily in the Collierville area. Halle Investment Company has been honored with various awards and proclamations for the development, charitable, and civic works successfully accomplished since the 1980s. The company was named an honoree in the 2003 Carnival Memphis Business and Industry Salute.

Some of the better-known projects are the company's involvement with the 500-acre Halle Plantation, one of the largest single-family residential, planned-unit developments in the Mid-South. Other developments include the 620-acre Almadale Farms, and Bailey Station, home of the FedEx World Technical Center. Halle Investment Company was host to the first Vesta Home Show for Collierville in 1995 and again in 1996. Due in part to the strong growth and economic boom of the Collierville area, Halle Investment Company has broken many of the county records in sales and appreciation percentages in their particular price range of residential properties.

David P. Halle, Jr., feels strongly about giving back to the community, and has

made donations of land, financial support, and time to better the Collierville area. Some of the gifts to the Town of Collierville include the sixty-acre Halle Park, home of the new Collierville Town Hall and Collierville Public Library, as well as land for a Collierville fire station. More recently, a gift of land for the permanent home of

the Page Robbins Adult Day Care Center was donated by Halle and his uncle, James G. Robbins. The Center was named in memory of Halle's maternal grandparents, Julia Page and Guy Robbins, of Osceola, Arkansas.

Halle's lifelong interest in history has been noted both locally and nationally. His participation in historical preservation as well as heredity and genealogical organizations have lead to membership and past and present board positions in more than twenty-five local and national societies. While serving as a Germantown Alderman (1988-1992) and member of the Germantown Historic Commission, Halle donated the historic John Gray House to Germantown. The Federal-style house, thought to be the oldest brick structure in Shelby County, is now a permanent feature behind the Germantown City Hall as part of the Germantown Civic Center Complex. With the participation of Germantown and Tennessee state funds, the house was moved from Highway 64 and renovated to its early grandeur.

Halle Investment Company continues to look toward the future and its involvement in Shelby County, while remembering the vital importance of the past.

✧

Above: Phil A. Halle Clothing Company occupied the first three stories of the Exchange Building located at Second Street and Madison for many generations. The photo was taken from the southeast corner of Court Square.

Below: Oak Hall was located at 55 North Main for over 100 years. Oak Hall was one of the first, if not the first, businesses on Main to have glass store fronts for display as well as electric lights. The photo was taken from the northwest corner of Court Square.

CRYE-LEIKE REALTORS®

Crye-Leike Realtors was established in December 1976, when realtors Harold Crye and Dick Leike decided to leave the firm they were with and open their own realty business. From its inception, they committed as partners to build a real estate company that would be like no other in the region. They were determined to establish a company that would be consumer-oriented, professionally operated, and would provide superior service "above and beyond" that provided by other real estate firms.

"We were naïve enough then not to know what wouldn't work so we went out and made it work," says Chief Executive Officer Harold Crye. "Our whole operating philosophy was—and is—that Crye-Leike is not in the real estate business; we're in the business of helping people achieve the American dream of homeownership."

The company began with thirty sales associates and first-year revenues of $19 million . As branch offices were added and more sales associates joined the firm, Crye-Leike became the largest real estate firm in Memphis within three years. The company is now the largest real estate company in Tennessee with more than 3,300 sales associates and 100 branches and franchise offices. In recent years, Crye-Leike has expanded into Arkansas and Mississippi, as well as portions of Florida, Georgia, and Kentucky. The company is now ranked number six among the country's largest residential real estate brokers and number five among independent firms.

Harold Crye and Dick Leike took real estate to a new level by providing a one-stop "home buying and selling experience." They were pioneers in building a full service real estate company focused on customer service and helping customers with more than just buying and selling their homes.

With a comprehensive approach to customer service, Crye-Leike expanded by opening a relocation division, a commercial division, a property leasing and management company, an insurance company, a home services division, and auction division. This allowed Crye-Leike to offer its clients a full menu of personalized pre- and post-occupancy services, including closing services, property, casualty and title insurance, and mortgage services. This "one-stop" shopping experience

❖

Harold Crye and Dick Leike.

still sets Crye-Leike apart from other real estate companies.

With the advent of the Internet, Crye-Leike introduced Crye-Leike Home Services, offering clients discounted services on home repair and such services as moving assistance. Hook-up of utilities, telephone, cable, and newspaper delivery may all be arranged over the Internet before the family moves into its new home.

As the company grew, Harold and Dick became well known within the real estate industry as innovators in commission structure and marketing, and are credited with bringing order and consolidation to an often-unstructured industry.

Crye-Leike instituted a fully computerized and staffed appointment center, the only one of its kind in the Mid-South, to capture every sales opportunity. The appointment center makes it easy for sales associates from other real estate companies to arrange an appointment to see Crye-Leike properties thirteen hours a day, seven days a week, from 7:00 a.m. to 8:00 p.m. The appointment center receives an average of 1,200 calls daily.

"Consumer-friendly marketing is a major focus at Crye-Leike," says Michael Frase, marketing director. "We believe marketing determines the speed at which homes sell, so we've positioned ourselves as the company that aggressively markets its homes to more buyers than any of our competitors."

Crye-Leike listings span sixty cities within Tennessee, Mississippi, Arkansas, Kentucky, Alabama, Florida, and Georgia.

To help maintain its number one position in the market, Crye-Leike has invested millions of dollars in technology and the Internet as a core part of its business strategy. A team of information technology specialists has harnessed the technical and global power of the Internet to reach homebuyers in a way that had not been done before.

The company's website (www.crye-leike.com) has unique on-line search capabilities that have contributed to increasing web traffic from 300,000 hits a month to well over 30 million and 500,000 unique visitors each month, and there's no end in sight notes Gurtej Sodhi, Crye-Leike's chief information officer.

As the Mid-South leader in real estate sales, Crye-Leike takes great pride in achieving a ninety-seven percent customer satisfaction rate, with more than ninety percent stating they were very satisfied with the overall services provided by Crye-Leike Realtors.

Harold and Dick have built a powerful, diverse, and influential real estate empire over the past three decades, but they feel they are just now beginning to reach their stride. "Just as each Crye-Leike division lends credibility and strength to the core business, that core business of providing the American dream of home ownership gives credibility and strength to each division, from insurance to property management, to relocation," says Harold.

Whatever the future may hold as the world of real estate continues to evolve, it is certain that Harold and Dick will be at the front of the pack, justifiably proud that their own American dream of building some thing special back in 1977 has come true beyond their wildest imaginations.

WILLIAM MATTHEWS

BY GARY WITT

Throughout its history, Shelby County has boasted more than a fair share of outstanding business entrepreneurs. Some say this is due to our central geographical location as the nation's distribution center. Others note that Memphis is perched atop the greatest waterway in the nation. And certainly the region's agricultural heritage of hard work at risky ventures has played a part. At any rate, Memphis and Shelby County have spawned many successful and highly recognized business men and women, from the cautious and conservative to the bold and brash.

Certainly William Matthews falls into the latter group. For a decade during the 1970s and early 1980s, he was a colorful, controversial visionary who attained a somewhat larger-than-life reputation as a highly original thinker, an advocate for progressive, even unheard of ideas in banking, and the president and chairman who saved Union Planters Bank.

Matthews was born in Georgia in 1933. After service in the U.S. Army, he set his sights on becoming a Wall Street investment banker. An uncle convinced him he needed to gain banking experience first, so he joined a major Atlanta, Georgia bank. In a remarkably short time, he was appointed president of the holding company which owned that bank.

In 1974, Matthews was offered the job of president of Union Planters Bank in Memphis. Amid a $17-million annual loss and rumors of closing, President Matthews soon became chairman and CEO of Union Planters as well, and was eventually recognized as the man who brought this historic banking organization back to life.

His leadership was controversial from the start, when he openly blamed poor management for the bank's problems and vowed to move in new and innovative directions. One of his first actions was to recommend the firing or forced resignation of many of the bank's top officers. He then took bold action to revitalize the bank, dramatically cutting its loan portfolio, closing unproductive branches, and cutting staff while raising salaries.

By 1977, Union Planters Bank was again in the black, posting an annual profit of a few million dollars. But Matthews always saw greater possibilities and potential, and declared this to be only the beginning. Describing himself as an "achiever" who craved new challenges, he introduced a steady stream of fresh and untried ideas, plans, products, and services. He developed automated teller machines, called "Annie, the anytime teller." He diversified the bank's activities into several new areas, including equipment leasing, and made a pioneering plunge into computer-based data processing services. As a result, Union Planters was soon recognized as the most technologically advanced bank in the region.

Matthews was a brilliant leader, given to flights of fancy and huge bursts of energy. He worked virtually around the clock, and often invited subordinates to 5:30 a.m. breakfasts before beginning their 6:00 a.m. meetings.

✧

Above: Bill Matthews.

Below: An aerial view of Union Planters Bank Branch in Memphis.

Ben Ward recalls Matthews' knack for new and bold ideas, such as when he suggested that the bank fund a life insurance company in Memphis. Understanding that other Southern cities had enjoyed greater growth by establishing such a long-term capital source, he loaned Ward $2.5 million to found Delta Life and Annuity in 1979. By 1990, Delta Life held $500 million in assets and became a great source of support for quality-of-life amenities such as the Memphis Zoo, the Pink Palace Museum, and LeMoyne Owen College. Matthews was also instrumental in providing Union Planters Bank support for the Orpheum Theater, Dixon Gallery, *Memphis* Magazine, and the University of Memphis Egyptian Museum, and many other organizations.

He also helped many struggling young businesses gain a good foothold, and was eager to take a chance on budding employee entrepreneurs. Gene Carlisle never knew what would happen when Matthews called on him, but it was usually good. Through Matthews, Carlisle became involved with the Beale Street Development Corporation and then developed Beale Street Landing. He later founded the Carlisle Corporation, which owns and operates ninety-five Wendy's restaurants and Carlisle Hotels and Properties, which consists of four Holiday Inns and 2,500 apartments.

Jim Vining also enjoyed Matthews' guidance and support, and went on to found Vining-Sparks, a huge player in the fixed income market, provide financial services to institutional investors.

Dan Palmer saw Matthews as a brave and understanding mentor, who funded Palmer's idea for an electronic funds transfer company. EFS Concorde eventually grew to become a world leader in electronic payment processing, credit and debit card transactions, and ATM transactions

These now successful entrepreneurs recall their own stories about Matthews with delight: Vining is still amazed at Matthews' brilliance at figuring out how to discount coupons on Treasury security bonds, an unheard of practice which is now commonplace. Others recall visiting an offshore bank at Grand Turk and circling the field while the mules were cleared from the

runway. Some of them recall operating a bankrupt life insurance company in California for two days a week, then flying back to Memphis overnight to begin another eight-hour workday at 7:00 a.m.

Matthews stayed ahead of the curve by reading and thinking constantly about applying new and often exotic ideas to the banking industry. He was outspoken, unorthodox, and highly creative, but many of his critics felt Matthews was moving the bank too far away from basic commercial practices. After returning to high profitability in the early 1980s, the bank began experiencing another serious downturn. Matthews left UP Bank in 1984, due to poor profits and "philosophical differences." He continued to work in Memphis for a few years and later became involved in business ventures in the Western United States until his death in 1994.

Over ten years later, Bill Matthews is still fondly remembered. He left a legacy of applying creative vision, inventive ideas, and unorthodox methods in an industry known for its caution and conservatism. His brash and colorful leadership remains an inspiration to many of today's most successful businessmen, who recall him fondly for both his bold risk-taking and for the great stories he left behind.

"This brief biography is intended as a memorial to William Matthews, in appreciation for his many contributions to Memphis' business and cultural institutions," Friends of Bill.

HOMEWOOD SUITES BY HILTON-MEMPHIS POPLAR

Homewood Suites by Hilton is a beautifully landscaped all-suite, residential-style hotel located in elegant east Memphis near Germantown.

Homewood Suites by Hilton are designed to allow you to feel closer to home whether you are traveling for a few nights, or longer. Every spacious suite features enough space for work, study or entertaining, plus all the comforts of being at home.

Featuring 140 suites, Homewood Suites by Hilton–Memphis Poplar includes two-bedroom suites, meeting facilities, outdoor pool, and exercise gym, remote controlled television with cable, irons and hair dryers.

In addition, you will find a microwave oven, two telephones with dataports, voice mail, and Internet access.

Guests also enjoy a complimentary Suite Start breakfast each morning and an evening Welcome Home reception with a complimentary light meal and beverages Monday thru Thursday evenings.

Nearby attractions include the Racquet Club, Southwind Golf Club, shopping malls, the Memphis Zoo, Graceland, and the FedEx Forum. Located on the east side of Memphis near Germantown, Homewood Suites is adjacent to nice shops, restaurants, and

business complexes. For your convenience, a complimentary shuttle to Memphis International Airport, which is located only twelve miles away, is provided.

Homewood Suites by Hilton now offer a special Suite Selection interactive tool that allows you to view hotel floor plans on your computer and book specific suite types.

With Suite Selection, you have the ability to view the hotel floor plan and select their preferred suite by viewing location photos and a description of each room. It can be as simple as selecting a suite facing east because you prefer waking up with the sun streaming in the windows, or choosing to be at the end of the hall, or booking a non-smoking King suite on the corner of the third floor. With this new technology, you are in control of the entire travel experience.

Homewood Suites by Hilton Memphis-Poplar is located at 5811 Poplar Avenue in Memphis, Tennessee.

Spacious suites have either one king size bed or two double beds.

NATIONAL GUARD PRODUCTS

Charles Foster Smith, Sr.

It was the year Persia became Iran. Hitler was preparing Germany for World War II, and United States unemployment exceeded twenty percent. It was 1935, and while duPont was introducing a product called Nylon, twenty-nine-year-old Charles Foster Smith was founding the Memphis Window Guard Company.

Smith had graduated from Southwestern College at Memphis (Rhodes College) and returned to his home in Canton, Mississippi, only to follow his older brother, Frazer, back to Memphis in search of a career. Frazer already was a prominent architect in the city.

During Frazer's architectural work throughout the region, he saw a growing demand for window "burglar bars." He suggested to Charles that they create a new company to manufacture them. With Frazer's financial backing, Charles organized and opened the company's doors for business on Madison Avenue in downtown Memphis.

Only seven years later, Charles was called to duty in the U.S. Navy and served in the Pacific. Lieutenant Charles Foster Smith left the Navy after the war and returned to Memphis to revive the company.

By 1950 the company was relocated to 540 North Parkway, near the center of what became the St. Jude Hospital Complex. It remained in that location for almost a half century.

Throughout the company's seventy-one years, it has epitomized adaptation, innovation and close customer relations.

As post-war construction grew and evolved, the company adapted to change. In addition to window guards, the now-maturing company began manufacturing retail hardware such as window sashes, kitchen linoleum nosing, "Shur-Lok" bed spring supports and bronze, residential weather-stripping.

Despite the demands of managing a growing company in a booming industry, Charles hardly could be described as all work and no play. An accomplished banjo player, Charles and a group of musician friends that included later-to-be Supreme Court Justice Abe Fortas, kept active nightlives playing gigs in the entertainment world of Memphis and Hot Springs, Arkansas.

During the 1950s, the company added residential door weather-stripping and bronze, exterior thresholds. By the early 1960s, and with a new name that reflected its more diversified product line, National Guard Products (NGP) began to test the commercial construction market.

It was National Guard sales manager, Lauren Watson, who first dabbled in the non-residential market. Watson had identified the need for better quality weather-stripping and thresholds in commercial construction, and NGP set out to develop those products.

In the 1970s, the world felt its first energy crunch. Energy conservation led to many changes in construction, and National Guard Products created new energy-saving products such as automatic door bottoms and nylon brush gaskets that eliminate drafts.

It was during the 1970s that Charles Foster Smith, Jr., "Chuck," joined the company and assured its continuing family ownership.

The Architectural Hardware Institute asked National Guard Products to develop the industry's first curriculum to teach the importance of weather-stripping for energy conservation. That NGP course is still taught by the institute over twenty-five years later.

In cooperation with Underwriters Laboratories, National Guard conducted the first tests of fire doors equipped with fireproof gaskets. The company's gaskets proved to be one of the most effective barriers to smoke and fire when installed around fire doors.

In 1983, and in the company's forty-eighth year, founder, Charles Foster Smith, died, and Chuck became president

As the company's product line grew and became more oriented toward commercial construction, National Guard assembled a strong force of independent sales representatives. Today, NGP is represented by twenty-four independent sales organizations throughout the U.S. and Canada.

With a continuing need for growing room, coupled with the space needs of its neighbor, St. Jude Hospital, National Guard acquired nine acres on East Raines Road. After a half-century on North Parkway, the company moved into its new, 100,000-square-foot factory in 1996.

While National Guard Products has competed in an industry category known for few, if any, product differences, NGP has differentiated its brand with marketing tactics that are unique in the industry.

Beginning in 1991, NGP began bringing customers to Memphis to visit its factory and see firsthand the attention to quality. The factory trips soon began to include a couple of days of duck hunting and "R and R" across the river. Hours in a duck blind, a John Boat or around a campfire turned buyer-seller relationships into lifelong friendships.

"There's a culture shock when you transplant a hard-charging businessman from Boston, New York, or San Francisco to a duck blind in Wabbaseka, Arkansas," Chuck says. "But it's never long after he's gone home before he wants to know, 'Have I bought enough for another duck hunt?'"

To which he expects to hear Chuck's standard response, "Not quite. Need a few more really big orders to make it this year."

The company that is differentiated by customer duck hunting trips has added to that brand image by special commissions to famous Memphis wildlife artist, Dr. Allen Hughes. For twenty years, Dr. Hughes has painted new watercolors of duck scenes for the covers of NGP catalogs. Lithographs of each new painting are sent to all 1,600 NGP customers. "There's hardly a customer office

without Allen's duck prints on the walls," Chuck says.

NGP took another major step in 2000 by expanding its product line with the addition of lite kits and louvers for doors. To accommodate the new products, 40,000 square feet were added to the factory, followed by an additional expansion of 20,000 square feet in 2002.

Seventy-one years after the Smith Brothers started a burglar-bar company in downtown Memphis, National Guard Products occupies a major role in the commercial door and door hardware accessory business throughout the U.S. and Canada.

Its products are known for quality and dependability. The company is known for integrity, quality, and the best duck hunting and duck watercolors in America.

✧

Above: Customers and NGP personnel after a business meeting in a duck blind.

Below: One of the many catalog covers by Dr. Allen Hughes, M.D.

BELZ
ENTERPRISES

A TRADE NAME USED BY VARIOUS BUSINESS ENTITIES

✧

Above: Chairman and CEO Jack A. Belz.

Below: Technicolor's Memphis facility at Belz's Southridge Industrial Park is the world's the largest home entertainment distribution center.

Philip Belz, founder of Belz Enterprises, took over the management of a South Memphis store at the age of fourteen when his parents became ill during the great influenza epidemic of World War I. His preparation for a building and real estate career, however, was circuitous. It included becoming an expert butcher, learning accounting and cotton classing, operating a cotton gin, and owning a dry goods business.

By the early 1930s, Philip was dabbling in small construction, building houses and stores. In 1936, he purchased four acres of land and built one of Memphis' first suburban shopping centers at Thomas and Firestore Streets. He also built several nearby duplexes, which he rented for $15 per month.

By the end of World War II, Philip had a good understanding of the vast untapped potential of the Memphis area. He and his son, Jack, turned their vision into warehouses, shopping centers, and neighborhoods to meet the needs of a growing city.

Today, most Memphians think of Belz Enterprises in connection with the redevelopment of the Peabody Hotel, which has become as much a Mid-South institution as Beale Street or the Mississippi River. But the Peabody is just one of many unique Belz Enterprises developments around the country. As one of Memphis' foremost developers, Belz has built a portfolio consisting of warehouse/distribution centers, industrial parks, offices, hotels, shopping centers, and

residential developments ranging from apartments to planned communities.

In the early 1950s, the industrial core of north Memphis was booming. Industry demanded infrastructure and large-scale warehousing, and Belz built some of the first warehouses and industrial parks in the Memphis area.

On the Mississippi River, Belz developed the 433-acre Rivergate Industrial Port, one of the largest privately owned industrial ports in the country. Since that time, Belz Enterprises has never lost sight of the importance of distribution and today offers more than eleven million square feet of warehouse, distribution, and industrial space. The company's efforts have played a big role in Memphis' emergence as North America's distribution center.

In 1979, Belz pioneered with the late Kemmons Wilson a new concept in shopping with the opening of the Factory Outlet Mall in Lakeland, Tennessee, which later became the Belz Factory Outlet Mall. Belz's second mall, the Belz Factory Outlet World in Orlando, Florida, was one of the busiest tourist destinations in Orlando and one of the largest non-anchored factory outlet centers in the world. Belz has developed more than three million square feet of factory outlet malls, including locations in Las Vegas, Nevada, St. Augustine, Florida, and Pigeon Forge, Tennessee. Belz has even taken the concept offshore with the Belz Factory Outlet World in Canovanas, Puerto Rico.

There are few places where the Belz commitment to Memphis is more evident

than downtown. Belz's reopening of the Peabody Hotel and construction of the massive Peabody Place mixed-use complex have been part of more than $2 billion in public and private funds put into the downtown area for development.

In 1981, Belz extensively renovated and reopened the Peabody Hotel, which was built originally in 1869. The hotel's lavish lobby, exquisite restaurants, and ceremonial daily duck march, have become perennial tourist favorites. The success of the Peabody led Belz to partner with Martin Marietta Corporation and to develop the Peabody Orlando, a 981-room luxury convention/resort hotel.

Peabody Place, one of the largest downtown mixed-use developments in the country, is comprised of a variety of multifaceted properties that have brought new vitality to downtown Memphis. These include Pembroke Square, 50 Peabody Place, and the Tower at Peabody Place.

The most recent phase of the Peabody Place project was the opening of a vast, multifaceted entertainment complex in the heart of the city's tourist district. The Peabody Place Retail and Entertainment Center included a twenty-two screen, state-of-the-art movieplex with a six-story-tall, large-screen format theater for special viewing options.

The third generation of the Belz family is now involved in the organization, and President Jack A. Belz says he hopes to have the fourth generation involved soon. "What we have done over the years is that family members have become active in either individual companies or projects and simply found their niche," he says.

He comments that the firm's management style has remained the same through the years, although it has become more structured. "I would say the main differences have been getting into larger and more varied projects by types and sizes," Belz says. "We strive to do projects which add to the value of the community and to our own pride in our activities. We like to be supportive of projects that we are carrying on, and to participate and justify the investment of time and capital."

Perhaps no part of Peabody Place demonstrates the Belz family commitment to

the city of Memphis more than the Belz Museum of Asian and Judaic Art. Jack and his wife, Marilyn, who wished to share their collection of Chinese art and sculpture with the city and its visitors, founded the museum in 1998. The collection has grown, and, in addition to including one of the largest collections of rare Oriental art in the country, now includes Russian lacquer boxes, European contemporary glass, a large group of exquisite carvings of the tusk of the woolly mammoth, and a large and elegant collection of Judaica.

✧

Above: The Peabody, Downtown Memphis.

Below: Peabody Place Retail and Entertainment Center has introduced a whole new dimension of entertainment, shopping, and dining to downtown Memphis.

I.M.C. SUPPLY COMPANY

A native Texan and World War II bomber pilot, Henry Hill founded Industrial Metal Cutters Supply Company (I.M.C.) in Memphis, Tennessee in 1959. After trying his hand at the cotton business and insurance adjustment, Henry became an industrial supply salesman and quickly realized there was a growing need for ready-access metal cutting tools. After receiving a small loan from his family, he went into business for himself, opening I.M.C.'s first location on Talbot Street in downtown Memphis.

In 1961, I.M.C. moved to 474 North Seventh Street, a location now occupied by St. Jude Medical Research Hospital. The company moved again in 1980, and in 1985 a new building was constructed at 3310 Commercial Parkway, where I.M.C. is presently located.

I.M.C. Supply Company is a true family business. Ann Hill, Henry's wife, began working with Henry soon after I.M.C. was founded. Henry's son, Mark, began working full-time for I.M.C. in 1978 and now serves as company president. Mark's wife, Janet, and Mark's five sisters, along with other extended family members, have all spent time working at the firm.

"Our business was started as a cutting tool specialty house and was different from the typical mill supply houses of the day," Mark explains. "I think my father was on the cutting edge of business trends of the time, realizing the need for specialization. Over the years we have continued to adapt to the changing business environments."

I.M.C. has served the Mid South for over forty-seven years and continues to be a cutting tool specialist, supplying high-speed steel and carbide drills, reamers, taps, dies, end mills, and blueprint special tools. I.M.C. offers its customers local availability, quality, and total cost, along with service and

✧

Above: I.M.C. founder Henry M. Hill and wife Ann, c. 1994. Henry Hill died in 1996.

Below: A group photo of I.M.C. employees: First row: Sally Pellegra, Tricia Patterson, Janet Hill (Mark's wife), Ann Hill (Mark's mother), Vicki Cronk, and Darlene Beake. Second row: Ernie Goad, Cary Rawlings, Mark Hill, Lester Giordano, and Bill Doty.

technical assistance. With a reputation for superior customer service, competitive pricing, access to a broad base of suppliers, and a well-stocked warehouse, I.M.C. serves the metalworking industry, including metalworking manufacturers, tool & die shops, machine shops, and contractors, to name a few.

"Our customers like us because they like doing business with someone they know and trust," Mark explains. "Cutting costs and increasing productivity are the top two concerns among our customers, and perhaps this explains in part why tool buyers prefer doing business with a local distributor like I.M.C. When pressure comes down from management to do things better, faster, and cheaper, they want to know they have someone nearby to turn to for assistance."

Realizing the growing needs of customers for additional services, Mark formed 1sourcesupplies, I.M.C.'s sister company, in 2003. Using the 1sourcesupplies business model and making it available to other distributors, 1sourcesupplies was designed to provide services to customers who wanted assistance with things such as inventory control and management, crib management, and detailed inventory reporting. 1sourcesupplies acts as a national distributor alliance that helps other independent distributors around the country provide the same solutions to their customers for inventory management and consolidated purchasing. Offering the products and services of a fully integrated supplier, the company's inventory management program incorporates the latest hardware and software technology in the industry.

1sourcesupplies has already secured contracts for I.M.C. with companies such as Medtronic, Flowserve Valve, Wright Medical, Thomas & Betts, and Intech Medical. 1sourcesupplies supports its alliance members in the generation of business opportunities from existing and new accounts. 1sourcesupplies allows the transactional cost-savings advantage of dealing with one source for order entry and consolidated billing, along with the technical expertise to satisfy the process, allowing improvement and cost savings initiatives in today's manufacturing environment. Through the use of cost-savings documentation forms, 1sourcesupplies initiates, tracks, and documents cost savings in all aspects of the operation. 1sourcesupplies uses the latest and lowest-cost web technology.

"We are very excited about the future of 1sourcesupplies," says Mark, "not just because of the growth it brings to I.M.C., but also because of the distributor alliances it is forming throughout the U.S." Helping distributors serve their customers more effectively and efficiently is our main goal. It's fulfilling to know that we are carrying on the tradition my father started forty-eight years ago."

For more information about I.M.C. and 1sourcesupplies, please visit the companies' websites at www.imcsupply.com or www.1sourcesupplies.com.

❖

I.M.C. facility in Memphis (1985-present).

MEMPHIS AREA TEACHERS' CREDIT UNION

As its modern, high-tech array of products and services demonstrates, Memphis Area Teachers' Credit Union (MATCU) has grown tremendously from its humble beginnings.

The credit union was founded in 1957 by a group of educators who kept the organization's records in a piano bench in the basement of East High School. The effort was led by James Brewster, who had been inspired by the success of a credit union in Portland, Oregon. The original goal of the credit union was to assist educators with financial success in an atmosphere of familiarity and trust.

While MATCU now boasts a membership of more than fifty-five thousand, its mission has remained the same: to give all its members the best value for their money.

MATCU's membership has grown from employees of educational facilities and companies related to education in Tennessee, DeSoto and Marshall Counties in Mississippi, and Crittenden County in Arkansas, to include other groups as well. Those now eligible to take part in the financial cooperative include federal government employees; residents of Cordova, Germantown and Collierville; students of higher learning; members of the Hispanic Business Alliance; employees of the Memphis Area Transit Authority; family members of current members; and anyone who works, worships, lives, volunteers, or attends school in the area of Memphis roughly bordered by I-240.

More than 200 MATCU employees serve members at fifteen locations around the Mid-South, including Southaven, Oakland, and Covington. MATCU offers a wide variety of services to meet members' needs. Auto, personal, business, and mortgage loans are provided at rates typically lower than traditional banks. In addition, MATCU offers credit and debit cards, checking and savings accounts, insurance products, and investment options.

For those with a strong credit history, the credit union's rates remain unbeatable. Members building or re-establishing credit may also qualify for many custom-designed products, including a secured Visa credit card and "Come As You Are" auto and home loans.

Members' First Financial Services, Inc. and MATCU have teamed to provide a one-stop financial institution. MATCU provides traditional banking services while Members' First Financial Services, Inc. provides investment opportunities, personal and property insurance programs, as well as financial planning, so members may take care of all their financial needs with an institution they know and trust.

MATCU is also making technological advances with enhanced products and services that allow members to take care of their financial needs anytime, day or night. MATCU's "CU@Home Internet Banking Service" and "Fast Line 24" telephone access provides members with free, twenty-four-hour access to account information. "My eZone" allows a member to view their account history, verify cleared checks, apply for loans, and offers many other account transactions and inquiries. With optional bill payment services, members can arrange to have bills paid monthly without the hassle of writing a check.

Above: Today membership at MATCU is open to many and not just limited to teachers.

Below: MATCU tellers in 1967.

MATCU differs from other financial institutions in that it is not-for-profit and the members are part owners. MATCU's Board of Directors includes a group of highly qualified and committed members who write policy and monitor services. The Board members are volunteers who receive no compensation for the countless hours they serve for the benefit of the organization and its members. This structure allows the credit union to offer higher dividends on savings and, in most cases, lower rates to members.

As a not-for-profit organization, MATCU uses profits gained from the interest on loans to cover operating costs and pay dividends to members' savings accounts. The more loans and services an individual has, the higher the profit margin is for credit union members. Since membership actually means ownership at a credit union, the concept of fully utilizing the cooperative financial institution is easy to support.

MATCU believes in community. With deep roots in the educational field, it is only natural that special attention is focused on two community projects that benefit educators. Future Teacher Scholarships and One Class At A Time Grants make a significant impact for those who are committed to education. $2,500 annual, renewable scholarships are offered to high school seniors and college students pursuing a career in education. Thus far, thirty-nine students have received a total of $263,750 through the scholarship program. The One Class At A Time Grant awards $500 to a deserving educator each month to help ease the financial strain of classroom equipment, supplies, or projects.

In addition, MATCU host free seminars on a multitude of subjects that include identity theft, car buying, home buying, and financial literacy, as well as youth savings seminars directed towards children and young adults. "CU Around Town," the credit unions' community involvement organization, reaches out to provide support for numerous programs and charitable events throughout the year.

"Helping the community is part of the credit union creed," notes Carlos Webb, president of MATCU. Recent projects have included raising money and doing volunteer work for The American Red Cross, Ronald McDonald House, WKNO Public Broadcast, the National Kidney Foundation, and others.

Looking to the future, Webb believes the credit union, which is the second largest locally owned financial institution in the Memphis area, will continue to be a strong consumer lender.

To learn more about the Memphis Area Teachers' Credit Union, call 901-385-5200, stop by any of the fifteen branch locations, or visit the website at www.matcu.com.

✧

Above: MATCU's tellers in 2006.

Below: MATCU's administration office and main branch is located at 7845 Highway 64.

BLUFF CITY BUICK COMPANY

On December 2, 2005, an article in *The Commercial Appeal* began with a simple sentence: "Bluff City Buick is closing." These words announced the end of Memphis' first Buick dealership—the oldest automobile dealership in continuous operation in Memphis history.

Buick Motor Company, the manufacturer of Buick automobiles, had been incorporated in 1903 by automobile pioneer David Buick. However, it was Will Durant, the creator of General Motors, who built Buick into the largest car manufacturer of the early 1900s. Buick Motor Company became a part of General Motors in 1908.

The period following World War I was one of manufacturing innovation and increased competition among automobile manufacturers. Bluff City Buick Company was one of many dealerships established throughout the country to meet the rising consumer demand for automobiles.

Wallace Claypool and Hugh Jetton founded Bluff City Buick Company in 1921. Later, their sales manager, Charles Creath, became a third partner. For most of its early existence, the dealership was located in downtown Memphis at 739 Union Avenue in a building originally constructed by General Motors as a regional showroom for Buick products.

On July 1, 1955, the founding partners sold Bluff City Buick to Joe H. Schaeffer, Jr., already a successful Memphis automobile executive. In 1961, Joe's brother Milton

Bluff City Buick was located at 1810 Getwell from 1972 until it closed in 2005.

joined the management team at Bluff City Buick after several years as a Lincoln-Mercury dealer in West Memphis, Arkansas, and in Mobile, Alabama. The 1960s were a time of great success as Bluff City Buick's sales and service to customers expanded to meet the needs of the growing car market in Memphis.

Buick was the dream car of many Americans. Only Cadillac was more prestigious. Buicks carried some of the best-remembered model names: Century, Limited, Special, Roadmaster, Super, Skylark, Electra, LeSabre, Riviera, Regal, and Park Avenue. The distinctive "VentiPorts" or portholes along their front fenders, as well as an adaptation of the Buick family crest known as the Trishield embellished many models.

In the late 1960s, Memphis, like many cities across the United States, began a program of urban renewal, and the Bluff City Buick building at 739 Union was slated for demolition. (A campus of Southwest Tennessee Community College currently occupies the site.) Milton bought his brother's stock in Bluff City Buick Company and began planning to move to a new location in East Memphis.

In July 1971 construction began on a fourteen-acre state-of-the-art facility for Buicks at Getwell Road and I-240. In March 1972 the new Bluff City Buick opened at 1810 Getwell Road with great fanfare. Among those in attendance was Memphis Mayor Wyeth Chandler. Buick automobiles were at the height of their popularity. Often, traffic on Getwell was blocked as trucks delivered and unloaded enough Buicks for Bluff City to sell 200 cars every month.

Throughout the 1970s and 1980s, Bluff City Buick continued to thrive. From 1973 to 1975, Bluff City Motor Homes operated the first dealership in the United States designed specifically to sell GMC motor homes.

The location at 1810 Getwell, which had expanded to include seventeen acres, became the home of Bluff City Jaguar in 1984 and Bluff City Nissan in 1987. Together the companies were marketed as Bluff City Autoplex with Buick as the flagship store. The next generation of the Schaeffer family became active in the business. Jill Schaeffer Broer in 1972, Harrell Schaeffer in 1973, and Joey

Schaeffer in 1981 joined their father in building Bluff City Autoplex into a very successful group of companies.

But by the 1990s, troubles were mounting for General Motors. Imported cars had made inroads into the American market as a younger generation turned more and more to Japanese cars, which had entered the American market in the 1960s. By the early 2000s, General Motors embarked on a policy of consolidation. It became increasingly common for Buicks to be sold from dealerships that also sold Pontiacs and GMC trucks. The days of the large, stand-alone Buick dealership were numbered.

In 2005, Milton made the difficult decision to close the eighty-four-year old Buick company where he had spent most of his life. After *The Commercial Appeal* announced the closing, tributes poured in from old customers, many of whom had bought cars at Bluff City for fifty years. For these people, "Bluff City" meant Buick, customer service, and local ownership. On November 30, 2005, the employees of Bluff City Buick gathered on the showroom at 1810 Getwell for the last time, marking the end of an era in the automobile business in Memphis.

The closing did not mean that the Schaeffer family abandoned the car business. Bluff City

Nissan became Wolfchase Nissan and moved from Getwell to join its sister store Wolfchase Honda, both owned by Joey Schaeffer and Jill Schaeffer Broer. Bluff City Jaguar, owned by Harrell Schaeffer, moved to a new location on Nonconnah Parkway. Milton Schaeffer, Jr., owns and operates Schaeffer BMW in Wilmington, North Carolina.

❖

Above: The old Bluff City Buick, 739 Union Avenue, c. the 1950s.

Below: Parts Manager Stanley Fisher, Milton and Joe Schaeffer in the Parts Department at 739 Union Avenue, c. the 1960s.

JOHN J. CAMPBELL CO.

John J. Campbell Co. (JJC) has been providing top-notch roofing services to the residential and commercial markets in the Memphis area since 1988. This award-winning company has earned the reputation as the area's best roofing company through hard work, excellent customer service, a commitment to employee training and cutting-edge technology, and a philosophy of working with only the best manufacturers in the industry.

The companies JJC works with have warranties that stand behind the products they sell. Their products have been tested in real-world situations over a number of years. Through extensive training, JJC crews keep up with the latest technology and are capable of installing many different types of materials.

Crews are constantly trained in each manufacturer's specific application methods, and the company's in-house quality control staff inspects each job as it is being installed and upon completion. That is followed by a manufacturer's warranty inspection to ensure that customers receive the highest-quality roof system.

JJC's consistent monitoring of every phase of a job translates into an efficient, productive and quality driven organization dedicated to serving customers. The company's comprehensive roofing departments work to give customers a dependable, long-lasting, weather-tight roof.

JJC can handle any size job from a 100-square-foot ATM canopy to a 1-million-square-foot distribution center. The company stays on the cutting edge of the roofing industry by utilizing the latest technology in digital estimating, cost accounting, database information systems, and state-of-the-art roofing equipment.

The company's new construction division specializes in commercial and industrial roof installations on retail centers, schools, hospitals, high rises, distribution warehouses, manufacturing plants, and office buildings. JJC's restoration/replacement division can handle jobs of any size or type and offers free estimates to customers within a 200-mile radius of Memphis. Its evaluation services provide customers with a full, professional report on a roof's existing conditions as well as recommendations to fit any budget.

JJC can handle any roofing repair service quickly and efficiently thanks to its fully dedicated service department and the largest fleet of committed service technicians in the region. Each of its service techs is highly trained in one thing: finding and repairing your leaks the first time. JJC uses the latest computer technology for work-order dispatching, tracking, and documentation. Its databases track each building's leak history and expenses, allowing customers to receive timely and accurate information concerning their roof expenditures and roof conditions. This allows customers to make better decisions regarding their roofs.

The company's maintenance/inspection division can uncover potential problems before they become emergencies and can reduce the total amount of expenditures on a roof system due to service calls. Roofs need periodic servicing and inspection to maximize return on investment. Owner maintenance is required under most roofing manufacturers' warranty conditions, and the National Roofing Contractors Association has determined that regular roof maintenance can add years of serviceable life to most roof systems.

In the event that an emergency does occur, JJC's Severe Weather Action Team (SWAT) swings into action. Minimizing damage to facilities, products, and equipment becomes the number one concern of each of the company's 250 employees. The JJC SWAT has extensive experience in handling emergency situations, and its response process is constantly analyzed to provide fast, experienced, and professional assistance.

JJC provides its services to customers in the educational, religious, office, retail, warehouse/distribution, government, and industrial/manufacturing sectors. The company is a founding member of RoofConnect, the Premier Independent Roofing Contractor Network. Only those roofing companies with long-standing reputations for quality and service are invited to join.

The company's commitment to quality workmanship has earned it numerous awards from the industry's largest manufacturers. JJC must pass rigorous inspections from manufacturers to be honored among the most prestigious roofing companies in the nation.

Each year since 1988, JJC has achieved the level of Master Contractor for Firestone Building Products, the largest manufacturer of EPDM products in the nation. This designation is awarded to the top contractors in each region. JJC also was named to the Firestone Building Products President's Club in 1996, 1997, 2000, 2001, 2002, and 2003. This award is presented to the top roofing contractors in each of Firestone's U.S. and international sales regions. JJC was one of a handful of firms internationally to receive this honor.

Firestone also awarded JJC the Inner Circle Quality of distinction in 2001, 2002,

and 2003. The "Q" award is based solely on the performance of previously installed roofing projects and reflects the company's dedication to high-quality roofing installation.

For several consecutive years, JJC received the Winners Circle distinction from GenFlex Roofing Systems. JJC also was named the GenFlex MVP from 1996 to 2000. The MVP award is given to the Top Roofing Contractor in each of its sales regions internationally. JJC also received the GenFlex All Star distinction from 2001 to 2003.

John J. Campbell Company has also received special recognition from the National Roofing Contractors Association for the design and construction of a copper baseball cap pavilion at AutoZone Park in Memphis.

FedEx Corporation

FedEx is a network of companies that share a rich heritage of innovation and industry leadership. Collectively they exhibit the "absolutely, positively" dedication to providing specialized solutions for every shipping, information, and global trade need.

The company is led by FedEx Corporation, which provides strategic direction and consolidated financial reporting for the operating companies that compete collectively under the FedEx name worldwide.

Those companies—FedEx Express, FedEx Ground, FedEx Freight, FedEx Kinko's Office and Print Services, FedEx Custom Critical, FedEx Trade Networks and FedEx Services—function under the motto of "operate independently, compete collectively and manage collaboratively."

Although subsidiary companies trace their origins as far back as 1913, the idea for the company most people think of as FedEx goes back to 1965, when Yale University undergraduate Frederick W. Smith wrote a term paper on the passenger route systems used by most airfreight shippers.

Smith, who viewed the passenger route systems as economically inadequate, expounded on the need for shippers to have a system designed specifically for airfreight that could accommodate time-sensitive shipments such as medicines, computer parts, and electronics.

In 1971, following a stint in the military, Smith bought controlling interest in Arkansas Aviation Sales, located in Little Rock, Arkansas. He quickly noticed the tremendous difficulty in getting packages and other airfreight delivered in one to two days and, after conducting the necessary research, founded Federal Express.

The company incorporated in June 1971 and officially began operating on April 17, 1973, with the launch of fourteen small aircraft from Memphis International Airport. Federal Express delivered 186 packages that night to twenty-five U.S. cities from Rochester, New York, to Miami, Florida.

The company moved its headquarters to Memphis, a city selected for its geographical center to the original target market cities for small packages. The Memphis weather, which rarely caused the airport to be closed, also proved attractive, as did the airport's available hangar space and willingness to make necessary improvements.

Though the company did not show a profit until July 1975, it soon became the premier carrier of high-priority goods in the marketplace and the standard-setter for the industry it established. Today, FedEx Express, as the flagship company has become known, is the world's largest all-cargo air fleet with a total daily lift capacity of more than 26.5 million pounds. In a twenty-four hour period, the fleet travels almost 500,000 miles—the equivalent of 100 trips around the world—and its couriers log 2.5 million miles.

Federal Express began to mature in the 1980s. Competitors were trying to catch up to the well-established leader, whose growth rate was compounding at about forty percent annually. In fiscal year 1983 the company reported $1 billion in revenues, making American business history as the first company to reach that mark within a decade without mergers or acquisitions.

International operations began in 1984 with service to Europe and Asia. The following year, FedEx marked its first regularly scheduled flight to Europe, and in 1988 the company began direct-scheduled cargo service to Japan. The acquisition of Tiger International, Inc., in February of 1989 turned the company into the world's largest full-service, all-cargo airline with

The FedEx fleet.

routes to twenty-one countries, a fleet of Boeing 747 and 727 aircraft, facilities throughout the world and Tiger's expertise in international airfreight.

Federal Express was granted authority to serve China through a 1995 acquisition from Evergreen International Airlines. Under its authority, Federal Express became the sole U.S.-based, all-cargo carrier with aviation rights to the world's most populous nation. The company's global reach has continued to expand since then, leading to an unsurpassed worldwide network. FedEx Express today delivers to customers in more than 220 countries.

The first evolution of the company's corporate identity came in 1994 when Federal Express officially adopted "FedEx" as its primary brand, taking a cue from customers, who frequently referred to the company by its abbreviated name. The second evolution came in 2000 when the company was renamed FedEx Express to reflect its position in the overall FedEx Corporation portfolio of services. This also signified the expanding breadth of the FedEx Express-specific service offerings, as well as a FedEx that was no longer just overnight delivery.

Through the years, FedEx has amassed an impressive list of "firsts," most notably for leading the industry in introducing new services to customers. Along with originating the Overnight Letter, the company was the first transportation company dedicated to overnight package delivery. It also was the first to offer next-day delivery by 10:30 a.m. and the first to offer Saturday delivery. Other firsts include being the first express company to offer time-definite service for freight and the first in the industry with money-back guarantees and free proof of performance; services that now extend to its worldwide network.

In 1990, Federal Express became the first company to win the Malcolm Baldrige National Quality Award in the service category and in 1994 received ISO 9001 registration for all its worldwide operations, making it the first global express transportation company to receive simultaneous system-wide certification.

FedEx values its employees and puts customers at the heart of everything it does. The company invents and inspires services and technologies that improve the way the world works and lives while managing its operations, finances and services with honesty, efficiency, and reliability. The company champions safe and healthy environments for the communities in which its employees live and work and earns the respect and confidence of FedEx employees, customers, and investors in everything it does.

Most of all, the company's "absolutely positively" spirit characterizes everything it does now and in the future.

✧

Above: FedEx Kinko's store.

Below: FedEx Operation Special Delivery is a year-round program designed to bring help and hope to local towns around the country. These specially designed trucks criss-cross the United States to provide transportation and logistics assistance at community events like Thanksgiving food drives, holiday toy collections, library book drives, and much more.

Memphis Home Improvement Company, Inc.

Faye Cook became a widow at a young age with two daughters to raise and educate alone. At the time, she was working as a teller at First National Bank and knew she had to change her vocation in order to make some money. She sold some rental property to obtain cash to invest in a business and put out the word that she was looking for an investment, with real estate sales her first priority.

As luck would have it, a gentleman who owned a home improvement company approached her and offered her a partnership for a substantial investment. But in the late 1960s and '70s, job opportunities were limited for women. The New Albany, Mississippi, native, who moved to Memphis at age seven-teen, was used to hard work, and this looked like a challenging opportunity.

In those days, in a male-dominated industry, it took ten years of hard work earning the respect among her male peers, even though they saw her at the lumber company every day and on her jobsites daily. The last thirty years has been much easier. In fact, she gets referrals from some of the larger builders that do not do remodeling and additions. Dedication, consistency and perseverance are what she believes has made her successful. She is dedicated to making any project she does be a good investment for her clients.

Through the years, MHIC has become a full-service new construction and remodeling company. Cook attributes her success to several things. It is impossible to have expertise in every area of the building industry, so she has surrounded herself with top professionals in the different fields. She also gives free professional decorating services to her clients. By doing this, it keeps her up on all the latest trends, and, as clients update their homes, it ensures them of a good investment.

Through the years, thanks to her hard work and help from friends and colleagues, Cook bought out her business partner (in 1971), and supported and educated her girls, as well as her granddaughters. Now in her seventies, she continues to own and operate Memphis Home Improvement Company, one of the Mid-South's top remodeling/builders and one of the largest remodelers in the country, offering all types of remodeling and building services.

Memphis Home Improvement Company is a full-service builder/remodeler. That means they can provide customers with any type of construction service from a small renovation to ground-up homebuilding. Services include design, kitchen and bathroom remodeling, home offices, theatre and media rooms, porches and sunrooms, and second-story expansions. They can also build garages and carports, vinyl siding and trim, replacement windows and roofs, decks and gazebos, pool houses, room additions, and complete indoor remodeling. Installation and remodeling

❖

Before (below) and after (bottom).

services include cabinetry, countertops, appliances, flooring, walls, windows, doors, electrical plumbing, HVAC, general carpentry, and extensions and alterations.

MHIC has successfully completed more than thirteen thousand projects in Memphis and Shelby and Desoto Counties. The company carries a $500,000 State General Contractor License in Tennessee and Mississippi and furnishes a certificate of insurance to clients on every project.

MHIC has received numerous awards through the years including selection in 1988, 1999 and 2000 as one of the "Top 50 Remodeling Companies in the United States."

Cook is active in the construction industry. She's past president of the National Association of the Remodeling Industry and in 1997 organized the Registered Remodelers Council under the Registered Builders Program of the Home Builders Association. She also serves on the Board of Directors of the Better Business Bureau of the Mid-South.

Eighty percent of Cook's business is from repeat customers and through referrals, a testament to her service and quality work. Cook ascribes to the professional remodeler's code of ethics to, among other things, conduct business operations in a manner that reflects credit upon the company, the Professional Remodeler's Council, and the remodeling industry.

Cook says she has no plans for retirement. Why should she? She loves her work, has earned the respect of family, friends, and colleagues and enjoys the challenge of staying abreast of industry trends and keeping her customers among the most satisfied in the building/remodeling industry.

Just goes to show you what can be done when opportunity meets determination.

Before (above) and after (below).

REGIONAL MEDICAL CENTER AT MEMPHIS

The Regional Medical Center at Memphis—The MED—has provided medical care for the Memphis region since 1829, making it the oldest hospital in Tennessee.

The hospital, known originally as the Memphis Hospital, was organized when the Tennessee State Senate appropriated $3,300 to enable the hospital to begin functioning in a small, wooden structure on Front Street.

The hospital was established to care for the hundreds of sick travelers on the Mississippi River. Memphis Hospital was a continuation of the Medieval Christian concept of charity, which took the form of the "hospice," a place for the sick and weary traveler to rest and recover before continuing his journey.

The cholera epidemics of 1832-1835 convinced the city and state that the hospital was inadequate and, in 1835, the legislature authorized the sale of the hospital building, with the funds to be used to purchase a better site. The building sold for $4,225, and an additional $5,000 was appropriated for construction of a new building. A ten-acre tract was purchased outside Forrest Park, and the new facility opened in 1841.

Clinical teaching of physicians began in 1846, and that tradition continues at The MED. The hospital has contributed to the education of over fifty percent of the physicians practicing in Tennessee.

The Memphis Hospital was converted to a military hospital during the Civil War. The

✤

Above: The interior of City of Memphis Hospital.

Below: The Regional Medical Center at Memphis—The MED.

facilities were expanded with the erection of four wooden wards, each with a capacity of twenty-five patients.

The hospital was returned to the state by the federal government in 1866, but the Legislature declined to appropriate funds for its operation and granted title of the hospital to the City of Memphis. The city supported the hospital with a special tax that yielded about $11,000 annually. From 1883-1885, the hospital had an average daily census of eighty patients with a per capita cost of 32.5 cents per day.

The hospital outgrew its Forrest Park site, and a new facility was constructed at St. Peter's Cemetery on the north end of Madison Avenue, just east of Dunlap. The new Memphis General Hospital received its first patient on July 3, 1898.

Several additions were added to the hospital as it continued to grow, including a new wing in 1911, a laboratory building in 1921, a maternity hospital in 1924, and a Children's Hospital in 1928.

By 1931, the total capacity of Memphis General Hospital was 400 beds but, although the hospital accepted paying patients, it was not self-sustaining. Deficits were made up from tax funds.

In 1929 the estate of Theresa Gaston Mann provided more than $300,000 for the establishment of a new hospital in memory of

her husband, John Gaston. Other funds were obtained from local and federal sources, and the former Memphis General Hospital became the John Gaston Hospital in 1936.

In 1964, the E.H. Crump Hospital, which had treated only black patients during the days of segregation, became a part of the John Gaston Hospital under the name City of Memphis Hospitals. Thus, in its long history, the hospital has been known as Memphis Hospital, Memphis City Hospital, Memphis General Hospital, John Gaston Hospital, and City of Memphis Hospital. In 1983, the hospital was officially renamed the Regional Medical Center at Memphis, or The MED.

Today, The MED includes five Centers of Excellence: Elvis Presley Memorial Trauma Center, Firefighters Regional Burn Center, Sheldon B. Korones Newborn Center, High Risk Obstetrics, and Wound Center.

The highly skilled staff at the High Risk Obstetric Center manages the care of patients when complications arise. They deliver more than 4,500 babies annually; most of them are high-risk births.

The Sheldon B. Korones Newborn Center, founded in 1968, is one of the oldest and largest intensive care units in the nation, treating approximately 1,300 premature or critically ill newborns yearly. The Newborn Center staff has saved more than 45,000 babies since it opened.

The Elvis Presley Memorial Trauma Center opened in 1983 and provides treatment for life-threatening injuries for the citizens of the Mid-South. It ranks as one of the busiest in the nation and is the only Level I Trauma Center in a 150-mile radius, which includes parts of five states.

The Firefighters Regional Burn Center, the only full-service burn center in the region, provides medical care and family support vital to the successful treatment of burn victims. Surgery, hydrotherapy, rehabilitation, and the best in restorative care are available to children and adults devastated by serious burns.

The Wound Center utilizes the most technologically advanced wound care equipment including a twelve-patient hyperbaric chamber. The dedicated staff provides specialized care for chronic, non-healing wounds and for trauma and burn patients. The Wound Center serves both inpatients and outpatients.

In 1999, The MED and the Memphis and Shelby County Health Department reached an agreement under which The MED manages the six health department primary care clinics along with the four MED-owned community based clinics. The consolidated primary care network, known as the Health Loop, has more than 60,000 patient visits each year.

For more information on what is available to you or the location of The MED, visit their website at www.the-med.org.

✧

Above: City of Memphis Hospital exterior shot with proposed structure drawn on rooftop.

Below: The Birth Place interior at The MED.

THE CRUMP FIRM, INC.
ARCHITECTS • PLANNERS
INTERIOR DESIGNERS

✧

Right: University of Memphis, FedEx Institute of Technology. The FedEx Institute of Technology serves as an incubator for a broad range of information technology including industry, government, commerce, healthcare, and other arenas. The Crump Firm/LRK, a joint venture, planned and designed the building with a maximum degree of flexibility to accommodate future changes in building systems, communications, and information technologies.

Below: International Paper, International Place Tower III. The design of the 11-story, 234,000-square-foot office tower with adjacent three story post-tensioned concrete parking garage and connecting underground tunnel was a challenge. The $25-million project was fast-tracked, with construction starting in early February 2001 and the core and shell completion in April 2002.

The Crump Firm, Inc., long recognized for design excellence, has earned a reputation as one of the leading architectural firms in Memphis. The firm, founded in 1970 and incorporated in 1985, is known for producing innovative, high-quality designs for a distinguished group of corporate, healthcare, institutional, educational, religious, and governmental clients, both locally and nationally.

The Crump Firm is a client-oriented, full-service architectural, planning, and interior design firm, and its 28 member staff has completed diverse projects in 29 states. With a staff of 10 architects and 8 interior designers, the firm is well known for working closely with its clients to produce award-winning designs within the client's budget and schedule.

"For more than thirty-seven years, we have served—and continue to serve—educational, religious, cultural, healthcare, corporate, and governmental institutions which help make Shelby County a better place in which to live, play, work, and worship," commented Metcalf Crump, FAIA, president of The Crump Firm. "In serving these repeat clients by providing cost-effective designs, we try to achieve our mission statement with each project: To create inspired architecture which will endure."

The Crump Firm specializes in designing corporate headquarters, tenant office buildings,

healthcare clinics and facilities, schools, colleges and university buildings of all types, performing arts centers, worship facilities and church additions, distribution centers, and a broad range of government projects.

Recently completed office buildings include the International Place Tower III and two three-story office buildings in the Shadow Creek Office Park at Southwind for Highwoods Properties. The Crump Firm's corporate headquarters designs include buildings for Allenberg Cotton Company, Hohenberg Cotton Company, Orion Packaging Systems, and Physiotherapy Associates.

The firm's healthcare clients include Baptist Memorial Health Care, Campbell Clinic, Semmes-Murphy Clinic, and the Stern Cardiovascular Center, for which The Crump Firm recently completed a new two-story clinic in Germantown. Recently completed school projects include a complete new upper school, campus center, and lower school expansion for Memphis University School; a new upper school and Early Childhood Center for St. Mary's Episcopal School; Millington Elementary School for Shelby County Schools; Craigmont Middle School for Memphis City Schools; and the new Federal Express Institute of Technology Building at the University of Memphis with LRK. The firm's design of college buildings includes seven new buildings and twelve renovations for Rhodes College.

The Crump Firm is also well known for its designs of new and innovative churches, fellowship halls, auditoriums and performing arts centers. Some of these projects include the Bartlett Performing Arts Center, the Rose Theater in the Buckman Hall Performing and Fine Arts Center at St. Mary's Episcopal School, and the Performing Arts Center in the recently completed St. Benedict at Auburndale High School. The firm's design of religious facilities include numerous and varied projects for the Catholic Diocese of Memphis, the Episcopal Diocese of West Tennessee, Second Presbyterian Church, Independent Presbyterian Church, Bellevue Baptist Church, Trinity Baptist Church and, most recently, major additions to Temple Israel.

The Crump Firm's governmental projects include numerous designs for the City of Memphis, Shelby County Government, the State of Tennessee and Memphis-Shelby County Airport Authority. The firm's services also include site analysis, master planning, feasibility studies, interior space planning, and a full range of interior design services with licensed interior designers. The firm is also recognized for assisting its clients with contractor selection and attentive project administration during construction.

The Crump Firm has completed numerous renovations and additions at the Memphis International Airport. This work began in 1988 and includes expansions throughout all three concourses, including the Federal Inspection Station for international arrivals completed in 1995. Presently, the firm is designing an expansion to double the current capacity for arriving international passengers and is completing its design of the new Tennessee Air National Guard Base at the Memphis International Airport. The Crump Firm is serving in the program management team on behalf of Memphis-Shelby County Airport Authority to assure the new base is built in accordance with the approved design.

Additional projects include several medical and corporate office buildings developed by Highwoods Properties, Inc., including the ThyssenKrupp Corporate Headquarters and the Wolf River Medical Complex Building Three, which will house Memphis

Orthopaedic Group. Other current projects include a new multi-sports stadium and athletic fields for Memphis University School; master planning and new recreational and education buildings for Lausanne Collegiate School; and multiple projects for FedEx, including the new Building I Administrative Building at Hacks Cross Road. The firm continues to plan and design over one million square feet annually of corporate, administrative, and healthcare facilities in existing buildings, including, most recently, the offices of the accounting firm Cannon Wright Blount and the headquarters of Wunderlich Securities.

Two principals, President Metcalf Crump FAIA, and Vice President David Hoback head the Crump Firm, Inc. More complete information about the firm may be found on the firm's website at www.crumpfirm.com.

✧

Above: Memphis University School Multi-Sports Complex. The 1,400-seat stadium at Memphis University School, a collegiate school for boys, will host football, soccer, and track and field events for its 650 member student body. The complex will feature a state-of-the-art press box and VIP seating.

Below: St. Mary's Episcopal School, Buckman Performing Arts and Fine Arts Center. This 300-seat performing arts center at St. Mary's Episcopal School serves 800 students and includes variable acoustics and lighting, a thrust stage, orchestra pit, orchestra shell and large storage areas for theatre sets, ship areas, and musical instruments. The theater is the resident venue for the Buchman Concert Series, featuring international performances, and the Memphis Vocal Arts Ensemble.

LUTTRELL BELTING & SUPPLY COMPANY, INC.

✧

Above: The second and third generation of the company (from left to right): Layton Luttrell's daughter, Rheba L. Turpin, and his grandson, Layton D. Turpin.

Below: Mr. & Mrs. Layton W. Luttrell, founders of Luttrell Belting & Supply Co., Inc.

Layton W. Luttrell, with the assistance of his wife, Madge, and his brother, Harry, opened Luttrell Belting & Supply Company, Inc. in 1957 with little capital but high hopes. "The business literally started on a shoestring," recalls Layton's daughter, Rheba Turpin, who is now president of the firm. "We started small, and were able to survive because the vendors agreed to work with us on consignment."

Today, Luttrell Belting & Supply has grown and expanded to become one of the leading industrial belting distributors in the region.

The company's first shop was at 743 Jackson Avenue, but, as the business expanded, it moved to larger facilities on Decatur Street, and then to more modern facilities at 311 Belz Boulevard, East.

"When the business started, industry was still using only leather and cotton belting," recalls Rheba. "My father used to put the belts on the famous 'Zippin Pippin' roller coaster at the Fairgrounds each year and make sure the ride was kept in good condition."

Rheba began her business career as an insurance clerk but joined the family firm in 1984. Her son, Layton, who serves as vice president, represents the third generation to be active in the business.

Luttrell Belting & Supply has state-of-the-art equipment and uses only the finest quality materials to supply customers with top-of-the-line belting and services. The company also offers an extensive line of items used to serve the baking, printing, sand, aggregate & gravel, catfish, food products, yarn and fiber, bottling, canning, and many other industries.

Luttrell's new semi-automated production disc skiver, supplied by Habisit, is used to skive the ends of numerous kinds of power transmission and conveyer belting. The rotary blade slitter with its twelve inch wide belt capacity can cut multiple belts out of a sleeve for matched sets of endless belts. With an electronically controlled press, Luttrell can do finger-splice and thermofix splice. This equipment makes Luttrell the most complete Habasit belt fabricator in the area.

Luttrell's 72" industrial belt slitter has a 72" wide, 96" diameter roll and up to 20,000 pound load capacity. The knife can be adjusted to between one-inch and full table width (72") and has multiple blade positioning. With the automatic side shift and tension drag brake, Luttrell can assure customers the width and length of the cut will be accurate.

Luttrell's hot vulcanizing process is invaluable for customers when their conveyer system is down for a belting splice job. Luttrell supplies experienced vulcanizing technicians to reduce down time.

The state-of-the-art Cleating and Vee Guide Department supplies quality work to get customers back up and running. Luttrell can cleat belts from 3" to 60" wide in white or black PVC up to ¼" thick with ½" high to 3" high cleats. Also, 2" white scoop cleats are available for custom order belt needs. If a customer is having a problem moving a product up an incline, Luttrell can solve that problem. In the Vee Guide Department, Luttrell makes belts from 1 ½" wide to 60" wide. Luttrell also has the capacity to fabricate belting for our customer's applications. With its top quality work and knowledgeable staff, the company can meet custom belting needs.

Luttrell Belting & Supply Company was built on service and that tradition continues to guide the company today. "My father built this business on fairness, loyalty, and customer service," says Rheba. "I consider this to be the key to our success now and for the future.

"All our customers are important to us, and we provide quality products and prompt service," she adds. "We have a highly qualified team of inside and outside sales people, along with well-trained belt technicians to serve our customer's production needs."

Employment at Luttrell Belting & Supply numbers about twenty, and the employees boast a total of more than 175 years cumulative experience. The company's regular office hours are from 7:00 a.m. to 5:00 p.m., Monday through Friday, and the sales staff and technicians are on call twenty-four hours a day, seven days a week.

Asked for the secret of Luttrell Belting & Supply's success, Rheba replies, "Stay strong and determined. Remember to be considerate of the people who work for you. There is a plaque on my desk that says, 'Lord, help me to remember that nothing is going to happen to me today that you and I can't handle together.' I consider those words to live by."

For more information about Luttrell Belting & Supply Company, Inc., check their website at www.luttrellbelting.com.

✧

Above: Shop Foreman J. R. Crouch and technician Nathan Durham lacing one of the many styles of belts that Luttrell Belts sells and services.

Below: The management and driving force of Luttrell Belting (from left to right): General Manager Lynn Hester, President Rheba L. Turpin, Vice President Layton D. Turpin, and Sales Manager Paul Sacco.

DUNAVANT ENTERPRISES, INCORPORATED

Although it has grown to become one of the largest cotton merchandisers in the world, Memphis-based Dunavant Enterprises, Inc. remains a privately owned company and is now operated by the third generation of the Dunavant family.

Although the Dunavant families' involvement with cotton dates to the late 1800s, the firm that became Dunavant Enterprises was first established in 1929 as a partnership between twenty-year-old W.B. "Buck" Dunavant and T.J. White.

William Buchanan "Billy" Dunavant, Jr. entered the business in 1952 while still in college and became a full partner with T.J. White and Company in 1956. Billy soon earned a reputation as one of the most aggressive businessmen among the cotton men of Front Street. While others were cautious in dealing with increased overseas competition and the growth of synthetic fibers during the '50s and '60s, he saw ways of prospering by lowering overhead and increasing volume.

The firm's senior partner, T.J. White, retired in 1960, leaving the father-and-son Dunavant team in charge of the business. However, Buck died the following year and control of the company passed to Billy, who was only twenty-nine years old.

The business Billy inherited was handling a respectable 100,000 bales a year, but, seeing an opportunity for expansion, Billy pioneered the idea of 'forward contracting' whereby cotton is bought from the farmer by the acre as it is planted.

Although speculating in cotton futures is risky, Billy had considerable success in the market, thanks to his legendary sense of timing and the professionalism of the organization he assembled.

The company's volume increased to an average of 250,000 to 300,000 bales a year during the mid-'60s and, by the early '70s, the figure had reached one million. Today, Dunavant routinely handles well in excess of four million bales of U.S. and foreign cotton each year.

Dunavant Enterprises was the first major firm to sell U.S. cotton to Mainland China in 1972, and today China has become the firm's largest customer.

In 1971, Dunavant moved its operations from cotton row to a modern, one-story office building on New Getwell Road. That same year, the company was reorganized as Dunavant Enterprises, Inc. All businesses owned by Dunavant were brought under the new organization's central management but kept financially separate. Although the company's business remains about ninety percent cotton merchandising, Dunavant Enterprises owns a commodities trading company, a cotton farming operation, and a trucking company that serves as agent for the 5,000 trucks used to haul cotton to domestic mills and ports for export.

Dunavant Enterprises, Inc. maintains offices in the major cotton producing areas of the United States, including Memphis, Jackson, and Brownsville, Tennessee; Fresno, California; Paragould, Arkansas; Lubbock, Corpus Christi, and Vernon, Texas; Mer Rouge, Louisiana; and Kill Devil Hills, North Carolina.

Domestic and export sales offices are maintained throughout the world, including Switzerland, China, Brazil, Mexico, Australia, and other countries. Dunavant cotton warehouses are located in California, Tennessee, South Carolina, Oklahoma, and Texas, and ginning operations are located in Australia, Uganda, Mozambique, and Zambia. The company owns a cotton-classing laboratory in Memphis and operates commodity-trading offices in New York and Memphis.

The company employs more than 2,000 persons worldwide and is ranked among the largest privately held companies in the United States by *Forbes* magazine, based on its billon-dollar-plus annual revenues. The *Memphis Business Journal* has ranked Dunavant Enterprises as the largest Memphis-area private company for three consecutive years.

Dunavant's global vision also encompasses multi-faceted investments in financial markets and real estate. Dunavant Capital Management develops diversified investment relationships that respond to both short and long-term public and private investment opportunities. Dunavant Development offers extensive land development capabilities and experience in large and small scale single and multiuse developments that include office, retail, industrial, recreational, and residential properties.

Chairman of the Board for Dunavant Enterprises, Billy Dunavant, and four of his sons are active in the firm's day-to-day management. William B. Dunavant, III serves as CEO and president; John Dobson Dunavant is senior vice president domestic sales operations; Buchanan Dunavant is vice president of Memphis operations; and Woodson Dunavant serves as assistant vice president, U.S. and foreign cotton operations.

The Dunavant family has been deeply involved in Memphis-area civic organizations as well as efforts to bring professional sports to the region. Billy Dunavant organized The Racquet Club of Memphis, considered one of the finest indoor tennis facilities in the world, as part of a desire to see Memphis develop a reputation for big-time sports.

In addition, the Dunavants have been supporters of the Boy Scouts of America, Youth Services of Memphis, Memphis Young Life, and many other organizations. Billy was King of the Memphis Cotton Carnival in 1973, and his daughter, Dorothy, has served as Queen of the Cotton Carnival.

Billy credits the success of Dunavant Enterprises to "people, timing, and flexibility," emphasizing that "we try to change ahead of the times, not with the times."

✧

Most of the earliest settlers to stop at the Fourth Chickasaw Bluff came by water, as illustrated by the often-reproduced painting of the "Jolly Flat Boatmen." In addition to settlers who had been present prior to the Chickasaw Cession, others stopped when they heard that West Tennessee would soon be opened to settlement.

MEDNIKOW JEWELERS

Mednikow owes its creation to Jacob Mednikow, who learned jewelry making from his father in Russia, sought a new life in the United States, and established a wholesale jewelry business in 1891.

With a base in Memphis, Mednikow had branches throughout the country. "At the time, a branch was located wherever a family member was willing to live and sell jewelry," explains Robert Mednikow. "Several family members had come to the United States, and we had branches in New York, Milwaukee, Oklahoma City, Chicago, and New Orleans."

A retail store for Mednikow soon followed, located originally on the south side of Union Avenue between Main and Front Streets, and later moving to 83 South Second Street across from the Peabody Hotel. At Jacob's death in 1935, his younger brother, John, took over the business and moved it to 5 South Main Street.

By the early 1950s, "Mr. M" as John became known, was approaching his seventieth birthday with hopes that his son, Robert, would return to the family business. In 1955, Lieutenant Bob Mednikow returned home from the Korean War and began putting his personal touch on the business by expanding services and merchandise. It was during this period that Rolex, Mikimoto, and Patek Philippe began their long association with Mednikow.

Another meaningful change occurred in December 1959 when Bob met his future bride, and Bob and Betty Mednikow began planning for the future of the business. By the time their children were born—Jay in 1964 and Molly in 1965—Bob and Betty were sensing a trend toward suburban growth, and opened the East Memphis location of Mednikow in 1968. Rapid growth created a need for Bob to acquire advanced management skills and he enrolled in the Owner/President Management Program at Harvard Business School in the 1970s.

Today, Mednikow is still run by Bob and son Jay, who joined the business and brought modern ideas to a traditional family business, but still continues the traditions of quality, service, and integrity that began 120 years ago.

Since the first non-family member joined Mednikow in the 1910s, employees have played a major role in the firm's success. "Our employees are among our most treasured resources. Many have given us a lifetime," says Bob. "Several have started to work here thinking it was stop in the road, and then stayed."

There are three traits employees of Mednikow must possess: integrity, enthusiasm, and a love of fine jewelry. Continuing education is also a stipulation. "Every person here is required to take professional courses of study through the Gemological Institute of America. All members of the sales staff are trained gemologists," notes Bob.

In accordance with the standards of operation specified by the American Gem Society's statement of purpose, employees of Mednikow are "genuinely interested in the establishment of a high level of business ethics for the jewelry industry."

✧

Below: Jay and Bob Mednikow.

Over the years, the Mednikow family has actively supported many community and charitable activities in the Memphis/Shelby County area.

Bob was a founding member of the Phoenix Club, a professional organization that supports the Boys & Girls Clubs of Memphis. The Mednikow Award, established by Bob's late father, John, is presented in his honor each year to the outstanding member of the Phoenix Club.

The Mednikow family also sponsors such worthwhile endeavors as the Memphis Symphony Ball, the Heart Gala, and the Orpheum.

Mednikow employees are encouraged to become active in at least one civic organization, and the firm sponsors their membership.

Although Mednikow represents the finest designers and watch brands in the world, the firm has never lost sight of the individual designs that distinguish it from other jewelry stores. More than half of Mednikow's jewelry is made in the firm's own workshops.

"We believe that our customers are entitled to fine quality, immediate delivery, and proper service. The only way to provide that is to make the jewelry ourselves," says Bob. "There are still some fine jewelers from whom we buy. The man who makes our wedding rings makes rings for Tiffany & Co., and another craftsman does special order work for Cartier. But by establishing our own manufacturing arm, we have assured our customers a continuing emphasis on quality as my son leads the firm into the new century."

Jay Mednikow is now president of Mednikow. Continuing the tradition of excellence in business management, Jay received a degree in Economics from Harvard University and a Master of Business Administration degree from Duke University's Fuqua School of Business, and worked outside the jewelry business before returning to manage the Memphis store.

Since Jay has returned to Memphis, Mednikow has added several designer jewelry lines, such as David Yurman, as well as new watch lines, such as Cartier.

Mednikow opened its Atlanta store in 1995, the first expansion outside the Memphis market since it was a wholesale jeweler at the turn of the past century where Molly Mednikow was living. Although Jay has since purchased his sister's interest in the business, Mednikow's Atlanta store is a modern example of the original location philosophy of its founder—"wherever a family member is willing to live and sell jewelry"—and that Mednikow wants its quality jewelry to sparkle throughout the south.

✧

Above: The employees of Mednikow Jewelers are among the firm's most treasured resources.

HomeForNow Corporate Housing

During a twenty-year career in the apartment industry, Angela Harris had frequent requests for short-time rentals from clients who did not want to spend weeks or months in cramped hotel rooms. To meet this need, Harris founded HomeForNow, a temporary corporate housing agency in July 2000.

Harris operated HomeForNow from her home for about a year, but the business has been profitable from the start, partly because the company does not rent an apartment until it has a client. HomeForNow has grown to five employees and annual sales of over $2 million.

"I had a lot of support and referrals from apartment communities," she says. "It grew from there. I started calling on corporations, insurance companies, realtors, and relocation companies."

Typical of those who rely on HomeForNow is Cole Lankford of Birmingham, Alabama, who spends 300 nights a year, on the road directing the construction of temporary facilities for golf tournaments. When he is in Memphis for the FedEx St. Jude Classic, he depends on HomeForNow to house his workers. "If I spent two-and-a-half-months in a hotel, you'd be taking me to the psychiatric ward," he says.

In addition to corporate clients, HomeForNow works with insurance companies needing temporary housing for families who have been victims of fire or natural disaster, and with consultants, professional athletes, and families of St. Jude Children's Research Hospital patients in town for treatment.

HomeForNow's efforts to house those left homeless by Hurricane Katrina earned Harris the Small Business of the Year Award in 2005. In presenting the award, Robert Staub, executive director of the Memphis Small Business Chamber, said, "HomeForNow was selected for its ability to maintain and provide exemplary service to their clients through the devastating influx of people with housing needs displaced by Hurricane Katrina. During this overwhelming housing period in the Memphis market, HomeForNow continued to be actively involved in the community and of service to others."

When HomeForNow acquires a new client, it leases an appropriately sized apartment in the Memphis metro area that the client has requested. If they are not sure where to live—though typically through word of mouth from co-workers, they have some idea—Harris and her crew will profile the client's desires, such as school needs, proximity to entertainment, and preferred length of commute.

Janet Palmer, relocation manager for ServiceMaster, relocates about 250 people each year and has worked with HomeForNow since 2003. "The times we've used HomeForNow, Angie has always come through for us," Palmer says. "She understands relocation can be a very stressful time, so she strives to make sure all the comforts of home are met."

✧

Above: Angela Harris, founder of HomeForNow

Another satisfied client is William Poynter, director of strategic recruiting and relocation for Smith & Nephew. When he purchased a new home, he had about six weeks between the close of his house and the close of the one he was building. "I was in a crunch, as I didn't expect a delay in the building of my new home," he says. "We stayed only six weeks at HomeForNow, but it was the easiest move we ever made. It sure made a stressful situation go away."

HomeForNow caters to extended business travelers, consultants and project managers, transferred employees, relocating families, corporate interns, professional athletes, training and short-term assignments, military and government travel, homebuyers between homes, insurance firms and adjusters, and hospital patients and their families in town for treatment.

HomeForNow offers a personal touch and attention to detail that reflects the company's ability to anticipate and satisfy individual needs. Each of the temporary homes is completely furnished and fully complimented with linens, house wares, cable television, utilities, unlimited local and long distance phone service, wireless Internet access, washer and dryer, and much more.

HomeForNow custom coordinates their client's needs exactly to their specifications. "Our promise is to provide you with superior service, unheard of flexibility, and a one hundred percent commitment to deliver a 'no surprises' leasing experience that will supply you with furnished temporary housing that is HomeForNow," Harris says.

Using the finest properties in the greater Memphis area—including Germantown, Collierville, Cordova, Bartlett, Downtown, and North Mississippi—HomeForNow offers the very best and most comfortable furnished temporary housing.

HomeForNow is the leading provider of temporary corporate housing for the greater Memphis area, and its lease terms are extremely accommodating, anything from less than thirty days to unlimited. "Looking at it from a cost standpoint, it can't be beat," Harris comments. "It usually works out to be about half the price of a hotel but with all the comforts of home. We offer the option of cooking in, which is a huge plus. When you are on the road, eating out every meal gets old very fast."

HomeForNow is located at 815 Exocet, Suite109 in Cordova, Tennessee. For more information about the company, go online to www. homefornow.com or call 901-737-1995.

MILLINGTON TELEPHONE COMPANY

Giving up twenty-two years' seniority with the Bell System and pledging their life's savings, Billy and Bessie Howard purchased the Millington Telephone System in October 1928. The couple paid $2,000 for the system, the amount of the company's indebtedness. The plant purchased by the Howards was in shambles, and the company had only forty customers, twenty of whom had ordered their telephones disconnected because service was cut off at night and on Sundays and holidays.

Despite the negatives, Millington was a community of neat homes and proud, hard-working people, and Billy and Bessie felt this was a community where they would like to live and where they could make a real contribution. Billy had been born on a farm near Enid, Mississippi, so moving to Millington was almost like coming back home.

From the time of the purchase, the Howards established twenty-four-hour service and began renovating the tumbled-down plant. While Billy tackled the plant problems, Bessie operated the switchboard and took care of the books.

✦

Billy Howard.

By 1932 the Millington Telephone Company had extended service to 165 customers, including Baughan Air College at Park Field, the first airfield in Shelby County.

Like most other businesses, the company struggled to survive during the great economic depression of the 1930s. When banks failed throughout the region and cash

was hard to come by, the Howards allowed their customers to use barter, exchanging telephone service for eggs, meat, and vegetables. Billy raised much-needed cash during the period by installing burglar alarms of his own design.

A severe sleet storm in 1933 leveled all the telephone lines and it took six weeks to restore service to all customers.

Prosperity began to return to the area when DuPont began construction of a power plant in 1940. Construction workers flocked to the community, and millions of dollars worth of construction materials had to be expedited by telephone. Millington Telephone Company met the challenge through long hours of hard work.

The Naval Air Station was built in 1942 and, realizing that time was of the essence for the wartime effort, Billy agreed that Southern Bell should serve the station for the duration of the war. The responsibility for providing telephone service to the influx of service and civilian personnel attached to the naval station fell to Millington Telephone. By the end of 1943, the company was serving 300 stations.

Billy turned to a new business venture in 1946 when he built the Howard Manor,

Millington's first motel, on the northwest corner of Highway 51 and Easley Street. Billy charged $3 for a room without air conditioning, $4 with air conditioning.

Billy, however, continued to operate the phone system and, by the late 1940s, the system had grown to 500 stations. The challenges of the depression and the war years had been met, but now the company had to meet the growing expectations of its customers.

In 1952, the company secured a loan from the Rural Electrification Administration to convert the phone system to modern dial operation and expand its plant to meet the increasing demands for service. Millington Telephone installed its one thousandth telephone in February 1954, and in October of that same year the Millington Exchange was converted to unattended dial operation, serving 1,700 stations. By 1961 the system had grown to 4,328 stations.

Billy died in 1953 and was succeeded as president and general manager by his son, W. S. "Babe" Howard. Four siblings of the third generation—Charlotte Barry, Stuart Howard, Holly Starnes, and Laura Rosas—are now involved in the business, and members of the fourth generation are beginning to take their place in the firm.

Never one to shirk his civic duties, Billy built the first facilities for Scout camping in the area and promoted the Shelby Forest area. He was a charter member and prime mover in the Millington Chamber of Commerce and encouraged several new businesses to locate in the community.

Babe has also been very instrumental in community affairs, serving in a number of capacities, including nineteen years as a Millington Alderman. He was first president of the Millington Chamber of Commerce, served eight years on the Millington Planning Commission, and was a member of the Shelby County School Board for seventeen years.

Babe sponsored many sports teams, including an American Legion baseball team,

and built USA Stadium, considered the top facility of its kind in the region.

Millington Telephone Company continued to thrive under the direction of Babe. The company purchased the Munford Telephone Company in 1955, acquiring 489 stations. In 1958 the company purchased the Mason and Stanton Exchanges with a combined total of 378 stations, and, in 1959, Millington Telephone acquired the Rosemark exchange with a total of 210 stations.

During 2005 more than $3 million was invested in digital equipment, and the outside plant distribution system to provide the new digital services that customers want and need. Ten miles of fiber-optic cable were put into service, and the build-out will continue for years to come. DSL (high speed/capacity data) services are available to virtually the entire serving area.

Millington Telephone Company continues to be a leading employer in north Shelby County and south Tipton County. The company provides a pension plan, a 401(k), and medical benefits to its 139 employees.

Currently, the Millington Telephone Company serves a total of 27,160 stations in Shelby, Tipton, Fayette, and Haywood Counties.

❖
Above: Bessie Howard.

Below: W. S. "Babe" Howard.

CDA INCORPORATED

The world has changed since the Oklahoma City bombing and the terrorist attacks of September 11, 2001. That's why companies like Memphis-based CDA, Inc., are sought after by private industry and government entities to safeguard facilities and people.

Clifton Dates, a former Memphis Police Department officer, state fraud investigator, and criminal investigator started his own private investigation business in 1976 and in the late 1980's performed investigative services for the Federal Defender's Office. After struggling for a few years as a private investigator, he began providing security services for special events and entertainers.

The company's big break came in 1988, when it received a twenty percent subcontract arrangement with a major guard company to provide security to Memphis Light, Gas and Water Division. The arrangement lasted through 1998, when CDA won the business as the prime contractor, a contract the company maintains to this day.

CDA began working with the federal government in 1989 guarding U.S. Army Corps of Engineers construction facilities along the Mississippi River. CDA has held contracts to protect federal employees and facilities in several states. These facilities range from government office buildings to military bases to historic facilities. As a GSA schedule holder, CDA has been awarded a significant contract as part of the Homeland Security Initiative.

Darryl Dates, the founder's son, joined the company in 1989 and has taken over from his father. Through the years, CDA has expanded its services to provide a full suit of security services to private sector and government agencies. The firm has provided armed and unarmed security services and dispatch services to various federal agencies in Washington, D.C.; Fort Knox, Kentucky; Arlington, Virginia; Fort Rucker, Alabama; and the states of Louisiana and Florida. The company is also a certified Transportation Administration Service Private Screening Partner.

CDA provides everything from traditional guard services to high-end video surveillance and GPS tracking. The company works with corporations and government agencies to assess risk, develops strategic plans, and implements systems in an integrated manner.

The company provides fully trained and screened officers and personnel. Armed personnel are drawn from civilian, law enforcement, and military professions. CDA's skilled investigative services help identify potential vulnerabilities to organizations and implement appropriate safeguards. These services cover a wide variety of situations including accounting fraud cases, tracing assets and goods, gathering intelligence for litigation, due diligence screening during acquisitions, vendor screening, and employee background checks.

CDA security consultants pinpoint security risks, set program goals, and help understand the variety of security solutions that can be used to mitigate security risks. Based on an intensive assessment process, experts will design an integrated physical and electronic security solutions optimized for each client's needs and budget. CDA works with clients on an ongoing basis to make sure their security system always matches their security needs. CDA plans to continue focusing on the government and private sector for growth opportunities.

CDA Incorporated is located at 203 Beale Street in Memphis and on the Internet at www.cdaglobal.com.

✧

Above: Darryl Dates.

Bttom: Clifton Dates.

E.J. Stengel was born in Colorado but never cared much for his home state's weather. He thought the winters were too long and cold and there was too much snow.

As a young man, Stengel heard there were plenty of jobs in Texas, where the weather was warmer, so he headed that way to seek his fortune. However, on the way to Texas, he learned that a company was bringing natural gas to Memphis and was looking for employees. Stengel detoured to Tennessee and spent the next fifteen years working for what is today the Memphis Light, Gas & Water Company.

In 1943, Stengel and four other men organized Automatic Heating & Service, Inc., which specialized in converting coal-fired boilers to natural gas, other heating repairs, and plumbing. By the late 1950s, air conditioning had become so popular the company dropped the plumbing division and replaced it with air conditioning.

The business was first located at 22 South Cooper in Memphis but relocated to larger quarters at 3470 Tchulahoma Road in 1965.

Over time, Stengel's son, Richard, and his wife, Carolyn, came into the business, and the Stengels bought out the other partners. E.J. died in 1971 and Richard brought his brother, Eugene, into the business. The company is still owned and operated by the Stengel family, with the third generation now being groomed to continue the family tradition.

Today, Automatic Heating and Air Conditioning is an authorized dealer for Carrier, the leader in home heating and cooling equipment. The company serves both residential and commercial clients and provides equipment retrofit and replacement, including boiler repair and replacement. Customers can count on Automatic to provide a system and solution that fits their unique needs, backed by a reputation for doing the job right the first time.

With nearly sixty-five years in business, Automatic Heating and Air Conditioning is dedicated to providing the best possible solution for each customer's needs. Each employee is thoroughly trained to see every job through from start to finish, making sure the unit or system performs to the customer's expectations.

AUTOMATIC HEATING & AIR CONDITIONING, INC.

Automatic Heating and Air Conditioning provides quick, professional service and complete service plans to keep systems operating at peak efficiency. In addition, the company offers free in-home estimates, planned service agreements, and radio-dispatched trucks. It is all part of Automatic's tradition of service—assuring your complete satisfaction.

For more information about Automatic Heating & Air Conditioning, Inc., check their website at www.automaticheatandair.com.

NATHAN BEDFORD FORREST HISTORICAL SOCIETY INTERNATIONAL, INC.

✧

Above: The equestrian statue of General Nathan Bedford Forrest in Forrest Park, Memphis.

Below: General Nathan Bedford Forrest in front of his Cavalry Corps battle flag.

The General Nathan Bedford Forrest Historical Society International, Inc., (FHS) is a nonprofit historical educational organization [501(c)(3)] dedicated to promoting the study and understanding of the life of General N. B. Forrest, advancing the general educational appreciation of the Civil War, and furthering the preservation of historic sites and related items of the War Between the States. The Society is a membership-based organization with headquarters in Memphis and a diverse worldwide membership.

The Society has its roots in the Forrest Monument Association that unofficially began its efforts in 1887 in Memphis to raise money for a befitting memorial to Confederate Lieutenant General Nathan Bedford Forrest. However, the Association actually incorporated on November 20, 1891, and its work culminated in the erection and dedication of Forrest Park and the Forrest Statue in May 1905. The Association was modeled after, and a derivative of, the post-Civil War 1867 Confederate Veterans Association, but with emphasis on preserving the legendary cavalry reputation of General Forrest. In succeeding years of the twentieth century, the Association was frequently overshadowed by the larger and more active Forrest Camp, Sons of Confederate Veterans. In April 1959 the modern-day organization became the Forrest Historical Society, and was sparked anew by long-time Forrest authority and enthusiast, Riley Gunter. More recently, the number of Forrest admirers—and War Between the States fans—has increased so dramatically that, over the last few years, the Society has grown in numbers and in scope. The Society's activities now encompass a wide range of historic preservation events as well as the central foundation of education and study of the life of General Forrest.

The Purpose of the Society is to honor and preserve the name and heroic deeds of our famed General; To guard and protect General Forrest's statue and last resting place; To identify, preserve and interpret historic sites and battlefields related to Forrest's life and military career and the War Between the States; To host special events, historical tours

and make available a speakers bureau of qualified Forrest historians; To publish manuscripts, articles, photos, books, and to make such available to our membership at special member's prices; To collect, preserve, maintain and display articles, artifacts, documents, weapons, uniforms, and related items of the Forrest family and War Between the States era; Also, to maintain the Forrest battle-related hiking trails in Tennessee and Mississippi; and to assist in the preservation of historic sites associated with General Forrest and with the War for Southern Independence.

Additional information on the Nathan Bedford Forrest Historical Society may be found on the Internet at www.nbforrest.org.

MEMPHIS FUNERAL HOME

Alvin Wunderlich, Sr., founded Memphis Funeral Home as National Funeral Home in 1931. The original location was 1038 Union Avenue, a central location near the trolley lines that provided transportation for most funeral attendees in the days when automobiles were still rare.

The funeral home moved a block away to 1177 Union Avenue in 1933 and served thousands of families from that location until 1998.

The name was changed to Memphis Funeral Home in 1962, the same year the firm became the largest funeral home in America under one roof. That year, Memphis Funeral Home served more than three thousand families.

Since 1970, the growth of Memphis Funeral Home has been managed by Lon Thurmer (now deceased), Paul B. McCarver, and E. C. Daves.

Under the continued leadership of E. C. Daves and Paul B. McCarver, Memphis Funeral Home has expanded to include five funeral homes, two cemeteries, a full-service crematory, and a floral service. This expansion has allowed Memphis Funeral Home to provide a total range of services to meet the needs and budgets of all families.

In addition to the Memphis Crematory Services at 4923 Summer Avenue, the firm offers the services of its Poplar Chapel at 5599 Poplar Avenue in Memphis; the Germantown Parkway Chapel at 3700 North Germantown Parkway in Memphis; Collierville Chapel at 534 West Poplar Avenue in Collierville; and the Brantley Chapel at 6875 Cockram

Street in Olive Branch, Mississippi. The cemeteries include Memory Hill Garden at 3700 North Germantown Parkway and Memphis Memory Gardens at 6464 Raleigh LaGrange Road.

Memphis Funeral Home has conducted as many as twenty-four funerals in one day and provided services for U.S. senators, governors and other notables, including Elvis Presley and the Presley family and Dr. Adrian Rogers, the beloved Memphis minister and president of the Southern Baptist Convention. Dr. Rogers' funeral, attended by more than 12,000 persons, was the largest ever conducted by Memphis Funeral Home.

In order to serve St. Jude Children's Research Hospital and other international clients, funeral directors are specially trained to transfer remains worldwide.

"Our plans for the future are to continue our heritage of care for each family we serve, meeting their needs one family at a time, and celebrating lives with dedication, excellence, innovation and dignity," says Daves, president of Memphis Funeral Home. "We are dedicated to the compassionate support of families during difficult times, helping them celebrate the significance of their loved ones' lives, and preserving memories that transcend generations."

WURZBURG, INC.

Wurzburg, Inc., traces its corporate history to 1908 when the Dillow Woods Company began supplying Memphis businesses with essential oils and flavorings. In 1909 the Tennessee legislature voted to ban the production of alcohol beginning in 1910. That year, a young salesman named Seymour Wurzburg was hired by the Dillow Woods Company to expand its offerings and sales.

When the hundred or so distilleries in the state were forced to move production to neighboring states, Seymour began to supply distilleries in the region with bottles, corks, cartons, and boxes. He became so successful that he bought the company from the Rosemore family in 1912. The company became a prosperous regional company but was shaken by the early death of Seymour in October 1917. His oldest son, Abe, resigned his job at the Specialty Manufacturing Company and took over his father's company on January 1, 1918.

One year later, nationwide prohibition was instituted via the Eighteenth amendment to the U.S. Constitution. Abe was forced to expand the company's packaging sales to regional cosmetic, pharmaceutical, and other manufacturers. Sales were so successful that Abe encouraged his brother, Reginald, to join him in 1925. The partnership became known as Wurzburg Brothers Company. This partnership proved to be a very successful one.

In 1958 the company incorporated as Wurzburg Bros., Inc., with offices and distribution in Memphis, Nashville, Birmingham, and New Orleans. For forty-two years the two Wurzburg brothers worked very closely until Abe's death in 1967. In 1980 the company changed its name to Wurzburg, Inc. In 1993, Reggie died.

Today, Wurzburg is owned and operated by the fourth generation of the Wurzburg family. As an industry leader, Wurzburg is committed to creating value in the marketplace through innovative packaging solutions and superior supply chain logistics. Wurzburg has grown to include two subsidiaries: ArtCraft, which offers full-service label design and production; and Wurzburg Print Services, which provides promotional products and print management. Wurzburg has twelve branch locations servicing the entire southeast. Products include tape, strapping, corrugated products, packaging films, poly bags, and protective packaging. Wurzburg also offers packaging equipment with installation and field services.

In its one-hundredth year, Wurzburg is committed to reinforcing its position of leadership in packaging. As Wurzburg enters its second century, its 400 employees remain firmly committed to the vision and values of its founders, Abe and Reggie Wurzburg—integrity, value, and innovation.

❖

Above: Abe (first individual) and brother, Reginald (fourth from left) standing in front of the Wurzburg building at 710 South Fourth Street in Memphis, c. 1926.

Below: Wurzburg's warehouse and shipping dock, c. 1926.

Since 1947, businesses across the Mid-South have trusted Dillard Door for facilities security and loss prevention.

Dillard Door's proud heritage spans six decades and began with John Dillard, Sr., whose Southern Glass Company at 556 Madison Avenue forged its first connection with the door industry. The firm represented Crawford Door Company, a manufacturer of sectional overhead doors.

In the 1950s, the Dillard Door Division of Southern Glass began operation. The company added such well-known names as Pella, ModernFold, and Slide-View doors to its product line. In addition to representing door manufacturers, Dillard Door began building custom industrial doors for special applications, such as "double-acting" doors and overhead one-piece doors.

In the late 1950s and early '60s, the company was known as Doors Incorporated and represented the Windsor Door Company.

John W. Dillard, Jr. joined the firm in 1964 and the owners soon formed J.W. Dillard & Company, which continued manufacturing and also represented the North American Door Corporation, a major manufacturer of coiling doors.

In 1974, the company name was changed to Dillard Door and Specialty Company. Manufacturing was discontinued, and the firm concentrated on representing North American Door Company and Atlas Door Corporation.

Dillard Door formed its Advanced Automated Entrances Division in 1981 and began its association with Horton Automatics, a major manufacturer of automatic pedestrian doors. Dillard Door also began installing and servicing automatic vehicle gates.

As the company's reputation for excellence grew, other manufacturers began to market their products in Memphis through Dillard Door, now located at 788 East Street.

In the 1990s, Advanced Automated Entrances was sold and, in 1998, the Entrance Control Systems division was formed to specialize in automatic gate systems, access controls, alarms, and closed-circuit television cameras.

In 2002, the Dillard family sold the company to Chris W. Bird, and the name

was changed to Dillard Door & Security. Today, Chris and his team continue the tradition of service excellence and integrity the Mid-South has come to expect from the Dillard name.

Dillard Door & Entrance Control services a 100-mile radius that includes west Tennessee, north Mississippi, and eastern Arkansas but the firm has done work as far away as New York. Satisfied customers have included AutoZone Park, Coors, FedEx, the Federal Reserve Bank, Memphis City Schools, Methodist HealthCare, Nike, the Pyramid, and UPS.

In today's world, physical barriers such as doors, gates and grilles, may be only part of a customer's needs. For this reason, Dillard Door's Entrance Control Systems division provides electronic barriers that control who can enter a building or parking lot, and who cannot. Visit Dillard Door's website at www.dillarddoor.com to examine the many services offered by the company.

Dillard Door & Entrance Control

✧

Above: In the 1950s, Dillard Doors product line included Pella, ModernFold, Slide-View and Crawford Overhead Doors.

Below: Today, Dillard's customers include AutoZone Park, where not only doors but alarm, access control, and surveillance cameras are part of the company's product offerings.

INMAN CONSTRUCTION CORP.

Inman Construction Corp. has grown in the past four decades from a two-man operation based in an upstairs bedroom to a company with annual revenues between $50 million and $80 million and an operating area that extends into twelve states.

The company got its official start on September 15, 1970, when Frank Inman, Jr., and Jim Johnson, who worked together at J. A. Jones, a large international construction company, decided to go into business for themselves.

They started the company under the name of Management/Construction/Inc. in Frank's house. To finance the company, Frank sold some property, Jim dipped into his savings, and they borrowed the rest from a local bank.

Their first major project was a $208,000 renovation of an intensive care unit at John Gaston Hospital. They hired Slim Buntin as their first superintendent. Not long after that they were hired to oversee tenant infill construction projects for First Tennessee Bank in their office tower in downtown Memphis. The working relationship with First Tennessee Bank spanned fourteen years.

The company focused on school and office building construction in its early years. Management/Construction/Inc. worked with Memphis City Schools on several design/build projects and, in 1980, began working with Baptist Healthcare. The company spent the next ten years working on multiple hospitals in the Mid-South area for Baptist Healthcare System.

It was during this time that Frank and his brother, George Inman, who owned a construction company in Houston, decided to merge their companies to create Inman Construction Corp. Through the years, the company has grown into one of the area's premier construction firms. The *Memphis Business Journal* consistently rates Inman Construction among the top contractors in the Memphis/Mid-South region.

Inman is dedicated to providing the best service and value to all of its customers in order to earn repeat business and differentiate it from the competition. The company has extensive experience in healthcare, commercial, institutional, and industrial construction.

The company has worked on many of the area's most well known projects including AutoZone Headquarters, AutoZone Park, Memphis International Airport, Methodist Hospital–Germantown, and the Campbell Clinic.

The company offers clients a complete range of pre-construction and construction services. Through sound leadership and the addition of talented field, office and supervisory personnel, Inman is dedicated to quality construction from concept to completion.

The owners and employees of Inman Construction Corp. have done a lot to make Memphis a great place to live and work, and that will continue to be among the company's most important goals as it grows and expands its area of operations.

Inman Construction Corp. is located on the Internet at www.inmanconstruction.com.

LAW OFFICES OF WEISS SPICER, PLLC

The beauty and integrity of a pre-Civil War townhouse in Memphis is being maintained thanks to the efforts of Weiss Spicer, PLLC, which maintains its law offices in the historic building.

Weiss Spicer, PLLC, composed of Arnold M. Weiss and Valerie Ann Spicer, was founded in 2005. However, Weiss had maintained offices in the building since 1965, when it was purchased by a partnership composed of Eulyse M. Smith, James D. Causey, J. Harold Ellis, and Arnold M. Weiss. Smith is credited with finding the building and realizing its potential.

The partners were successful in having the Italianate Victorian townhouse at 208 Adams Avenue placed on the National Register of Historical Places. "Not only did we consider the building worthy of the selection, but we also wanted to prevent it from being demolished and turned into a parking lot, the fate of other beautiful Victorian homes along Adams Avenue," Weiss explains.

Because of the expansion of the law practice, which now has a support staff of more than thirty employees, Weiss purchased an additional office building at 243 Adams Avenue, which is in close proximity to 208 Adams.

Sterling Fowlkes, who came to Memphis from Virginia before 1840 and became a cotton factor and merchant, built the handsome townhouse in the 1850s. One of his sons, Sterling, Jr., was educated in Virginia and was already head of his own cotton broker firm when the Civil War broke out. He served as a Captain in the Confederate Army and was killed in the Battle of Perryville at the age of twenty-five.

Sterling Fowlkes, Sr., died in 1872 at the age of sixty-nine. Records in Elmwood Cemetery note that Sterling Fowlkes and his cousin, Austin Fowlkes, were "alike distinguished for probity and sterling integrity. They bent neither in the presence of adversity nor of prosperity and were ever the same honest, truthful, industrious merchants."

After Fowlkes death, the house was sold to Thomas Raymond Boyle, who was born in Ireland. He and his family lived in the townhouse until he died of typhoid fever in 1890. His wife, the former Margaret Owen, and their children lived in the home until 1920.

The characteristics of the downtown area changed over time, and the townhouse eventually became a bordello, until Hillsman Taylor, who converted the building to law offices, purchased it.

The town home is painted brick with brick quoins emphasizing the corners and limestone belt courses indicating the first and second floors. The cornice is supported by large paired brackets and incorporates cast iron ventilation grills in its design. The long windows on the front façade have ornate hoods. The structure has two stories, an attic, and a basement.

❖

Above: (From left to right) Attorneys Arnold M. Weiss, Eulyse M. Smith, James D. Causey, and J. Harold Ellis.

Below: Law Offices of Weiss Spicer, PLLC.
PHOTOGRAPH COURTESY OF BRAD JOHNSON.

ST. AGNES
ACADEMY–
ST. DOMINIC
SCHOOL

St. Agnes Academy-St. Dominic School has been providing students academic excellence in a Catholic environment for 155 years. A Catholic college preparatory day school, St. Agnes enrolls girls in Pre-Kindergarten through grade twelve and St. Dominic enrolls boys in Pre-Kindergarten through grade eight.

Having served the Memphis community since 1851, St. Agnes Academy is the oldest continuously operating school in Memphis. Founded by the Dominican Sisters of St. Catherine, Kentucky, St. Agnes was originally located at Vance Avenue and Orleans Street. The first class included twenty boarders and fifteen day students. Today the school enrolls over 850 students. The Dominican Sisters played an important role in Memphis' history, caring for the sick during the yellow fever epidemic, operating an orphanage, and supporting the civil rights movement.

The school moved to its present site on Walnut Grove Road in 1951 and, in 1956, ground was broken for St. Dominic School. Campus growth over the years has included construction of the Buckman Math and Science Building in 1991 and the Davis Early Childhood Center and Tot Lot in 1998. Siena Hall opened in 1999, providing a double gymnasium, 300-seat performing arts center, art/music studios, administrative offices, and St. Catherine Chapel.

The school's mission is to educate young people in a principle-based program designed to prepare them for advanced formal and personal studies while deepening their faith and relationship with God. In the Dominican tradition, the school actively encourages academic excellence and promotes spiritual and moral growth, social and ecological responsibility, leadership skills, multicultural

awareness, emotional maturity, artistic expression, and physical fitness.

Classes are co-educational in early childhood and junior high and single gender in lower and upper schools. This unique configuration helps provide the school's teachers with ways to individualize and customize curricula to match the students' developmental and gender-specific needs. St. Agnes–St. Dominic builds strong minds and hearts by establishing brain-based learning research as the organizing principle for all that it offers its students. The curriculum and programs reflect research on multiple intelligences, learning styles, and teaching styles, and the facilities and technology enhancements support the teaching and learning processes. The first school in the area to provide laptops to every student from grades one through twelve, the school is a leader in the integration of technology into the curriculum. Strong fine arts and athletic programs enrich the curriculum.

St. Agnes–St. Dominic attracts and retains a very qualified and dedicated faculty. More than half the faculty members hold advanced degrees, and many have served the school for twenty years or longer.

Intellectual and personal disciplines are standards for the traditional education at St. Agnes–St. Dominic. Students learn to integrate prayer, study, community, and service with academic excellence...learning values that stand a lifetime.

DENNIS ELECTRIC, INC.

Dennis Electric, Inc. has operated in Memphis since 1947, but its roots go all the way back to 1930, when Byrd Electric Company was founded by R.M. Byrd, a native Memphian.

In 1945, Charles H. Dennis, Sr. began working for Byrd Electric and, two years later, became a partner in the firm. Byrd died in 1950, and the Dennis family purchased his share of the business from the Byrd family. The name of the firm was changed to Dennis Electric, Inc. in 1986.

Although the business name and address have changed over the years, the Dennis family has retained ownership of the firm since 1950. Today, Charles H. Dennis, Jr. and his children; Robert M. Dennis, Susan Dennis Crawford, John C. Dennis, Phillip A., and Cole H. Dennis are stockholders in the family firm and active participants in the daily activities of the corporation.

A recent article in the *Memphis Business Journal* noted that, "Dennis is proud that the company has remained in the family and that the family extends to every employee of the company, including his sister, brother-in-law, niece and grandson, who also work for the company."

"It makes you feel good that you can provide your family with something they want to do," he was quoted by the paper. "If they didn't enjoy it, they wouldn't be here."

Business has grown tremendously over the years, and DEI currently operates from two locations. The corporate office is located in Memphis with a second office in Rogers, Arkansas.

DEI specializes in new construction, renovations, and continuous service for commercial and industrial clients. The firm's service area includes Tennessee, Mississippi, Arkansas, Missouri, and Alabama.

DEI performs electrical maintenance work for hospitals, office complexes, retail stores, churches, schools, data centers, restaurants, and clubs. DEI service trucks are on call twenty-four hours a day and are available for any emergency situation. If an installation is required after hours while the facility is closed, or

during a specific time period, DEI will gladly accommodate.

A good example of DEI's ability to respond to any situation was the severe windstorm that hit the Memphis area in 2003. Although the storm tested the company's ability and stamina, DEI secured large and small generators for its customers and had them safe, secure, and operating quickly.

The function of the Arkansas office is primarily to support DEI's work with the world's largest retailer, Wal-Mart. DEI has performed electrical work for Wal-Mart since 1985, including new construction and service to the data centers and various office buildings, as well as local stores.

DEI customers routinely request a particular electrician because of the confidence he instills and his familiarity with their facility. The primary service electricians at DEI are Steve Campbell and Charlie Davis, who have been with the company since 1986; Mike Smith, since 1996; and Michael Bradley, who joined the company in 2000. They are valuable, educated, and trustworthy team members, and we are pleased to call them DEI employees.

For more information abut Dennis Electric, Inc., please visit the company's website at www.denniselectric.com.

❖

Back row (from left to right): Cole Dennis, Robert Dennis, and Phil Dennis. Front row (from left to right): John Dennis, Charles Dennis, and Susan Crawford.

WEST
TENNESSEE
HISTORICAL
SOCIETY

The West Tennessee Historical Society is one of the Mid-South's least conspicuous educational and recreational amenities. It is the umbrella heritage organization for the Western "Grand Division" of Tennessee and a true cultural gem. Through its antecedent organizations, it dates back to 1857 when "The Old Folks of Shelby County" began meeting for regular programs. Residents who had arrived in the 1820s and 1830s told the stories of their pioneer days.

In the Civil War's aftermath, three successive local history groups had a Confederate historical emphasis. In the 1910s, the last of these groups morphed into the Memphis Historical Society. In 1935 the MHS broadened its geographical scope to include all twenty-one counties of West Tennessee. Reflecting this area's population distribution, however, somewhat more than half of the society's historical emphasis has stayed focused on Memphis and Shelby County. Consequently, there is no separate historical society for either Memphis or Shelby County.

From its inception, WTHS has sponsored and scheduled periodic regional history programs. Since 1996, Memphis University School has hosted the society's monthly meetings in Memphis. The November and March meetings are held in the Martin and Jackson, Tennessee areas, respectively.

Since 1947, WTHS has published an annual anthology of formal papers, notes, documents, and book reviews relating to West Tennessee. Almost the entire run of the

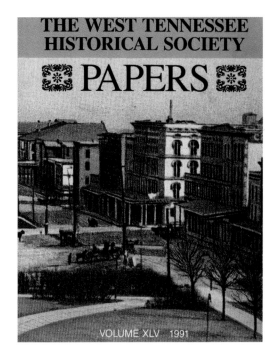

society's annual journals is available on the *Shelby County Register's* website.

Probably as important as publishing *The WTHS Papers* is the society's work in sponsoring and publishing books and reprints related to the area's history. Such books include: *The Old Folks Record*, J. Harvey Mathes' *The Old Guard in Grey*, Judge J. P. Young's *Standard History of Memphis, Tennessee*, James D. Davis' *The History of the City of Memphis* (facsimile reprint, edited by James E. Roper), and John E. Harkins' *Metropolis of the American Nile* and *Historic Shelby County*. WTHS has also bought up inventories of "remaindered" books, keeping them available for purchase. Examples include Robert A. Sigafoos' *Cotton Row to Beale Street* and Paul R. Coppock's six-volume set of Memphis-area historical anthologies.

The society's other major functions include sanctioning and erecting historical markers, helping preserve historic structures and sites, and collecting and preserving publications and documents bearing on West Tennessee history. The WTHS manuscripts and rare books' collections are permanently housed in the Special Collections Department at the University of Memphis Libraries.

Finally, WTHS serves as a referral network and a clearinghouse for sharing information about events bearing on West Tennessee's past. To learn more about WTHS, please visit our website at www.wths.tn.org.

The history of St. Mary's Episcopal School, one of the nation's most distinguished girls' schools, spans three centuries. Its story began in 1847, when Mary Foote Pope, a woman with a strong Christian faith, started a small school at Calvary Episcopal Church in Memphis.

Pope believed that girls should have the same educational opportunities as boys, a belief shared to this day by St. Mary's faculty, staff, Board of Trustees, and alumnae. The St. Mary's experience allows girls to learn in an atmosphere that combines the pursuit of excellence in all areas, the nurture and guidance of gifted teachers, and an Episcopal community that encourages spiritual and moral development.

The school hasn't always been located in Memphis.

In 1862, Pope moved St. Mary's (although it operated under another name at the time) to Hernando, Mississippi, until the end of the Civil War. After the war, she returned to Memphis and set up shop at the corner of Poplar and Alabama Streets.

From 1873 to 1910, the Sisters of the Order of St. Mary ran the school and gave it the name that it carries today. One of St. Mary's most treasured traditions—Springfest—began under the sisters' direction. To this day each senior class, as a reminder of the sisters' dedication, visits St. Mary's Episcopal Cathedral.

St. Mary's later relocated to 1257 Poplar Avenue, where it operated until 1949, when it relocated again to Grace-St. Luke's Episcopal Church. The school stayed there until 1953, when it relocated to the Church of the Holy Communion at Walnut Grove and Perkins, its current location. The school incorporated in 1958, and by the fall of 1959, enrollment had nearly doubled to 400 and faculty had increased to 30.

The first edition of the school's yearbook, *Carillon*, was published in 1961, and the next year, the school received accreditation from Southern Association of Colleges and Secondary Schools.

Dr. Nathanial Cheairs Hughes, who served as headmaster from 1962 to 1973, is credited with launching St. Mary's into prominence as a school that was outstanding for preparing girls for college. During his tenure, St. Mary's

graduated an increasingly high percentage of National Merit Scholars, incorporated as an independent Episcopal school and became the first independent school, in Memphis to integrate its student body.

The tradition of excellence that Hughes cultivated continues at St. Mary's. The National Merit Scholarship Program recognized 36 percent of the 2006 senior class. The school fields more athletic teams than ever before, and the creative arts program includes drama, dance, vocal and instrumental music, and art. St. Mary's success is unquestioned.

Now under the leadership of Marlene Shaw, the school has no plans to rest on its laurels. A $30 million master plan will address future needs in the areas of facilities, people, and programs. St. Mary's Episcopal School will continue to maintain a low pupil-to-teacher ratio and maintain an educational environment that develops self-discipline, integrity, and honorable behavior.

For more information about St. Mary's Episcopal School, visit them on the internet at www.stmarysschool.org.

ST. MARY'S EPISCOPAL SCHOOL

❖

Above: The St. Mary's Episcopal School Class of 1909.

Below: The state-of-the-art Early Childhood Center opened in the fall of 2005.

MEMPHIS UNIVERSITY SCHOOL

Memphis University School is a college preparatory school dedicated to the development of well-rounded young men of strong moral character, consistent with the school's Christian tradition. MUS was founded in 1893 by two energetic young educators who, at the suggestion of the University of Tennessee's president, came to Memphis and opened a small college preparatory school. Since then MUS has been committed to the highest standards of academic performance, extracurricular activities, and personal honor for each of its students. In addition to its engaging curriculum, the school provides an exceptionally able and dedicated faculty, which nurtures critical thinking, challenging discussion, and lively exchanges of ideas. More than seventy-five

percent of the MUS faculty hold advanced degrees, including two JDs and five PhDs. MUS teachers have an average of twenty years experience in challenging young minds.

The original MUS opened with only seven students, but it grew rapidly. It thrived into the 1920s, grooming numerous young men for leadership roles of various sorts in the Mid-South and beyond. In 1936, however, the Great Depression and shrinking enrollments forced the school's closure.

The new MUS, patterned closely on the methods and values of its namesake, opened in the fall of 1955 with ninety boys on a ninety-four-acre wooded campus at 6191 Park Avenue. In the ensuing fifty years, its enrollment has grown to 650 students. Its college-preparatory program thoroughly grounds each student in traditional disciplines of the humanities, fine arts, and physical sciences. The campus includes state-of-the-art laboratories and classrooms and a library that rivals those of many colleges.

MUS focuses on preparing boys in grades seven through twelve to enter some of the nation's most competitive colleges. Its students have a one hundred percent college acceptance record, and each graduating class earns several million dollars in merit-based scholarships. Mastering critical-thinking skills and self-discipline, MUS students consistently score well above national averages on standardized tests, Advanced Placement examinations, and National Merit Scholar recognition.

From its inception, MUS also has emphasized physical fitness and athletic competition. Both boys and teachers played on the earliest MUS athletic teams, at times defeating even college squads. Today, approximately seventy percent of the student body participates in a total of twelve sanctioned sports. In recent decades, MUS teams have won numerous city, county, district, regional, and state champion-ships, earning the enthusiastic support of fellow students, faculty, and alumni. More important than simply winning, however, are the life lessons that the boys internalize in the areas of self-discipline, teamwork, leadership, and personal responsibility.

The school's extracurricular activities are not limited to athletics. MUS also provides an exceptional climate for student achievement and extension of individual talents in the areas of choral music, dramatics, the graphic arts, and student publications. Moreover, MUS government club teams consistently dominate such activities as Model UN, Youth Legislature, and mock trial competitions. Civic service to the Mid-South community is yet another area of profound student involvement.

Most important of all, however, is the school's student-operated and student enforced Honor System. An integral part of school life from the beginning, the Honor Code epitomizes the firm bonds of faith and trust among students and faculty. Lying, stealing, and cheating simply are not tolerated.

For additional information about Memphis University School, visit www.musowls.org.

BAILEY,
CLARKE &
BENFIELD

MOSBY-
BENNETT
HOUSE

The Mosby-Bennett House in East Memphis has come a long way from the 5,000-acre plantation house Samuel and Joseph Mosby built in 1852. The three-story, rectangular structure combines Greek Revival simplicity with Victorian ornamentation and serves as an office for Bailey, Clarke & Benfield, a civil litigation firm that represents infants who suffer brain damage during birth due to medical malpractice.

The house now sits on a small lot amid an office park, serving as a reminder to Memphis residents of its historical roots. The Mosby-Bennett House is a rectangular building with a brick foundation, weatherboard siding, and a slate-covered gable roof.

Although built in the Greek Revival style, a subsequent owner added a variety of Victorian details. One of the Mosbys and his wife lived in the house from 1852 to 1863, when the Civil War forced them to move to Memphis, twelve miles to the west, for safety. They rented the house to William Lawrence Hall and his wife, who had moved from Kentucky when their son joined Morgan's Kentucky Raiders, a Confederate cavalry unit. General Ulysses S. Grant is said to have spent the night at the house following the Battle of Shiloh.

In 1870 the Mosbys sold the house and about 1,900 acres to Bennett, a well-known racehorse breeder, who built a racetrack on the property. Bennett added curvilinear bargeboards, porches on each side with bracketed posts, perforated railings, and gingerbread trim. He also added scrollwork above the window cornices and the peak of the facade's central gable. On the inside, Bennett added a heavily carved newel post to the stair, two marble mantelpieces and picture rails. He built a banquet hall in the basement and installed a Delco lighting system, an early electric generator. Bennett also built three gazebos in back of the house. One twelve-foot octagonal gazebo with pointed arches is still standing. In 1979 the home was sold to be the centerpiece of a modern office complex.

Sadler Bailey, who started the firm as a solo practitioner with a single secretary, has seen his practice grow to include five attorneys and a support staff of seven.

The firm's attorneys are: R. Sadler Bailey; Andrew C. Clarke; J. Mark Benfield; Eric H. Espey; and Thomas R. Greer.

With an eye toward preservation and historical accuracy, Bailey has overseen renovations to the building, including changing its color from yellow to the original white with green shutters. Future plans call for a chandelier in the entryway and alterations to accommodate the handicapped.

The Mosby-Bennett House has found a benefactor in Bailey, Clarke & Benfield that is dedicated to preserving this Memphis landmark.

GRIMES TIRE STORE

Grimes Tire Store opened for business in 1958 when Ward Grimes, who had worked for International Harvester for several years, decided to go into business for himself. He and Marvin Steele, who had a decade of experience managing Firestone stores, became partners in 1970. Twelve years later, Steele bought out Grimes when he decided to retire.

Steele later took on a partner, Jay Guiltner, and together they opened Guiltner-Steele Tire Center at 100 North Missouri Street in West Memphis. Through their efforts, the business has grown in more ways than one.

For instance, Grimes Tire Store does more than sell and maintain tires. It also provides customers with oil changes, tune-ups, alignments, and brake work, shocks, alternators, and air-conditioning service. In fact, Grimes offers customers all kinds of automotive services with the exception of engine overhauls and transmission work.

The company has grown in one other way as well: Its single location has grown to three. Along with the original store and the Guiltner-Steele Tire Center, the company operates a second Grimes Tire Store at 4285 Hacks Cross Road. The staff includes Steele's son, Mike, who manages the Lamar store, and Marvin's son, Toby, who manages the West Memphis store. Jay Guiltner's son, Jason, is service manager of the West Memphis store, and Larry Speck manages the Hacks Cross store.

The company's success is founded on the belief that every person who comes in the door should be treated the way the company's employees would want to be treated. Grimes Tire employees, who work with the latest equipment and attend automotive schools to enhance their skills, inform customers exactly how much the work will cost before work begins. They also have another employee independently verify a diagnosed problem to make sure the trouble has been correctly identified.

Grimes Tire Store owes its success to its hard-working employees, many of who have been with the company for years. It also owes a debt of gratitude to its loyal customers, who return to Grimes year after year, bringing friends and family members with them. Some of today's customers are the children and grandchildren of the original Grimes Tire Store customers, and there's no greater testament to a business than that.

The company's owners and employees believe it is important to give back to their community. Marvin served as a state representative in Arkansas from 1998 to 2002 and has served on the Delta Regional Commission for Arkansas. He and Jay Guiltner are members of the West Memphis Rotary Club.

Grimes Tire Store has donated money and tires to many area groups, including the Boy Scouts of America Chickasaw Council and the American Heart Association in Crittenden County. The company's owners and employees are always involved in something designed to help the community. They plan to continue that tradition and continue giving Memphis-area customers the best service and products in the industry.

❖

Top: Grimes Tire Store's Hacks Cross Road location.

Below: Grimes Tire's original 1958 location.

Bottom: Grimes Tire Store's Lamar Avenue location.

Prominent attorney Lee A. Hardison, Jr., who practiced civil and criminal law in Memphis from 1937 until his death in 1983, founded the Hardison Law Firm. As a tribute to the founder, the firm began operating as The Hardison Law Firm, P.C. in 1985.

The firm has grown from a professional staff of two in 1983 to a current professional staff of twenty and a total staff of more than forty. The Hardison Law Firm concentrates its practice on the defense of physicians, hospitals, and other healthcare practitioners, and provides alternative dispute resolution services. The firm also focuses on the defense of legal malpractice claims, the defense of other professionals, and other types of insurance defense.

Although most of the firm's practice is centered in the Memphis area, the firm also represents clients, and has lawyers licensed, in a territory encompassing West Tennessee, Eastern Arkansas, and Northern Mississippi. The firm's lawyers are licensed in the U.S. District Courts in the Mid-South area, including those in Arkansas and Mississippi.

David M. Cook, who serves as president, and Jerry O. Potter, vice president, head the Hardison Law Firm. Cook, a Memphis native, received his B.A. degree from the University of Tennessee and graduated from law school at the University of Memphis. He began his career with the Law Offices of Lee A. Hardison, Jr., in 1977. Cook is active in a number of professional organizations and currently serves as President of the Memphis Bar Association. He is also a Fellow of the American College of Trial Lawyers.

Potter received his B.S. degree from the University of Tennessee at Martin and his law degree from the University of Memphis. He is also active in several professional organizations and is a Fellow of the American College of Trial Lawyers.

THE HARDISON LAW FIRM, P.C.

The Hardison Law Firm, P.C. is located in a beautifully restored historic building at 119 South Main Street in Memphis. The building, constructed in 1901, once housed the famous Goldsmith's Department Store and is now referred to as Peabody Place's Pembroke Square. 119 South Main Street is part of the Gayoso-Peabody Historical District and is listed in the U.S. Department of the Interior's Register of National Historic Places.

The staff of The Hardison Law Firm is active in many Memphis-area civic and charitable organizations and provides *pro bono publico* legal representation for a number of clients each year.

The firm maintains a tradition of high quality, aggressive representation, and a common sense approach to its clients' needs and sensitivity to its clients' economic concerns.

For more information about The Hardison Law Firm, please visit its website at www.thehardisonlawfirm.com.

❖

Lee A. Hardinson, Jr.

CATHOLIC DIOCESE OF MEMPHIS

"As we look to the future, and we are future bound, to the months and years that lie before us, what kind of Church shall we be? What kind of Church do we want to be?" Bishop Carol T. Dozier, the first Bishop of Memphis, spoke those words during his installation ceremony as Bishop on January 6, 1971. He urged those listening to become a Church that was noted for being "a Good Samaritan on the banks of the Mississippi."

Bishop Dozier's years as Bishop of Memphis were marked by reconciliation of the races, by a search for unity among the churches, by efforts to recognize and begin to fill the needs of the poor and downtrodden, to protect the life of the unborn, and to crusade for peace and disarmament.

When Bishop Dozier came to the diocese it comprised approximately 50,000 Catholics in twenty-one West Tennessee counties, the vast majority of them within Shelby County. Outside the Memphis metropolitan area, much of the rural area was mission territory. There were a total of 30 parishes, 28 Catholic schools with slightly more than 10,000 students, eight hospitals, orphanages and similar facilities, all served by 77 priests, 20 seminarians, and 131 nuns. There were also a number of Christian Brothers who ran Christian Brothers High School, and a college which has since become Christian Brothers University.

When ill health forced his resignation in 1982, Bishop Dozier was succeeded by Bishop J. Francis Stafford, who had served a number of years as Auxiliary Bishop of the Archdiocese of Baltimore. With his administrative skills and winning personality, he quickly revised the structure of the Pastoral Office and improved the fiscal health of the diocese. However, Bishop Stafford served only a short time in Memphis. He was appointed Archbishop of Denver in 1986 and was subsequently called to Rome by Pope John Paul II and appointed a Cardinal.

Monsignor Paul J. Morris served several months as Diocesan Administrator, after which Most Reverend Daniel M. Buechlein assumed the title of Bishop, becoming the first Bishop of Memphis to be installed at ceremonies at the Cathedral. He came to Memphis from St. Meinrad Seminary and brought great faith and tremendous planning and fund raising skills to his new assignment. When Bishop Buechlein left the diocese in 1992 to become Archbishop of Indianapolis, the diocese was in good financial and strategic shape.

Bishop J. Terry Steib, SVD, the current Bishop of Memphis, is the inspiration for a vision that established the Jubilee schools, a group of Catholic schools in urban neighborhoods designed to provide an education for disadvantaged children. The Diocese has grown under Bishop Steib's direction. Along with a growth in the number of new churches and other buildings, Bishop Steib is responsible for overseeing the construction of a home for retired priests that was completed in 2004, and a retreat center for all the people of the diocese, which was opened in 2005.

Currently there are twenty-nine parishes in the Memphis Deanery, and fourteen parishes and five missions in the Jackson Deanery. The Memphis Diocese has a total of 28 schools, including seven Jubilee schools, with a total of more than 8,000 students. There are more than 65,000 Catholics in the diocese served by more than 80 priests, 135 religious sisters, 24 brothers, and 55 deacons.

❖

The Cathedral of the Immaculate Conception, Memphis.

HVAC Sales & Supply Co., Inc.

In 1982 Memphis native William D. Bomar was a partner in a successful contracting business when he decided to start HVAC Sales & Supply Co., Inc. Another Memphis native, Dale C. Smith, was the first hire, and the two men started the business with confidence, determination, and a taste for hard work.

The company began operations as a small wholesaler of duct pipe and fittings. At first, HVAC Sales & Supply Co., Inc. operated out of an aged abandoned metal building on Old Summer Road. For the first few years, Bomar and Smith worked many sixteen hour days as the business grew.

Now in its twenty-fifth year of operation, HVAC Sales and Supply Co., Inc. takes pride in delivering the highest quality and best value to its customers. "This commitment goes all the way back to our roots," says Bomar. "It is our history, as well as our future."

Today, the firm is a leading wholesale distributor of heating and air conditioning parts, equipment and supplies for the Mid-South region of Tennessee, Mississippi, Arkansas, and Missouri. The staff has grown from the original two men to fifty highly trained employees.

The business philosophy at HVAC Sales & Supply Co., Inc. is simple, yet effective, and its marketing strategy is essentially the same today as it was in 1982—offer quality products at competitive prices with unparalleled service. HVAC has always been a "people business" focused on building and strengthening mutually beneficial long-term relationships with its customers.

HVAC Sales & Supply Co., Inc. currently operates six warehouses in Tennessee, Arkansas, and Mississippi. The corporate office and central distribution center is located in Memphis.

The company operates a large fleet of delivery trucks, equipped with GPS tracking, assuring that customers always have what they need, when they need it.

HVAC Sales & Supply Co., Inc. has always been on the cutting edge of the latest business technology and was the first wholesaler in its market area to offer real-time inventory control and order entry via computers. With the increasing awareness of 'total indoor air quality' and ever-changing governmental standards, HVAC is spearheading efforts to offer its

contractor customers the most advanced products available. HVAC's role is changing from 'supplier' to a 'business partner' offering training that ranges from technical service analysis to business administration to marketing.

The founder of HVAC Sales & Supply Co., Inc. William D. Bomar, serves as president of the firm and was a finalist in the *Memphis Business Journal*'s "Small Business Executive of the Year" in 2001. Dale C. Smith serves as vice president. Kevin DeBord, a West Virginia native who moved to Memphis in 1993, is the firm's sales and marketing manager. Bomar was one of five finalists for the *Memphis Business Journal*'s Small Business Executive of the Year award in 2001.

For additional information on HVAC Sales & Supply Co., Inc., visit them on the Internet at www.hvacsalesandsupply.com.

LESS, GETZ & LIPMAN

Less, Getz & Lipman was established in 1980 as a construction, fidelity, and surety law firm. Since its inception, the firm has offered owners, contractors, architects, engineers, sureties, and insurers quality legal services in connection with their projects. This representation includes drafting and negotiation of design and construction agreements and the representation of clients in complex disputes through trial and appellate litigation and alternative dispute resolution procedures.

The founder and senior partner of Less, Getz & Lipman is Michael I. Less. Partners include Joseph T. Getz, Clifton M. Lipman, Christopher M. Caputo, Elizabeth B. Stengel, and John D. Willet.

- Less received his B.A. degree from the University of Missouri and his J.D. degree from the University of Memphis. He is a fellow of the American College of Construction Lawyers and a founder and past president of the Tennessee Association of Construction Counsel. His numerous publications include *Place Your Bets—Your Insurance—on a Casino Construction Project* for the American Bar Association, *Law of Payment Bonds,* and *Improving the Odds for a Well Managed Project* for the Gaming Lawyer publication.

- Getz received his B.B.A. degree from the University of Mississippi and his J.D. degree from the University of Memphis. Getz is a member of the American Bar Association Forum Committee on Construction, Fidelity and Surety Law Committee, and a founder and board member of the Tennessee Association of Construction Counsel. Getz has written and lectured on construction law topics to numerous national groups. His written publications include *Pyramids and Privity*, a Discussion of the Miller Act for the Defense Research Institute; and *Advanced Construction Law in Tennessee* for the National Business Institute. Getz has also co-authored *Handling Fidelity & Surety Claims*, Wiley Publications; *Building and Construction Agreements*, West Publication; and *Construction Law Handbook*, Aspen Publications.

- Lipman received his B.B.A., M.B.A., and J.D. degrees from the University of Memphis. Lipman is a former adjunct professor of law at the University of Memphis Herff School of Engineering. He is a member of the Memphis and American Bar Associations and also belongs to the Construction Specifications Institute and the American Subcontractors Association.

- Caputo received his B.A. degree from Colgate University and his J.D. degree from the University of Miami School of Law. A member of the Tennessee, Rhode Island, Massachusetts, and American Bar Associations, Caputo has authored several construction related publications and lectured extensively on construction related topics.

- Stengel received her B.A. degree from the University of Tennessee and her J.D. degree from the University of Memphis. She is a member of the Memphis, Tennessee, and American Bar Associations, the Tennessee Trial Lawyers Association, and the Tennessee Association of Construction Counsel.

- Willet received a B.S. degree from the University of Southern Mississippi and a J.D. degree from the University of Memphis. He is a member of the Tennessee Association of Construction Counsel and American Bar Association and serves on the Technology Committee of the American Bar Association's Forum on the Construction Industry.

Less, Getz & Lipman is located at 100 Peabody Place, Suite 1150, in Memphis, Tennessee and on the Internet at www.lgllaw.com.

Shelby Electric Co., Inc. began in 1919 as a small motor repair shop operated by Thomas Kramer. The young firm prospered and soon outgrew its original location on Union Avenue and moved to larger facilities at 390 South Main Street.

The company again outgrew its location and, in 1930, relocated to its present headquarters on E.H. Crump Boulevard. Meanwhile, a fully-staffed Construction Department was organized to serve the firm's steadily growing customer base.

Shelby Electric has been known as 'Electricians for the South' for nearly ninety years, but the slogan is only part of the Shelby Electric story.

As an electrical contractor, Shelby Electric has been an integral part of the growth of new business and industry in the Memphis/Shelby County area. The firm has taken a strong supporting role in servicing customers throughout the region through its Construction Department, Sales Department, and Motor Shop, and as a distributor of electrical and industrial supplies.

The Sales Department represents nationally known lines of power transmission equipment. The department has expanded into various other mechanical lines not commonly associated with the electrical industry such as hoists, rubber goods, and tools.

The Parts Department maintains a complete stock of replacement parts so that costly breakdowns are minimized. Customers can rely on Shelby Electric's parts inventory to help maintain equipment at peak performance long after installation.

All types of motors are rewound in the Motor Repair Shop. The shop specializes in DC Motors and in rebuilding heavy motors and repair services for industrial installations. Emergency standby equipment is often rushed to the site while on-the-job repairs are completed.

Much of the growth of Shelby Electric can be attributed to the skill and loyalty of its many key employees. Many of the companies employees have devoted their entire business careers to the company, and their experience and 'know-how' are a vital part of the firm's success.

Shelby Electric has been associated with a wide range of major projects throughout the South. Some of these installations include the Psychiatric and Research Hospital in Memphis, the main office of Memphis Light, Gas, and Water Division, the Naval Air Station in Millington, the Research Tower at St. Jude Hospital, the North Memphis Wastewater Treatment Plant, the new intermodal facility for Canadian National Railroad, and lighting for the I-240 and I-55 Expressway in Memphis.

Furthermore, the company is poised to expand its horizons and continue its growth in the Tri-State region by participating in new technology projects, such as the Memphis Smartway System for the Department of Homeland Security. With its eighty-seven years of local history, Shelby Electric is proud to continue its presence as a leading force in the region's construction industry.

SHELBY ELECTRIC CO., INC.

❖

Above: Originally located on Union Avenue and later on South Main Street, Shelby Electric expanded its services and moved to its present location at 96-118 East E.H. Crump Boulevard in 1930. Today, Shelby Electric offers electrical contracting, commercial and industrial sales, electrical motor and apparatus repairs, and crane and hoist services. Serving the industry since 1919.

Below: Shelby Electric's current owners include (from left to right): Treasurer Bob Hunolt, Secretary Pat Walkup, President Al Quarin, and Vice President Ken Stevens.

FIRST TENNESSEE BANK

It was March 1864 and Memphis was struggling through the Civil War. After two years of strict military control by federal troops, development in the city had come to a halt. A once proud and prosperous city was now dormant.

Despite the hard times, business leader Frank S. Davis recognized the many advantages offered by a system of national banks, which had been authorized by Congress in 1863. Davis called a meeting of those favoring the organization of a national bank and on March 10, 1864, the First National Bank of Memphis was formed. Davis was elected president, a position he would hold for eighteen years.

First National, which grew into today's First Tennessee Bank, opened for business in one room of a building on North Court Street.

Memphis was in economic ruin following the Civil War, and First National Bank played a major role in rebuilding the city.

The bank grew along with Memphis and, in 1913, following passage of the Federal Reserve Act, First National was one of five banks involved in incorporation of the Federal Reserve Bank of St. Louis, of which the Federal Reserve Bank of Memphis is a branch.

As Memphis continued to grow, First National opened its first suburban branch, the Crosstown Branch, in 1942 with a staff of two officers and fifteen employees. Although growth slowed during World War II, First National operated seven branches by 1952.

A need for additional space became a priority as the bank approached its one hundredth anniversary. In 1961, plans were announced for construction of a twenty-three-story bank and office building on Madison Avenue at Third Street. First National moved into the new facility in 1964, and it remains First Tennessee's headquarters to this day.

By 1967, First National had become the largest bank in the Mid-South and, in 1969, First National Holding Company was organized. The holding company paved the way for acquisition of banks throughout the state and, eventually, national expansion.

The company opened its inaugural First Horizon Bank in Northern Virginia in 2003 and then expanded into Georgia and Texas. Meanwhile, the company's capital markets division, FTN Financial, expanded to become one of the nation's top underwriters of U.S. government agency securities.

During the 1990s the corporation also began to develop a national mortgage division that now operates in more than forty states under the name First Horizon Home Loans.

In 2004 the name of the parent company was changed to First Horizon National Corporation, and today First Horizon is one of the thirty largest banking companies in the United States. First Horizon companies have been recognized for being among the nation's best employers by *AARP, Working Mother* and *Fortune* magazines. First Horizon was also named one of the nation's 100 Best Corporate Citizens by *Business Ethics* magazine.

❖

Above: The First Tennessee Bank building in the late 1880s.

Below: The headquarters of First Tennessee Bank.

Trezevant is a unique Lifecare retirement community that has been dedicated to enriching the lives of seniors for thirty years. In 1973, Edward H. Little gave a $1-million gift to The Reverend Brinkley Morton, then rector of Grace-St. Luke's Episcopal Church, asking that a senior living community be built and named in honor of his late wife, Suzanne Trezevant Little. Trezevant is a not-for-profit community governed by a board of directors dedicated to upholding the valued and timeless principles of its founders.

Located in the heart of Memphis, Trezevant is a gated community situated on a campus surrounded by beautiful gardens and trees. Residential apartments in Trezevant Manor and Trezevant Place, as well as Garden Homes, are offered to active seniors. Assisted care in Trezevant Terrace and nursing care in Allen Morgan Health Center are available to residents needing healthcare.

The assisted living program includes support with daily activities, twenty-four hour staff on duty, medication supervision, three nutritious meals a day, an emergency call-response system, and group activities. Allen Morgan Health Center offers intermediate and skilled nursing care, physical and occupational therapy, memory support care, special diets, and recreational and social activities.

Life at Trezevant can be as active as our residents choose. A wide range of activities is offered to satisfy an array of interests suited to their lifestyles. All activities at Trezevant are devoted to enhancing wellness, socialization, culture and spirit. Planned cultural programs, trips, exercise highlight residential activity and fitness programs as well as spiritual and religious programs. Although our residents may be retired, they are far from retiring. Residents may

TREZEVANT MANOR

volunteer their time to participate on various resident committees as well as taking part in two of our biggest fundraisers: the annual fashion show and the Trash and Treasure Sale. All proceeds from both events are donated to the Trezevant Manor Foundation.

Trezevant is the only retirement community in the Mid-South area accredited by the Continuing Care Accreditation Commission. Accredited communities must meet standards of distinction in three areas: governance and administration, financial resources and disclosure and resident life, and health and wellness. Official recognition is based on the premise that certification promotes and maintains quality and integrity in the retirement industry. Trezevant maintains this outstanding reputation because of its well-recognized emphasis on quality healthcare for all residents.

Trezevant Manor is located at 177 North Highland Street in Memphis, Tennessee and on the Internet at www.trezevantmanor.org.

MEMORIAL PARK FUNERAL HOME AND CEMETERY

Most people wouldn't put a cemetery on their itinerary when planning a vacation. But each year more than 100,000 people visit Memorial Park Funeral Home and Cemetery in Memphis to view one of the most beautiful and architecturally significant cemeteries in the world.

The cemetery, in fact, has been listed on the *National Register of Historic Places* since 1991, thanks to the foresight of Memorial Park's founder and the artist he hired to create a truly unique environment.

E. Clovis Hinds started Memorial Park in 1924 after selling his Cotton States Life Insurance Company. The North Mississippi merchant and cotton factor moved to Memphis in 1916, had founded the life insurance company. He sold his business and began creating what he called "a perpetual garden of promise" that became Memorial Park Funeral Home and Cemetery.

Hinds, influenced by Hubert Eaton of California's Forest Lawn Cemetery, employed engineers and landscape architects to create a park on the gently rolling terrain that was both beautiful and unique. Hinds also commissioned Mexico City artist Dionicio Rodriguez to give it the distinctive qualities that have made it both a national treasure and a popular tourist attraction.

Rodriguez used Arkansas fieldstone, semiprecious stones, and concrete to create realistic replicas of rustic scenes, legendary sites, and Biblical shrines. Opened in 1925, Memorial Park includes such sights as the Sunken Garden, the Covered Bridge, the Wishing Well, Annie Laurie's Chair, and the Fountain of Youth.

Biblical replicas include the Pool of Hebron, Abraham's Oak, God's Garden, and the Cave of Machpelah (Abraham's Tomb). Visitors marvel at the Crystal Shrine Grotto featuring ten scenes from the life of Christ. All these creations are set amid thousands of flowering annuals, shrubs, and trees.

Hinds, who died in 1949, left his creation in the capable hands of family members devoted to carrying on his legacy. In 1974 the family dedicated a large hillside mausoleum and began offering crypts and crematory services. Katherine Hinds Smythe, who was elected president in 1976, built the park's own funeral home and flower shop to provide total interment services.

The company expanded its business in 1983 when it purchased Treadwell-Norris Funeral Chapel and Cosmopolitan Funeral Home. The company also opened the 126-acre Memorial Park South Woods at 5485 Hacks Cross Road, southeast of Memphis, and employed the same character and quality as the original site.

Memorial Park continues to adhere to its founder's principles by creating beautiful sites that combine nature's beauty with the best buildings that architect and builder can create. The atmosphere, services, and attitude found at Memorial Park Funeral Home and Cemetery continue to make it the preferred choice among Memphis residents seeking a final resting place for those they love.

Methods of road and railroad grading probably did not change much during the nineteenth century. Men and mules working in the Raleigh area about 1910 are removing stumps from the right of way for what would ultimately become Highway 51.

COURTESY OF MEMPHIS & SHELBY COUNTY ROOM, MEMPHIS PUBLIC LIBRARY & INFORMATION CENTER.

HYMAN BUILDERS SUPPLY, INC.

Hyman Builders Supply, Inc. represents a heritage that dates from the company's founding in 1896, when it was known as Jordan Lumber Company. The 10,000 square foot store is located on a four-and-a-half acre lumberyard at 40 West McLemore in Memphis.

Hyman Builders Supply specializes in lumber and building material, selling everything needed to build or remodel a house. The customer base includes roofing contractors, general contractors, remodelers, and intercity builders. The company has enjoyed an excellent relationship with residents of the intercity communities for many years.

Billy Z. Hyman, president and majority stockholder of Hyman Builders Supply, Inc., has been with Hyman Builders Supply for more than fifty-seven years. In addition, he served as a member of Memphis City Council for twenty years.

Hyman began supervising home construction in 1956, overseeing the building of a house on Trigg Avenue, east of Mississippi Boulevard. He has been active in home building in Arkansas, Mississippi, Missouri, and Tennessee for nearly half-a-century. His specialty has been low to moderate income affordable housing.

Hyman Homes, Inc. was established in 1971 and since that time has completed a wide range of homes in all price ranges. The majority of the firm's work is in the low to moderate income, affordable, first-time homebuyers market.

In the last decade, Hyman has concentrated on land development ventures. These include a house subdivision in Phillips County, Arkansas; Turrell Heights in Crittenden Country, Arkansas; Central City in Henderson, Tennessee; Magnolia Heights, Olive Ridge Subdivision, Bell Ridge subdivision, and Braybourne subdivision in Desoto County, Mississippi; and Bayou Vista in Marion, Arkansas. Hyman has also built out several distressed or abandoned subdivisions for mortgage companies and banks.

In the intercity of Memphis, Hyman has completed the subdivisions of Wilbert Heights and Gracewood, and the Graves Village project. He recently completed College Park Phase I and is currently working on College Park Phase II and Uptown Village subdivision.

The management team at Hyman Homes has nearly 120 years of combined experience in the construction business, led by Billy Hyman's more than fifty years. R. Dean Tutor, Sr., president of Hyman Homes, came into the construction business in the early 1960s.

In the last seventeen years, Hyman Homes has built more than 450 houses with sales in excess of $26 million. Eighty-five percent of the homes are classified as low and moderate income affordable housing.

Hyman Homes is a member of the Memphis Area Home Builders Association, which offers a warranty program the firm offers to its buyers. Hyman Homes has been honored as a thermal-crafted builder by Owens Corning, and has been awarded by TVA and Memphis Light, Gas, and Water for its Energy Efficient Homes programs. The firm is a builder in good standing in the EcoBuild program sponsored by Memphis Light, Gas and Water.

COLEMAN TAYLOR TRANSMISSIONS

In 1961, Larry Coleman and his brother-in-law, Bill Taylor, opened a transmission shop in Memphis and established a tradition of quality that continues today.

Coleman, president of Coleman Taylor Transmissions, completed two years of Engineering at Christian Brothers College and began his career in the transmission industry when he went to work for a transmission shop in Memphis. His experience there motivated him to open his own business. "I thought that if someone could do this job honestly, they could make a good living at it," he says.

Originally, Torque Converters, Inc. (TCI) was part of Coleman Taylor, but in an amicable transaction, Coleman bought out Taylor's interest in the transmission business in 1969 and his brother-in-law kept TCI.

In the forty-five years since, Coleman Taylor has grown to fifteen retail centers in fives cities and three remanufacturing centers. Larry's son, Nick, worked his way up the ranks and is now the vice president of the company, which builds about 25,000 to 30,000 transmissions a year.

In addition, the firm markets specialty products under the Life Automotive Products name. Life Automotive Products division of Coleman Taylor is under the direction of Larry's son, Marty. Life Automotive offers a line of lubricants, flushers, cleaners, and additives for transmissions to be rebuilt.

Coleman Taylor's roots were in racing, with both founders owning drag racing cars. In 1986, Alan Kulwicki won Rookie of the Year honors on the NASCAR Winston Cup circuit driving the Coleman Taylor owned T-Bird at Daytona, Talladega, Charlotte, and Atlanta.

Coleman Taylor has always focused on excellent customer relations and is one of the few companies to offer a maximum up-front price after diagnosis and with no obligation whatsoever. It was the first to offer a twelve-month warranty, and today's Coleman Taylor warranties range from 24 to 36 months or up to 100,000 miles.

Coleman Taylor's policy is to hire employees without experience and train them from the ground up, making managers eventual partners. The company has 150 employees, and one-third of them have been with the company more than fifteen years.

In the early nineties, Coleman Taylor was selected by SASCO, a prominent Mid-East operation, to establish a turnkey transmission plant in Saudi Arabia. This helped expand the SASCO auto parts division, which had large facilities throughout the kingdom.

A major reason for Coleman Taylor's sustained growth through the years may well be in the company motto, which was instituted from the very first: Whatever It Takes for Customer Satisfaction. "Always give more than you promise," says Coleman. "If you do that, customers have nothing more to ask for."

Shelby Residential and Vocational Services (SRVS) began with a simple goal: a sheltered work environment where very special people could earn a competitive wage and become more independent. It was an idea for which a group of parents sacrificed their time and energy to bring to fruition. It was a dream that became reality through love and determination.

Established in 1962, SRVS has provided programs, services and support to people with developmental disabilities. SOS Industries, Inc., the agency's oldest program, introduced basic job skills training to eight adults that year. In the early 1970s, the Mid-South Association for Retarded Children (MARC), started residential services and a day center. In 1983, SOS Industries and MARC merged to form SRVS.

The chairman of the fundraising effort for SOS Industries in 1962 was attorney and civic leader Charles M. Crump. Other prominent Memphians involved from the onset included Persia Buck Williams, city chairman of the Memphis Shelby County Council for the Aid of Retarded Children; W. S. Easterling, campaign committee chairman; Colonel Hugh Richbourg, a member of the committee and the first Director of SOS; and William Brammer, chairman of the Council of Aid for Retarded Children. Mrs. Kemmons Wilson was volunteer coordinator for the initial fundraiser when parents canvassed door-to-door to raise funds for the new facility. Many of those involved in the initial startup of SOS have remained with SRVS over the years and have helped steer the organization through its developmental stages.

Since 1962, SRVS has grown to be the largest and most comprehensive service provider in West Tennessee, supporting more than 800 individuals. SRVS' programs include residential services, a day center, SOS Industries, employment services, a family support program, community activities, and a personal assistance program. Ancillary services include nursing, behavior supports and therapy.

As a nonprofit United Way member agency serving people with developmental disabilities, SRVS works daily to support people who need assistance and help in becoming more self-reliant. Through SOS, more than 180 individuals are employed. SRVS also helped find jobs in the community for fifty-four individuals who work at Pizza Hut, McDonald's, Wal-Mart and other companies, and fourteen who are employed through the Mobile Work Crew and Enclaves programs.

The agency's residential services consist of five community living departments. Together these departments provide direct support professionals to assist 142 individuals in supported living homes, 30 individuals in group homes, and 48 individuals in eight Intermediate Care Facilities. SRVS' Personal Assistance service is a growing area in the Community Living IV Department. Currently, eighteen individuals utilize this service in their family homes.

In addition, more than seventy families are able to keep their loved ones at home through activities offered by the Kramer Activity Center. This day center features a classroom environment focusing on teaching social skills, self-care skills, and prevocational training. The organization's newest service, the Ambassadors Club, supports individuals who desire to do community and volunteer work.

The Family Support Program provides funds for 350-400 families per year to maintain the care of their loved ones at home by helping them with home and vehicle modifications, supplies, respite care, and other needed items not covered by insurance.

SRVS' mission is a commitment to excellence in providing options and opportunities to people with developmental disabilities. Throughout its history, SRVS has remained steadfast in its dedication to helping the agency's individuals lead meaningful and productive lives.

SHELBY RESIDENTIAL AND VOCATIONAL SERVICES INCORPORATED

MCLEMORE MARKETS

McLemore Markets have served the Memphis/Shelby County area for more than sixty years, beginning during the Christmas season of 1945 when W. F. and Colleen McLemore opened their first grocery on Lamar Avenue in Memphis. Family members recall that Colleen sold her sewing machine to purchase merchandise for the first store.

During its early years, W. F. and Colleen operated the store with the help of two sons, Billy and Gerald. The McLemores, who grew up on farms near Corinth, Mississippi, were also involved in farming and raising cattle during this period.

The McLemore's two other sons, Shannon and Dennis, worked in the family business after college but later decided to pursue careers in travel and farming. Gerald, meanwhile, retired.

After graduating from the University of Tennessee in 1960, Billy returned to Memphis to assist his father with an expansion program that included twenty-one stores at one time. Billy, a civil engineering major with a contractor's license, drew the plans for the new stores and supervised their construction. He also participated fully in the operational side of the business, assisted by his wife, Jackie. Their daughter, Dana, and son, Todd, are also involved in the family business, while another son, David, was involved before going into business on his own.

McLemore Markets provide gas pumps, a full-service Deli, and fresh produce, as well as a complete line of basic grocery items. The markets are open 6:00 am to midnight, 365 days a year.

In an interview with *Convenience Store News*, Billy noted that, "We want to make McLemores an alternative to going to the huge supermarket, without forcing customers out of our store with high prices. We want to be easy to shop, with everything a customer would want."

Although the emphasis remains on groceries, food service has become a more important part of the business in recent years. About seventeen percent of inside sales are attributed to food service, with 400 to 500 square feet, including a seating area devoted to fast food. The menu includes deli sandwiches and salads, hot entrees, fried fish, and whole meals.

Billy's contributions to the grocery industry were recognized with the Spirit of America award from the National Grocers Association. The award is presented to those who have shown outstanding effort in promoting the grocery industry and improving government relations.

The McLemores are strongly committed to giving back to the community and have sponsored a number of Little League sports teams, both male and female. In addition, Billy is an active member of the Tennessee Grocers Association and the University of Tennessee Alumni Association.

✧

Above: W. F. and Colleen McLemore.

Below: Billy M. McLemore.

MORGAN KEEGAN & COMPANY, INC.

Morgan Keegan & Company, Inc. is the securities brokerage and asset management arm of Regions Financial Corporation.

Morgan Keegan was founded in 1969 when Allen Morgan opened the first locally based investment firm in Memphis. With $500,000 in equity capital, Morgan, Jim Keegan, Joe Weller, and Robert Gooch, Jr., launched Morgan Keegan as a securities research boutique that focused on identifying investment opportunities with companies based in the South.

In 1970, Morgan Keegan became the first Memphis firm to purchase a seat on the New York Stock Exchange. Over the next two decades, the firm would develop the largest fixed income capital markets operations outside of Wall Street, and one of the country's most widely respected equity research departments by providing coverage of Southern companies like Wal-Mart, AutoZone, and FedEx.

In 1983, Allen Morgan's vision led Morgan Keegan to list its own stock on the NYSE. After eighteen years of continued growth and success as a public company, Morgan Keegan was acquired by Regions Financial Corporation in 2001 and today has 3,500 employees, including more than a 1,000 in the Memphis community. Headquartered in the Morgan Keegan Tower in downtown Memphis, Morgan Keegan is the twenty-fourth largest full-service brokerage firm in the nation, with over 1,100 licensed financial advisors. The firm operates more than 300 branch offices in 18 states throughout the South, Midwest, and Texas.

As a full-service regional investment firm, Morgan Keegan serves the diverse financial needs of individual investors through its Private Client Group division and institutional clients throughout the United States and abroad. After nearly four decades in business, Morgan Keegan is recognized as a leader in the financial services industry with a list of acknowledgments and achievements to its credit:

- The firm's Fixed Income Capital Markets Division was ranked the eleventh largest senior manager of competitive long-term municipal bond issues in the nation in 2005, underwriting more than $8.8 billion.
- The Fixed Income Division has been ranked the number one municipal underwriter in the South Central U.S. (Alabama, Arkansas, Kentucky, Louisiana, Mississippi, and Tennessee) for thirteen consecutive years.
- Morgan Keegan's Equity Capital Markets Division has underwritten $38 billion in 331 equity-related securities since 1991.
- The *Wall Street Journal* and Forbes.com have honored our equity research analysts for their stock picking ability and accuracy of earnings estimates.
- Regions Morgan Keegan Trust manages assets of $37 billion. Morgan Asset Management, the investment advisory arm, manages $6.6 billion in the Regions Morgan Keegan Select Fund mutual fund family.
- Regions Morgan Keegan Timberland Group manages over 1.2 million acres in 14 states.

Morgan Keegan has been profitable for thirty-five consecutive years and, in 2005, reported its fourth consecutive year of record revenues and earnings. Annual revenues for the year were $810 million, with earnings of $102 million. The firm's equity capital stands at more than $600 million.

Morgan Keegan is an established leader in the financial services industry. Guiding the firm's direction in the future will be our mission to advance the financial interests of our clients through sound financial advice, comprehensive and timely research, and responsive service.

✧

Above: Morgan Keegan founder Allen Morgan (seated) meets with the firm's executive committee in 1970.
COURTESY OF MORGAN KEEGAN & COMPANY, INC.

Below: Allen Morgan (center) rings the closing bell at the New York Stock Exchange with a team of Morgan Keegan financial advisors.
COURTESY OF MORGAN KEEGAN & COMPANY, INC.

MEMPHIS AREA ASSOCIATION OF REALTORS®

The Memphis Area Association of REALTORS® (MAAR) was founded in 1910 as the Memphis Real Estate Association through the efforts of seven individuals with the mission to get a mandatory licensing law passed in Tennessee. Several months later, the Association was asked to join the National Association of Real Estate Boards (now known as the National Association of REALTORS®), founded in 1908 in response to the rapidly growing speculation, exploitation, and disorder in the real estate industry.

The Memphis association's first offices were located in the Business Men's Club, and four subsequent moves preceded MAAR's settling into its current location in 1979 at 6393 Poplar Avenue. Over the years it also underwent a number of name changes until it acquired its current name in 1992. Since its beginnings in 1910, MAAR has realized many significant accomplishments on behalf of its members and the real estate consumer. Some of these include:

• The Multiple Listing Service (MLS), an information-sharing and cooperative marketing network to foster the purchase and sale of real estate and establish means for participants to make unilateral offers of compensation to other participants for effecting real estate transactions, was started in 1954. Originally an exchange of paper with listing information and photos, the MLS is now computer-based to give property maximum marketing exposure to all members and the public through the REALTOR.com website.

• The REALTORS® Political Action Committee, established in 1969, is the sole grassroots and issues mobilizing force protecting and promoting private property rights. In Tennessee, MAAR has been instrumental in advocating for the passage of key legislation, including an anti-predatory lending law enacted in 2006.

• The MAAR Commercial Council was created in 2003 to unite those in all commercial real estate fields for the betterment of the industry, to provide a property information database of commercial properties and to monitor legislative and public policy issues of interest to the industry.

• Developed jointly with the City of Memphis, "Welcome Home Memphis" was introduced in 2006 to identify, develop, advocate and promote homeownership assistance programs available for low- to moderate-income families.

• Offering a variety of real estate courses and seminars every year, MAAR has been a strong advocate for the professional designations and continuing education that help REALTORS® stay current in a changing marketplace and achieve greater success in their business.

Today MAAR is the Mid-South's largest real estate trade association serving approximately 5,000 members and working to ensure that every REALTOR® is highly skilled and ethical in the delivery of service to all real estate consumers. To learn more, visit www.maar.org.

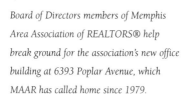

✧

Board of Directors members of Memphis Area Association of REALTORS® help break ground for the association's new office building at 6393 Poplar Avenue, which MAAR has called home since 1979.

Bill Morat Insurance Services is a story of community involvement, building a business, and raising a family. It is also the story of a couple of high school sweethearts who have been married fifty-five years, as of August 2005.

William Robert "Bill" Morat was born in Memphis in December 1928. He graduated from Messick High School in 1947 and was voted by his classmates as "Most Likely to Succeed." He also served as president of his Speech Class, earned All-Memphis in football, was the Outstanding Third Year ROTC Cadet, and Outstanding Debater.

Jeanette "Jan" Baker moved to Memphis and began school at Messick in the seventh grade. She was a member of Sigma sorority.

Following graduation, Bill and Jan attended Memphis State, where she became a member of Alpha Gamma Delta sorority. Bill graduated with a B.A. degree in business with an accounting major and went to work selling life and hospital insurance.

The couple was engaged in 1949 and married in 1950. Their first son, William R. Morat, Jr., was born in October 1951. A second son, Michael T., was born in August 1953, and a daughter, Jan Marie, was born in September 1956.

In 1960, Bill left his original job and began selling additional coverage of auto, homeowners, and group insurance. He incorporated his own firm in 1965.

Bill joined the Memphis Jaycees in 1952 and was elected president in 1957. Meanwhile, Jan was appointed by Mayor Henry Loeb to serve on Memphis City Beautiful as Christmas Lighting Chairman. In 1957, the family joined Kingsway Christian Church (Disciples of Christ). Jan has been a choir member and soloist for at Kingsway for thirty years. Bill has served as Deacon, Elder, and Treasurer and as Sunday School teacher.

The Jaycees selected Bill as Memphis' Outstanding Young Man in 1962. He entered politics and ran for State Senate on the Republican ticket. In 1992, he joined the Napoleonic Society of America and was elected to the National Board of Directors for six years.

Jan has been hostess of the Christmas party for the Memphis Oral School for the Deaf for twenty-five years, rising money for toys, party favors and everything that goes into a children's party. In 2001, Jan and Bill started the Morat Foundation and contributed funds to the school for equipment to test the Cochlear Implant for hearing aides.

The Morats' children are now grown and have raised their own children, and all three have worked for the insurance agency as licensed agents. The agency represents more than fifteen companies, has more than 3,000 customers and does approximately $4 million in annual premium volume.

Because of their children, Jan and Bill have been able to enjoy life and its advantages. The Morats have two mottos: "Do it right the first time" and remember "God's gift to us is our mortal life; what we do with it is our gift to God."

BILL MORAT
INSURANCE
SERVICES, INC.

❖

Bill and Jan Morat.

REGIONS BANK

The history of Regions Bank dates from 1856 when the First National Bank of Huntsville, Alabama was chartered. In 1971, First National united with two other venerable Alabama banks, First National of Montgomery and Exchange Security Bank of Birmingham to form a multi-bank holding company, First Alabama Bancshares.

By 1994, First Alabama Bancshares had expanded to cover seven states and a more appropriate name, Regions Bank, was adopted.

Meanwhile, Union Planters National Bank of Memphis was on a growth course of its own. Union Planters was founded in 1869 when the DeSoto Insurance Company was converted to a bank. By 1929 the bank had received a national banking charter in the name of Union Planters National Bank and Trust Company.

The bank qualified for federal deposit insurance in 1935, and, by the mid-1940s, the Union Planters National Bank of Memphis was the largest bank in Tennessee and one of the Top 100 in the United States.

Regions Bank merged with Memphis-based Union Planters in 2004 and, today, Regions provides banking services to more than five million customers in sixteen states across the South, Midwest, and Texas. Regions is one of the Top 15 financial service providers in the nation, with $85.3 billion in assets. The bank operates 1,400 offices and a 1,600 ATM network.

Locally, Regions Bank in Greater Memphis covers Shelby, DeSoto, and Crittenden Counties, including fifty branches and 140 ATMs. The bank's customer base is a mixture of commercial and small business clients and retail households across the Mid-South Area. And, the corporate offices for Morgan Keegan, Regions Insurance Group, and Regions Mortgage are also based in Memphis, Tennessee.

"Our strong partnerships with Morgan Keegan, Regions Insurance Group, and Regions Mortgage means our customers benefit from the diverse set of products and services we can offer them from across our banking, mortgage, brokerage, trust, investment banking, and insurance units," says Curt Gabardi, Regions president in Memphis-West Tennessee Region.

Throughout the company's growth, Regions Bank has made customer service and community focus its top priority. The bank's stated mission is to help its customers and communities by anticipating, understanding, and meeting their financial needs through responsive associates who have the ability to provide effective solutions.

For Gabardi, the entire package of service and product offerings is really about "doing the right thing." He cites the bank's response in helping its employees who were disrupted by 2005's Hurricane Katrina as a prime example. The company provided the food, water and financial resources they needed to get back on their feet and back to work. The bank also worked with customers who were impacted by the hurricane, providing them with loan extensions and fee waivers.

"It's all about doing the right thing for our customers," adds Gabardi. "The right thing, done the right way, and at the right time, leads not only to lasting prosperity but to pride in your work, to peace of mind, and the ability to sleep well each night."

✦

President Curt Gabardi, Memphis West Tennessee Region.

From the Chucalissa Indian Village to Graceland, Memphis and Shelby County are rich in history. The responsibility for preserving and marking these priceless treasures lies with the Shelby County Historical Commission, which works on behalf of historical awareness, preservation, and history.

Few places in the nation can boast a history as storied as Memphis and Shelby County. The explorer Hernando de Soto discovered the area in 1541, the French arrived in 1739 and built Fort Assumption, and the British took control of the bluffs following the French and Indian War. The four-block wide city of Memphis, population fifty, was founded in 1819.

Memphis grew rapidly and became the cotton capital of the world. Today, Memphis is home to the world's busiest cargo airport in terms of tonnage, still leads the world's cotton market, and has become a leading manufacturing center for textiles.

The Shelby County Historical Commission helps preserve and recognize this long history by reviewing and approving requests for historical markers and maintaining a reference book on all historical markers in the county. The Commission recognizes area historical authors and literary works, directs media and public attention to historic preservation issues, and awards area high school and college historical scholars.

In addition, the Commission participates in historical commemorative events and provides knowledgeable speakers for community organizations.

The Shelby County Historical Society is comprised of a thirty-member board appointed by the county mayor. Current members of the Commission include: Nancy Bassett, Dr. Beverly Bond (treasurer), Mariessa Bridges, Dr. Marius Carriere, Jr., Dr. Charles Crawford, Dr. Doug Cupples (secretary), Alan Doyle, Robert Dye, Ed Frank, Dr. John E. Harkins, Elizabeth P. Hughes (county genealogist), Fred D. Johnson, Bill Kelsey, Earnest E Lacey, Sylvester Louis, Perre Magness, Lee Millar (chairman), Mary Louise Nazor, Faye Osteen, Andy Pouncey, Clarene Russell (vice chairman), Dr. Janann Sherman, Martha Tibbs, Greg Todd, Elaine Lee Turner, Ed Williams, III (county historian), Walter D. Wills, III, Dr. Cathy Wilson, and A. Sid Witherington.

SHELBY COUNTY HISTORICAL COMMISSION

❖

Right: The latest historical marker erected by the Commission.

Below: Chairman Lee Millar.

SPONSORS

INDEX

ABOUT THE AUTHOR

DR. JOHN E. HARKINS

Dr. John E. Harkins teaches history at Memphis University School, which has hosted the meetings of the West Tennessee Historical Society since the mid-1990s. John is a fifth-generation Memphian, descended from Irish immigrants who came to Shelby County in the early 1850s. John and Georgia, his wife of forty-two years, are both active members of the Descendants of Early Settlers of Shelby County and Adjoining Counties. Georgia has served as Registrar of the Descendants and John is a past-president of the group. Georgia has critiqued and edited virtually all of John's published works.

John served as Memphis and Shelby County archivist for six years and as president of the West Tennessee Historical Society for eight years. He served eight years on the Tennessee Public Records Commission, and for a similar term on the Shelby County Historical Commission. He currently serves on the Tennessee Historical Commission. John is also a member of Memphis Heritage, the Tennessee Historical Society, the Association for the Preservation of Tennessee Antiquities, the Tennessee Preservation Trust, the Jackson Purchase Historical Society, and the Bartlett Historical Society. Moreover, he has served for a number of years as an involved member of the Davies Manor Association, which preserves and operates a log cabin, museum home complex in northeast Shelby County.

Dr. Harkins has written widely on topics related to Memphis, Shelby County, and Tennessee history. His other books include *Metropolis of the American Nile, an Illustrated History of Memphis and Shelby County*, *The MUS Century Book*, and *The New Orleans Cabildo*. *Metropolis* and the *Century Book* have both been republished in second editions. Harkins also writes a monthly local history column for *The Best Times*.

For more information about the following publications or about publishing your own book, please call
Historical Publishing Network at 800-749-9790 or visit www.lammertinc.com.

Black Gold: The Story of Texas Oil & Gas

Historic Abilene: An Illustrated History

Historic Albuquerque: An Illustrated History

Historic Amarillo: An Illustrated History

Historic Anchorage: An Illustrated History

Historic Austin: An Illustrated History

Historic Baldwin County: A Bicentennial History

Historic Baton Rouge: An Illustrated History

Historic Beaufort County: An Illustrated History

Historic Beaumont: An Illustrated History

Historic Bexar County: An Illustrated History

Historic Birmingham & Jefferson County: An Illustrated History

Historic Brazoria County: An Illustrated History

Historic Charlotte:
An Illustrated History of Charlotte and Mecklenburg County

Historic Cheyenne: A History of the Magic City

Historic Comal County: An Illustrated History

Historic Corpus Christi: An Illustrated History

Historic Denton County: An Illustrated History

Historic Edmond: An Illustrated History

Historic El Paso: An Illustrated History

Historic Erie County: An Illustrated History

Historic Fairbanks: An Illustrated History

Historic Gainesville & Hall County: An Illustrated History

Historic Grand Prairie: An Illustrated History

Historic Greenville: An Illustrated History

Historic Gregg County: An Illustrated History

Historic Hampton Roads: Where America Began

Historic Hancock County: An Illustrated History

Historic Henry County: An Illustrated History

Historic Houston: An Illustrated History

Historic Illinois: An Illustrated History

Historic Kern County:
An Illustrated History of Bakersfield and Kern County

Historic Lafayette:
An Illustrated History of Lafayette & Lafayette Parish

Historic Laredo:
An Illustrated History of Laredo & Webb County

Historic Little Rock: An Illustrated History

Historic Louisiana: An Illustrated History

Historic Midland: An Illustrated History

Historic Montgomery County:
An Illustrated History of Montgomery County, Texas

Historic Ocala: The Story of Ocala & Marion County

Historic Oklahoma: An Illustrated History

Historic Oklahoma County: An Illustrated History

Historic Omaha:
An Illustrated History of Omaha and Douglas County

Historic Ouachita Parish: An Illustrated History

Historic Paris and Lamar County: An Illustrated History

Historic Pasadena: An Illustrated History

Historic Passaic County: An Illustrated History

Historic Philadelphia: An Illustrated History

Historic Prescott:
An Illustrated History of Prescott & Yavapai County

Historic Richardson: An Illustrated History

Historic Rio Grande Valley: An Illustrated History

Historic Scottsdale: A Life from the Land

Historic Shreveport-Bossier:
An Illustrated History of Shreveport & Bossier City

Historic South Carolina: An Illustrated History

Historic Smith County: An Illustrated History

Historic Texas: An Illustrated History

Historic Victoria: An Illustrated History

Historic Tulsa: An Illustrated History

Historic Williamson County: An Illustrated History

Historic Wilmington & The Lower Cape Fear:
An Illustrated History

Iron, Wood & Water: An Illustrated History of Lake Oswego

Miami's Historic Neighborhoods: A History of Community

Old Orange County Courthouse: A Centennial History

Plano: An Illustrated Chronicle

The New Frontier:
A Contemporary History of Fort Worth & Tarrant County

The San Gabriel Valley: A 21st Century Portrait

The Spirit of Collin County

Valley Places, Valley Faces

Shelby County Growth Plan

Miles
3   1.5   0   3

- Memphis
- Millington
- Lakeland
- Germantown
- Bartlett
- Collierville
- Arlington

Reserve Areas

- Memphis Reserve
- Millington Reserve
- Lakeland Reserve
- Bartlett Reserve
- Collierville Reserve
- Arlington Reserve
- Not Reserved
- Rural

Prepared by Memphis and Shelby County
Division of Planning and Development
February 07, 2007.

Rural Area amended in 2003 by consent decree.

The map is for representation only, and
may not be considered a legal document.

RURAL

RURAL

RURAL